Wall Construction and Finishing

Elizabeth and Robert Williams

TAB BOOKS Inc.
Blue Ridge Summit, PA

FIRST EDITION
FIRST PRINTING

Copyright © 1989 by TAB BOOKS Inc.
Printed in the United States of America

Library of Congress Cataloging in Publication Data

Williams, Elizabeth, 1942-
    Wall construction and finishing / by Elizabeth and Robert
  Williams.

        p.   cm.
    Includes index.
      ISBN 0-8306-9087-5 — ISBN 0-8306-9387-4 (pbk.)
  1932- . II. Title.
  TH2201.W55 1989   88-32318
  690′.12—dc19   CIP

TAB BOOKS Inc. offers software for sale. For information and a catalog, please contact:
TAB Software Department, Blue Ridge Summit, PA 17294-0850.

Questions regarding the content of this book should be addressed to:

    Reader Inquiry Branch
    TAB BOOKS Inc.
    Blue Ridge Summit, PA 17294-0214

Edited by Nina E. Barr

Contents

Introduction

At least half the cost of a house on the market reflects the payment to the carpenters and other members of the construction crew. House construction is not an easy job, and these people earn their money. Seen from the other viewpoint, however, they are actually earning *your* money. They get paid because the typical person either cannot, will not, or simply does not want to cut building costs by doing part of the work on the house.

Many contractors will agree to complete the work on the footings, foundation walls, frame, and roof. You can be your own contractor and sublet the work on the foundation, footings, subflooring, and other parts of the house. Then you can do the work you feel comfortable with, such as framing and wall construction.

Perhaps you feel that you are not qualified by your training and experience to do wall construction work. If, however, you will approach the work in a simple. logical, and guided fashion, you will find that wall construction is relatively simple and highly enjoyable work.

It is more than enjoyable. It is exciting! You can buy your own materials and, therefore, see that you get what you paid for. Most building supply houses will grant you contractor's prices when you buy lumber and the other supplies you will need for the work.

When you buy your own materials, you can inspect and reject any timbers that you do not want to put in your house. When you do your own wall construction work, you can save considerable amounts of money simply by using sound judgment in the use of the lumber you have bought.

You need no particular experience, training, or expertise to get started in wall construction. You need the ability to drive a nail, measure accurately, saw along a straight line, and use a few basic tools capably. You can learn the rest, partially through the help of this book. In a surprisingly short time you can be installing siding, hanging wallpaper, painting, and putting up paneling.

This book will provide you with direct, simple, easy-to-follow instructions on every phase and step of the work you will need to do. These instructions will be in everyday language. All technical or esoteric terms will be defined and explained, so you will not need to consult friends or reference books.

You will find, as all do-it-yourselfers learn, that a major part of the job is finding a starting point. You also will learn that tiny problems left unsolved at the beginning of a particular step in the building process can lead to significant and costly correctional steps. This book will show and tell you what to look for before you begin work and how to correct most of the problems that are likely to be present.

Although your own tastes and judgments will be the determining factor in what types of materials you put into your walls, you will also be shown many of the advantages and disadvantages of the possible options you have. You also will be introduced to several new and delightful products now on the market.

Wall construction is a very old process. While many of the materials and techniques have changed radically over the decades, many steps are still being carried out as they were half a century ago—or longer.

As a case in point, wall framing has changed very little in the past few years. You still need a good foundation, subflooring, sole plates (for the studs to rest upon), common studs (usually 8-foot 2 × 4s), cripple or shorter studs under windows, top plates over the studding, and a top cap over the plates. This top cap actually results in a double layer of 2- × -4 timbers—to add strength and to allow partition walls to be tied to the frame for the greatest strength and durability.

Many years ago, corner bracing was done largely through what is called *cut-in bracing* and *let-in bracing*. This first style consisted of a series of shallow cuts in the studding to permit a 1- × -4 or 1- × -5 board to be nailed diagonally into the cuts. The board would then be connected to the corner post, so that the entire corner of the room was braced and supported by the cut-in bracing. The second style of bracing was let-in bracing. In this fashion, short lengths of 2 × 4s would be angle-cut and installed between studs to form a diagonal line.

These two forms of bracing are excellent. Nowadays, however, many home builders use 4- × -8-foot sheets of plywood nailed vertically on both outside sides of corners, or they use thin strips of steel bracing. Builders have learned that plywood is not only good for insulation but it is also excellent to prevent *racking* (or twisting of the corners).

Before you get ready to do any serious wall construction, you should investigate fully the task before you. You should make a thorough visual examination of the wall frame to see if it is ready for the wall covering. You should check to see that the corners are square at the bottom, at the top, and horizontally and vertically. You should be prepared to examine insulation to see that it is properly installed and that a good vapor barrier is also installed.

This book will lead you through these investigations and many others before you start to buy materials or drive nails. You will be shown and told how to determine if corner posts are plumb and if studding is correctly installed and, if not, how to make the needed corrections.

For instance, if a stud has been installed improperly, it might protrude to the inside wall and create problems with plasterboard or paneling. If the edge of the stud protrudes to the outside wall side, it can create similar problems with siding. If it is not nailed in straight, problems can arise when sheathing or plasterboard or paneling is installed.

Similarly, if sole plates or top plates are defective, you can later experience sagging and sinking in your walls. The problem, if it exists, should be corrected before you begin to nail up wall coverings.

Many of the walls in a house are *load-bearing walls*, or *bearing walls*. This means that the wall supports a large part of the weight of the roof and all that is above the top plates and cap plates. The bearing wall must be strong and durable.

Another function of the wall is to provide protection from unwanted intruders such as insects, moisture, fungus growth, and hot or cold air. A wall that is improperly constructed can be deficient in its protective qualities. The result might be cost, irritation, discomfort, or all of the above.

A third function of the wall is to provide sound and sturdy frames for windows and doors. If the wall is not correct, the doors might stick or scrape and windows might jam or be so loose that they rattle or will not stay up when raised.

A fourth function of the wall is aesthetic. An outside wall that is drab and uninteresting detracts significantly from the beauty of the house and, by extension, from the value of the house when it is put on the market. The same holds true for interior walls.

The converse is also true, however. If a wall is neat, colorful, functional, and generally pleasing to the eye, then the value of the house is markedly increased.

One of the most exciting aspects of wall construction is that your knowledge, imagination, skills, and creativity can produce walls that are in all respects commendable. You can choose all of the lumber, install all of the sheathing to keep the house cool in summer and warm in winter, nail up the siding to give the house its distinctive properties, complete all the decorating inside the house when you select and install paneling or wallpaper, and in the final but by no means an unimportant step, paint or stain to create an impression of beauty, balance, and taste.

The format of this book is a simple one—you will be shown where and how to start and then how to complete every step until the wall construction is completed.

Initially, you will be given a list of tools and other types of equipment to help you in your work. Some of these items are absolutely indispensable while others are desirable or merely handy. You will be told how to spot and correct problem areas while they can still be corrected easily. Several check points for electrical wiring and plumbing will be cited.

Other chapters will deal with installation of insulation and sheathing: what to buy, how much to buy, how to install, how to avoid waste, how to save time.

Starting points are generally crucial in all types of modern construction. Particular attention is given to corners as the starting points for paneling and other wall coverings. A good start does not assure you of a happy finish, but it is definitely an indication of a satisfactory job, so particular attention is paid to creating perfect corners.

As in many other areas of specialized work, your work in wall construction will hinge largely on the small, unnoticed points that make the difference between a wall and a great wall. You will find an abundance of information on the small, but important, points in wall construction in this book.

This book is geared for the do-it-yourself person ranging from the total apprentice to the serious hobbyist, the weekend carpenter to the accomplished home-repair person. If you know virtually nothing about wall construction, this book will meet your needs;

if you are experienced in carpentry, you will find some new ideas, approaches, or methodology that will benefit you.

The language of the book is directed toward the beginner, and detailed instructions are given. Perhaps almost equally important, the reasons for doing things in a particular way are also given.

Finally, a comprehensive index is provided at the back of this book. Technical terms are defined in the text when the terms are first used. In short, every effort has been made to assure you that when you follow the instructions in this book, you will be able to complete a wall that will be a source of future pleasure to you.

1
Preparing to Work

WALL CONSTRUCTION IS ONE OF THE MOST ENJOYABLE ASPECTS OF home construction projects. It is also one of the most challenging areas of work. Among the greatest pleasures is seeing amazing and rewarding amounts of work completed each day. Among the challenges is seeing the work completed expertly and professionally.

Another rewarding aspect of the work is found in the wide variety of materials you can use. These materials range from traditional paneling to plywood, plaster, plasterboard or wallboard, wallpaper, wainscoting, and wide-board covering on the inside. The outside wall covering materials include sheathing, building paper, plywood, cement blocks, bricks, sidings of vinyl, aluminum, and asphalt, clapboard, and others.

With these materials, you have a wide choice of how much work you plan to do yourself, how much you need to subcontract, and how simple or difficult you expect the job to be. Some of the building materials can be installed very quickly, while others require considerable amounts of time.

Time is a very important consideration. With some types of building materials, you can work only a few minutes and stop, if you wish. With others, you need to work until the mortar is used, for instance, or you will have a great deal of loss and waste. With some materials, such as plaster, you cannot leave a job that is partially done, at least until you reach a logical and convenient stopping place.

If you live where the work project is being done, you can be more relaxed concerning theft and vandalism; but, if you reside some distance from the worksite, you have to prepare yourself to deal with the possibilities of deliberate loss or damage. This possibility of loss means that you will need to have a convenient method of securing the premises and a way to protect your supplies, tools, and other equipment.

Here, again, time is a factor. You will want to complete the project to a point where proper security measures can be taken. If you are installing plywood panels, for instance, as outside wall covering, you should not leave large amounts of paneling stacked in open

1

view and unsecured. Each panel might cost as much as $20, and rain, vandals, or thieves could damage, ruin, or haul off respectively several hundred dollars worth of your property.

Your work schedule should be planned as efficiently as possible, not only to protect your property but also to complete the most work in the time allotted. It is false economy, for instance, to drive several miles and 30 minutes one way in order to work 15 minutes. You should plan your work schedule so that you can have blocks of several hours at a time, unless you live very near your work.

Another part of work planning is the consideration of how much available help you will have—free or hired. If you are paying helpers, plan your work to receive the maximum service from these employees during any given work period. For example, if you have a choice of nailing siding to the upper areas of the house walls; or nailing cedar shakes or shingles to the lower reaches of the wall, by all means use your hired assistants to help you with the siding because for this job you will need someone else on a ladder or scaffold to hold one end while you nail or to assist you in moving ladders, passing up wall covering, or helping do the other things you would have great difficulty doing alone. You could, on the other hand, nail up shakes or shingles unassisted without difficulty. There is no need to pay someone to help in this process, unless time is a highly important factor.

One extremely important element of your readiness to work is the planning that will determine just how much of a do-it-yourself project your work will be. If your primary need is to get the house or spare room completed in the shortest possible time, it is wise to use your helpers to the maximum. If your project is more along the lines of hobby work and time is of no consequence, then plan your work so that you can do as much of it as possible, at your own convenience.

Just how much of the work in wall construction can one person do, working totally alone? In truth, one person can do virtually all of the work without undue stress and exertion. Several years ago a 90-year-old woman built an entire house herself except for installing roof rafters, the ridgepole, and a few isolated areas of work where she did not have access to needed equipment. With a little foresight and planning, and with sound judgment and the help of hints from this book, you should be able to construct a complete wall, inside and out, working alone.

Admittedly, there are areas of work that will tax your energy and strength; but, the vast majority of the work is such that you can do it while working at a very leisurely pace. If you are working alone, pace yourself intelligently. It is commonplace for one person to work, unconsciously, at a much faster rate than he would if he had someone nearby with whom to chat or with whom to take coffee breaks while working.

This pacing is even more important if you are not accustomed to rather strenuous, manual labor. You run the risks of pulled or strained muscles, injuries, or extreme fatique when pacing is not considered.

Weather is always a factor in outdoor construction projects. You have to plan your work projects for a particular day often in conjunction with weather forecasts. You would have difficulty laying bricks if the weather is so cold that your mortar freezes, although some masons have been known to mix antifreeze with their water when they are mixing mortar. If the temperature is at the other extreme, you might be wise to delay the installation of siding on the sunny side of the house and work inside where it is shady and cooler. When the forecast is for heavy rain the following day, you should weatherproof your house or spare room instead of nailing up paneling.

NECESSARY AND DESIRABLE TOOLS

Any job is easier where you have the proper tools. Conversely, you will spend more hours and damage more materials if you try to do the job without the right tools.

In wall construction, the list of necessary tools includes several items; before you buy them, you should investigate the feasibility of renting them. Most tools can be rented, but some are extremely expensive. In case you need to dig footings, you have a choice of using a pick, mattock, and shovel, or renting a ditcher.

Working manually, you can dig footings 18 inches deep at the rate of 10 feet per hour; however, it is unlikely that you will wish to dig eight hours per day. The work is very hard and dirty, and it can be complicated immeasureably by the presence of large underground rocks and hard soil. You need to decide which makes better economic sense to you: spending several days digging the footings or spending the money needed to rent a ditcher.

You can rent a ditcher for about $50 for 3 hours, plus the usual deposit fee of $50. You have to drive to the rental agency to pick up and return the equipment. If you have a 30 minute drive to the agency, you have used 1 hour of your rental time in driving, and the 2 hours of use will cost you $25 per hour. On the positive side, you get your $50 deposit returned when you deliver the ditcher in good condition, and you can dig the greater part of the footings for a house in that amount of time. Your question is whether you can afford to rent the equipment easier than you can spare the time digging the footings yourself.

In many areas, you can rent an entire toolbox filled with nearly every kind of tool you would need for constructing a wall. You must keep in mind that if you are going to be working only an hour or two after work each day, you will soon have the cost of buying the tools tied up in rental fees. If you decide to buy the basic tools, you should consider the following:

A good hammer: You can buy an excellent hammer for about $12.95, and it will last for years. You can also buy hammers that are cheaper and of lower quality for $7.95, but the hammer might not last through the project you are planning.

You have a wide choice of hammers. You can buy hammers with handles made of wood, steel, or fiberglass. You can get them with a bell-facing or plain-facing. They are available with straight or curved claws. For daily use, the bell-faced hammer with a good wooden handle and curved claws is hard to beat.

You can also buy ball-peen hammers, straight-peen hammers, and cross-peen hammers, but the use of a peen hammer is so rare in wall construction that there is no need to buy one. Choose instead a traditional carpenter's hammer—a claw hammer—with a good handle, a bell face, and curved claws.

Metal-Cutting Tools: You will probably need some type of metal-cutting tool if you plan to install termite shields between foundation and sills. Straight hand snips, large enough to permit you to cut metal easily, work well. You can find these snips in hardware stores in sizes from 6 to 16 inches. Mid-range snips will be sufficient for nearly all of your metal-cutting needs. These snips will cut tin sheeting and aluminum alloy metals without difficulty. They are very safe to use and very durable as long as you do not attempt to cut heavier metals with them.

One tool that has limited, but often essential use, is the hacksaw, which can be used to cut through very thick metals. You can cut angle iron with it, if you need to cut lintels for doorways or fireplaces. The work is slow but certain, and you can find a variety of blades to fit a hacksaw frame. If you are going to be cutting heavy metal, such as steel, buy a blade that has 18 teeth per inch. If you need the hacksaw for cutting angle iron, you will need one with 24 teeth per inch. Blades are inexpensive, so if you plan to cut a variety of materials, you can buy blades with 14, 18, 24, and 32 teeth per inch. You will also be able to cut all kinds of materials with the same blade; the major difference in blades is that you will cut faster with the proper blade.

You can also make relatively small wood cuts with a hacksaw blade. The hacksaw has the advantage of being adjustable to several angles. You can use the blade without the frame, if you need to do so.

A unique tool, with minor but important uses, is the rod saw. This saw is made with a handle and a straight bar or rod sticking out from it. The rod saw has hundreds of tungsten-carbide particles permanently bonded to the rod. The best qualities of the rod saw is that it cuts on forward and reverse strokes and is so hard that it cuts through stainless steel, files, and other metals so hard that hacksaw blades are totally ineffective against them.

The Punch: A small and inexpensive tool that has several important uses is the punch. The major use of the hand punch is in installing tongue and groove siding or flooring. You can use the punch to sink nails flush with the wood surface by holding the punch so that the point is against the head of the nail and then striking the nail, or you can lay the punch flat across the head of the nail and parallel with the tongue of the lumber and then strike the punch.

Saws: A saw is absolutely essential. You have a choice of handsaws or power saws. Even with handsaws, you can have a crosscut saw or ripping saw. If you plan to use the saw almost exclusively for crosscutting (cutting across a board), then you will not have much use for a ripping saw, which does a very poor job of crosscutting. The ripping saw is used to saw lengthwise down a board (with the grain), but the teeth are not arranged properly for crosscut work.

You might want to buy a power saw, if you have electrical current at your worksite. These saws, while more dangerous, are infinitely faster than handsaws and easier to use. You can buy blades that will crosscut or rip: you can also buy combination blades that will do both. You can purchase blades that will cut stones, metal, and other materials normally much too hard for any type of power saw to cut.

The Bench Plane: A fine tool used often in window installation and in door fitting is the bench plane, which comes in three basic types: the jack plane, smooth plane, and jointer plane. The three have common qualities, but the jack plane probably has greater versatility in an overall sense. It can cut deep, plane a long, smooth surface, and provides great trueness. You can use a fourth type, the block plane, for squaring or smoothing end cuts in lumber: but, there is not enough use for this type of plane to justify buying one. You will need only one plane, and the jack plane is the one most likely to meet everyday carpentry requirements.

Augers and Drills: Any work that involves boring holes in wood generally requires an auger or drill. You can buy a hand auger, often called a brace-and-bit tool. You can hold the handle in one hand and turn the auger with the other to bore holes. An electric drill is also an inexpensive and handy tool, if you have electrical power. The drill is inexpensive and it will save you incredible time and effort. You can also buy drills or bits that will cut through all types of wood and some metals.

Wood Chisels: An inexpensive wood chisel is a welcome addition to your toolbox. This small device will enable you to cut away wood in places that a plane or auger cannot reach effectively.

Screwdrivers: Depending upon the nature of your wall construction work, you might find that a pair of screwdrivers will be useful. You need one slot-head screwdriver and one Phillips-head screwdriver. You can buy traditional screwdrivers with handles made of plastic, wood, or metal. The shank will be made of steel or similar metal. For lighter work, the shank is usually made round. Square shanks are available for heavier work. The square shank permits the use of a wrench on the shank to help turn it when greater force is needed.

You can purchase other types of screwdrivers, including the offset screwdriver, which can be very handy. They are usually not needed often enough to justify buying them.

Pliers: You can purchase a good pair of pliers inexpensively. Here again, the choice is wide. You can find round-nose, needle-nose, short-nose, diagonal, slipjoint, channel-lock, vise-grip, water-pump, long-nose, and cutting pliers. Perhaps the most useful and universal is the channel-lock pliers, which have very long handles and provide a powerful grip. In addition, they can be set in a variety of grip openings so that they perform almost like an adjustable wrench.

Clamps: If you do not think you will need both a vise and a C-clamp, buy the C-clamp. This clamp is one of the most useful devices you can purchase, particularly if you are working alone. Buy one that is at least 6 inches wide at the opening.

Protective Eyewear: Goggles or protective glasses are also recommended. In many kinds of work there will be sawdust, metal shavings, dirt, grit, and tiny metal fragments that can damage, if not put out an eye. You should always use protective glasses when working with a drill, power saw, or chain saw. You should wear them also when you are working directly overhead, particularly if the work involves hammering, grinding, filing, or sawing.

Rulers: You will need some reliable method of measuring. You have a choice of a folding ruler, a tape rule (or ruler), hook rule, steel rule with holder, or steel or fiberglass tape. Perhaps the handiest choice would be to buy a 6-foot folding rule and a steel-tape rule that is at least 50 feet long. You might also want to have a 10-foot tape rule that can be stuck in your pocket or hooked over your belt while you are working.

Plumb Bob: A plumb bob with cord and target can also be on your list of tools and equipment often needed in carpentry and construction work. The *plumb bob* is used to determine a plumb or vertical line from the point where the bob is held to the ground or floor. This tool is indispensable when you must assure yourself that your work line is perfectly vertical.

Levels: Do not start to work seriously until you have secured a good, clear, and reliable level. This tool is used to show the true vertical and true horizontal lines in building work. You can buy levels that are calibrated to show in degrees, minutes, and seconds, the angle of a wall or other surface in relation to true horizontal or true vertical.

Levels are simple devices which have glass or plastic tubes containing alcohol, chloroform, or other similar liquid plus a bubble that appears between lines when a surface is true vertical or horizontal. The tube is mounted in a wood, plastic, or often aluminum frame. Some levels have two or three readings so that you can see at a glance at either end or the middle whether a surface is level or horizontal.

Square: Numerous other tools are available which are either completely necessary or highly desirable. One of these is a square, which is an essential piece of equipment. A square can be a simple piece of metal or plastic, even wood, that is shaped at a right angle. Each arm of the level is marked in inches and fractional inches, and the edges are perfectly straight. You can also buy a combination square, which contains a level and a scribe.

Pocketknives: Finally, secure a good pocketknife. You can buy knives that have lock blades and spring-released blades, not to be confused with the notorious switchblade associated with criminal activity. A spring-released blade is very handy, particularly if you need to locate and use the knife while one hand is occupied. You can hold the knife in the palm of your hand, release the spring, and the blade opens with a gentle, smooth motion: the knife is ready to use.

The tools listed here will be sufficient to take care of most of your carpentry or construction needs, unless you need to do some work in mortar, such as brick-laying or cement-block laying. In this event, you will need a good trowel.

Proper Use of Tools

No matter how well equipped you are, if you do not know how the tools were designed to be used, you are not prepared to work effectively. Worst of all, you can be seriously injured, or the tools can be damaged or ruined. Following are some basic guidelines for the most efficient use of the tools listed previously.

The Hammer: This tool, which appears to be the simplest tool on the market, is one of the most abused pieces of equipment. To use a hammer correctly, you need to grip it correctly.

The correct grip is holding the hammer at the end of the handle so that the very end of the hammer extends beyond your grip by no more than 1 inch. Do not *choke* the hammer; that is, do not grasp it at the midpoint of the handle and try to hammer effectively. If you do so, your blows will lack power and accuracy. You will bend a large number of nails because the head of the hammer, called the *face*, will strike the nail at an acute angle and cause the nail to bend in the direction of the blows.

If you hold the hammer properly, you can lift it so that your fist comes to a point even with your ear and the head of the hammer extends beyond the back of your head. Never lift the hammer so that the head comes toward your face or any other part of your body. When you start to strike a nail or other object, bring the head of the hammer sharply downward so that the full face of the hammer is in direct contact with the head of the nail.

Never use both hands. This motion will cause the hammer to be unbalanced and inaccurate. Do not use the side of the hammer to drive nails. The thinnest part of the hammer is between the neck and the wedge part of the hammer. There is a chance that the hammer can crack, particularly if you are striking a metal target. The hammer, which is sideways under these conditions, is more likely to hit your face as you start the blow downward or you might hit an object near the nail you are trying to drive. You will bend more nails and damage the surface of the material you are installing if you use the hammer in a sideways fashion.

When you are using the claws of the hammer to extract nails, always use a thin piece of wood under the *technical head* of the hammer. This area is midway between the claws and the wedge. By using a section of board or other type of wedge, you create a fulcrum affect that will make your job a great deal easier and you will not risk breaking the handle out of the hammer.

One special word of caution is necessary concerning pulling nails. Many times when a nail is suddenly released by the wood fibers, it will fly into the air at a considerable speed and will soar for 10 to 20 feet. If the nail should strike you or one of your helpers in the face, permanent damage can result. Eyes particularly are vulnerable to this kind of damage.

To prevent the nail from flying upward, use the wood for a fulcrum and, as soon as the nail starts to give slightly, place one hand in a cuplike fashion over the claws and nail so that the nail will be cushioned and stopped by your palm. Your hand will not be injured because the shank of the nail will hit your palm flat so that no penetration can occur.

Tin Snips or Metal Shears: When you are using tin snips or metal shears, you should realize that they do not remove any part of the metal in the cutting process: You will create minute fractures in the metal. These fractures are tiny and very sharp slivers of metal. The sharp metal can easily puncture flesh and rip your hand badly. To prevent accidents, always wear heavy gloves when cutting tin or any other kind of metal.

Because there is no metal lost, (no kerf is created as the shears pass through the metal), you should make the cutline just outside the mark you have made. In this way, you will make the cut exactly the right length or width.

When cutting heavier metals, always cut with the back part of the blades. There is more power here because there is greater leverage and your cuts will be more accurate because the shears are under better control. As you move further out on the blades, your control over the cutline is decreased considerably.

Never try to cut metal that is too thick for the shears. If you do, you will spring the shears. As a result, the shears or snips are permanently ruined and should be thrown away.

Hacksaws and Rod Saws: Hacksaws, used properly, are among the handiest tools in the toolbox. Used improperly, the hacksaw can be laborious to use and you can bend or break the blades easily.

The first step in using a hacksaw is to select the best blade for the job. Coarse blades with fewer teeth should be used to cut heavier metals. These blades cut faster and with less energy. If you are cutting thinner metals, you should use a finer blade with more teeth per inch.

When you install a hacksaw blade, turn the blade so that the teeth point away from the frame. Hook the hole in the blade over the peg at the end of the frame and then hook the end closer to the handle in the same fashion. You will find a wing nut at the handle end of the blade. Tighten the wing nut until the blade is very taut. It should not move at all when you apply slight pressure with your fingers. The blade might bend slightly, but, it will not move at the ends.

To cut metal, you should remember that the hacksaw blade cuts only on the forward stroke. On the return stroke there is no cutting. Start the stroke forward and lean slightly forward as the blade moves. At the end of the stroke, lift the blade slightly and move it back to the starting point. Keep swaying back and forth as you saw, exerting slight but steady pressure on the blade with each forward stroke. For best results, keep a steady stroke pace. One stroke every two seconds is a good speed.

Hold the saw so that one hand in on the handle, with the top of your hand high against the handle ridge. You can extend one finger parallel with the top of the frame and rest against it; the other hand should be on the other end of the frame with the thumb and upper palm resting on the curve of the frame and the fingers wrapping around the end of the frame.

If you need to make a long cut, one that is too long for the depth of the frame, you can remove the blade and turn it so that the frame is horizontal and the blade is vertical. The portion of material to be cut off is inside the frame; that is, it is between the frame and the blade.

If you are working with very thin metal or if you must saw very near the edge of the metal, you should secure two smooth and even blocks of wood, sandwich the metal between the wood, and then place the sandwiched metal in a vise. With the vise tightened securely, you can saw without fear of ruining the metal and you will not scrape or cut your hand on the raw edge of the metal.

Hacksaw blades usually break because the blade is not tight enough, because you twist the blade, or because you are sawing too fast. To prevent breakage, which can cause serious harm to your hands and forearms, saw with a slow, rhythmic movement. You should stop from time to time to check blade tightness, and you should saw with an even stroke so there is no twisting movement to the blade.

A rod saw is made very similar to the hacksaw, and the same general observations apply. The major difference is that the rod saw cuts on both forward and return strokes and you can exert the same pressure in both directions.

The Punch: Using a punch is very simple. When you wish to sink a nail without damaging the wood, place the point of the punch in the center of the nail head and tap the end of the punch lightly. For this use, choose only a punch with a blunt point. Use a center punch but never a prick punch, pin punch, or starting punch.

If the head of the nail extends $\frac{1}{4}$ to $\frac{1}{2}$ inch or more, lay the punch flat so that the thickest part of the punch is atop the nail head. Never hit the punch unless it is being held. Never hold the punch so that your fingers are close to the point of hammer contact. Wear gloves and hold the punch by the squared or flat-sided end and strike it at least an inch from your fingers, or more if space permits.

If you are drilling a hole in metal, use the punch to mark the starting point. Hold the punch erect with the point where the hole is to be drilled. While holding the punch firmly, tap the end sharply with a hammer. Start the drill in the indentation you have made. If you do not punch the starting point, your drill will have a tendency to move erratically across the surface of the metal until enough penetration is made. Therefore, keep the drill tip in a stable position.

The Handsaw and Circular Saw: When you are working with no electrical power handy, the handsaw is the tool needed to make board and timber cuts. Of the many people who have seen handsaws used frequently, the majority have never used a handsaw to any real extent. Daily, people who are inexperienced in carpentry are joining the ranks of the millions who are engaged in some form of do-it-yourself construction or repair work. Many of these newcomers have little or no experience with a handsaw.

One mistake frequently made by beginners is to place the saw too close to a horizontal position. When the saw is nearly flat, the teeth cover more territory; that is, the teeth cut a longer kerf. The amateur sees this elongated groove as evidence that he is making great progress. Actually, when the heel of the saw is too low and the toe too high, you have much less control over the saw, and your kerf (groove) will become too wide in places and the saw line will be crooked.

The proper way to use a handsaw is to place the lumber to be sawed upon a work surface, such as a sawhorse or sawbuck, so that the lumber is about 30 inches high (the height depends upon your own height). Stand, if possible, so that you can rest one hand and one knee on the lumber. Hold the saw firmly by the grip and let the saw and your forearm form a straight line that is maintained in the sawing motion. Your forearm moves up and down in perfect alignment with the saw. Extend your first finger along the handle of the saw, parallel with the blade, as you did with the hacksaw.

Short boards can be sawed easily on one sawhorse, but, if you are sawing long boards, place the boards over two sawhorses. Never attempt to saw a line between the sawhorses. Extend the board so that the saw line extends over the edge of one sawhorse. If you try to saw between the sawhorses, your weight will cause the board to bend and pinch the saw so that you cannot move it.

A saw will occasionally bind even if there is no weight on the board. This problem is usually caused by sawing a crooked line. The blade of the saw becomes caught in a slight arc and is wedged there. To correct this problem, lift the saw from the groove and position it so that it is nearly in a horizontal position. Saw lightly, letting the weight of the saw provide the needed pressure, along the top of the saw line until the saw line has been straightened. Or, you can stop cutting, mark a new saw line, and start over, if you can do so without shortening the board too much to serve its purpose.

Other reasons for binding are wet wood, dull blades, and your tendency to lean the saw to the left or right as you start the forward or return stroke. Occasionally, you find that no matter how diligently you try, your cutline is not straight. One way to help remedy the situation is to take very short strokes and to saw very slowly, so that you can watch the penciled cutline at all times. You might need to pause to blow or brush away sawdust in order to keep the saw line visible at all times. If you realize that the cutline is going astray, pull the saw slightly in the direction opposite the variant cutline, and very gradually bring the cutline back into its accurate direction.

If the saw continues to bind or drag more than usual, even if your cutline is perfectly straight, you can help the saw to move more freely if you put a little oil on the sides of the blade. Oil sometimes discolors the end of the board at the cutline. If this is a problem, you can use a clear mineral oil. The time-honored method of preventing bind or drag was to rub the saw with a chunk of meat fat or "fatback." This home remedy worked beautifully. Any form of grease will help the saw move better.

Using a circular saw is much different from using a handsaw. The circular saw blade turns backward, or upward, and the teeth slash in a vertical direction. This fact means that when you are using a handsaw, the ragged edge will be on the bottom side of the board, but, if you are using a circular saw, the jagged edge will be on the top of the sawed board. So, keep in mind, if you are sawing paneling or similar materials, turn the panel upside down and make the cut with a circular saw. The splintered edge will be on the back side, rather than on the face side.

When you are using a handsaw and come to the end of the cut, saw very slowly and use your free hand to hold the waste end. As the saw nearly completes the cut, allow the waste end to sag slightly, but continue to hold it firmly so it will not drop suddenly and splinter the bottom side of the board. When you are using a circular saw, do not allow the revolutions to slow as you reach the end of the cut. The speed of the saw's cutting action is so great that the final part of the cut is made before any splintering action occurs.

One way to start a cut with a handsaw is to place the teeth of the saw on the cutline and at the edge of the board. Rest your hand against the side of the saw blade so the blade will not slip from the saw line and pull the saw slowly toward your body. This slow movement will cause the saw to cut a shallow groove. Now move your hand away from the blade and push the saw forward slowly and with very gentle pressure. Make several slow, short strokes until the teeth move smoothly and easily in the groove, at which time you can assume your normal sawing stroke.

Starting a cut with a circular saw requires you to take special precautions. Your fingers or any other part of your body should not be near the cutline. Instead, hold the saw so that the blade is an inch from the starting point. Squeeze the trigger so that the blade is moving at full speed when it comes into contact with the wood. Never let the teeth of the blade be in contact with the wood when you squeeze the trigger. If it is in contact with the wood, the saw will buck severely and could cause damage to you or, the saw, or the wood.

When a handsaw is bound in a long cut, you can insert a small wedge to keep the wood gapped slightly and you will free the saw.

The Plane: A plane is very simple to use, with only two adjustments likely to be made. Many planes have two nut adjustments: the adjusting nut and the rear adjusting nut. The adjusting nut moves the cutting edge up or down for a deeper or more shallow cut. The rear adjusting nut tilts the cutting edge to the right or left. (See Fig. 1-1.)

If you need to adjust your plane for better cutting action, turn it upside down and sight along the bottom of the plane as you turn the adjusting nut until the cutting edge appears. You do not want the blade to stick out very far, because it will take too big a bite and will consequently gouge your wood surface. When you have the blade set, turn the rear adjusting nut until the blade appears in perfect alignment with the bottom of the plane.

Some newer models of planes have only the one adjustment. You can loosen the nut, remove the blade completely, reseat it as you want it to be, and then retighten the nut. Again, do not let much blade show or you will gouge and gap your wood.

The Electric Drill: You will drill or bore holes occasionally in your carpentry work. If you have access to electricity, you will probably use an electric drill. To do so, use the chuck key that came with the drill to open the chuck. You will find three locations where the chuck key will fit. Turn the key counterclockwise two or three times and then slip the shaft or shank of the drill bit into the open chuck. Tighten the chuck by turning the key clockwise in all three locations until the bit is firmly secured.

To drill a hole, choose the proper bit. Some bits are used to drill in wood; others are used to drill in metal. If you need to drill a hole in metal, use a punch to make the starting point, and then proceed to drill. Keep firm, but medium pressure, on the top of the drill. Do not apply excessive pressure. If you do, you can burn up the drill motor, risk breaking the bit and cause injury and damage. You might add a drop or two of oil at the point of the bit when you start using the drill. If the metal is very thick, you might need to remove the bit and add a drop of oil into the hole every minute or two.

Drilling a hole in wood is much easier than drilling one in metal. If the wood is a thin board, you can mark the starting point, squeeze the trigger, and touch the drill bit

Fig. 1-1. A good plane with adjustable blade is a vital tool for most construction jobs.

lightly to the wood to ensure that you have started accurately. When you are assured that the start is a good one, and if the hole is to be ½ inch or smaller, give the bit full power and drill straight through the board.

For larger holes, you need to drill slower and exert less pressure on the drill. You might find that it is easier to start with a smaller drill and drill a hole through the wood, then change to a larger bit and ream out the hole to the needed size.

You can purchase drilling attachments that will drill a hole virtually any size you need up to 2½ inches. These attachments are useful for drilling holes in lumber which is no thicker than two inches. For thicker wood, you will need to use a solid bit, and drill slowly and with medium pressure. (See Fig. 1-2.)

If you do not have electricity, you might need to do your boring or drilling with the old-fashioned auger or brace and bit. This tool consists of a chuck which can be opened by hand pressure, a bit, offset shaft, and handle. The bits have very sharp points that flare out quickly. They are within an inch of the size of the hole you are planning to drill.

Fig. 1-2. You can buy inexpensive drill attachments that will bore larger holes in a matter of seconds.

Start to drill or bore by placing the sharp point on the starting point mark. Apply slight pressure to keep the point in place as you straighten the auger, until it is vertical. Place one hand on the handle and the other hand on the cap. While holding the cap firmly, turn the handle clockwise. The bit will start to bite deeper into the hole. Keep the pressure steady until you feel the tip of the bit start to emerge from the bottom of the board. Turn slowly until the entire bit emerges, then turn the handle counterclockwise and back the bit out of the hole. There will be some splintering on the bottom side of the board, so always start to drill with the face side upward.

To remove the bit, hold the screw sleeve tightly in one hand and turn the handle counterclockwise until the bit is free. You insert a bit in the opposite fashion; you hold the screw sleeve as before, place the bit in the chuck, then turn the handle clockwise to tighten the chuck.

Some braces have ratchet action which will permit you to turn the handle halfway, then reverse, then turn halfway again. This feature is especially useful if you must drill a hole very near a wall or stud or other obstruction which would keep the handle from making a complete turn. If the brace does not have ratchet action, you will find that you cannot drill extremely close to obstacles.

Pliers: While everyone is familiar with the action of pliers, some people might not know how channel-lock and vise-drip pliers work. The channel-lock pliers are very much like water-pump pliers; they have long handles and have a similar physical appearance. The method of adjustment differs considerably, however. The channel-lock pliers have one side with grooves in one jaw and lands or stops in the other jaw. You can change the opening by changing the position of the lands and grooves. Do not try to use channel-lock pliers when you need an adjustable or open-end wrench or socket. The channel-lock pliers provide a very sturdy and strong gripping action. On the other hand, if you release the pressure slightly while you are attempting to turn a nut or bolt, the pliers will slip around the head of the bolt, or around the nut, and start to "round" the corners so that it is almost impossible to free the nut later.

Vise-grip pliers are extremely handy tools. They usually have clamp-jaw action that adjusts to fit any size possible for that particular model. You can tighten the grip by squeezing the handles together and then tighten a set nut on the end of the handles. The pliers will retain their grip, leaving both of your hands free to do other work.

The C-Clamp: The C-clamp works in a very obvious manner, but you might not be aware of some of the many uses of this device. You use it by simply placing the bottom of the clamp in position, then you tighten the operating screw which has a swivel head at the end. As the swivel head moves into contact with the surface of the object to be clamped in place, you turn the handle until it bites into the surface enough to hold the material securely in place while you work.

One of the best uses of the C-clamp is using it to hold materials while you work. If you need to hold a timber in place while you nail, but the timber is too heavy to hold with one hand, simply clamp one end of the timber in place and then nail it easily. When you are sawing short pieces of lumber, you can lay the lumber flat, then clamp it to the sawhorse or workbench and saw easily. (See Fig. 1-3.)

One of the handiest uses of the C-clamp is in the leveling of timbers, particularly if you are working alone. You will find it extremely difficult to hold the timber, keep the level against it for a proper reading, and nail it in place, all at the same time. The C-clamp will help you remarkably in this respect if you will position the level against the edge of the timber and, while you are holding it, place the swivel head against the recessed edge of the level, then tighten the operating screw so that the clamp closes over the timber and the edge of the level. The level will remain stationary while you take care of the nailing, and you can get a reading while you are at the nailing point.

In many respects the C-clamp is like a vise. The major differences between the C-clamp and the vise are that a vise is more powerful and has wider holding surfaces. The C-clamp, however, is much easier to use. A vise must be mounted and secured with nuts and bolts for the most serviceable use. A C-clamp can be used virtually anywhere and under nearly all conditions.

Tapes and Rulers: Tapes and rules, or rulers, are commonplace in nearly every work area in the nation, but, if you are a newcomer to home-repair work or do-it-yourself projects,

Fig. 1-3. A C-clamp is one of the most versatile tools you can buy. One of its major uses is to hold materials while you saw them.

you need to be familiar with some of the characteristics of good tapes and rules. A folding rule can be very useful because it is stiff and can be extended 6 or 8 feet. Consequently, you can stand on the ground, or floor, and still measure distances considerably beyond your reach.

If you need to measure the space between rafters, to cite one example, you can bend the folding rule at the 2-foot mark, then stick the rule up to the bottom ends of the rafters and get your measurement without having to go to the trouble of finding, moving, and climbing a ladder. You can also measure angles by folding the rule so that it conforms with the angle then, leaving the fold as it was when you measured, laying the rule against the board you will be cutting at an angle and marking it accordingly.

Some of the steel tapes have hooks on the end. You can drape the hook over the end of a board and the end of the tape will remain in position while you measure to the desired point. Many tapes are marked metrically in addition to being marked in traditional inches and feet.

The usual tape rule also has many advantages. Some are so flexible that you can wrap them around a pipe to get perfect outside circumference measurements, and yet these flexible tapes are strong enough that they can be extended without support for several feet.

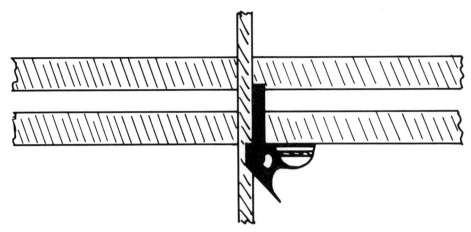

Fig. 1-4. The combination square is a series of tools in one instrument. It has many uses in construction, particularly in the task of marking plates and caps.

One very useful characteristic of some tapes is the thumb set. You can extend the tape to the desired point, push the set button, and the tape remains set. This feature is most helpful when you are spacing cross-bridging or similar timbers and they must all be spaced accurately. You can set the tape, stand it on edge, and then position the timbers so that the bottom of the timbers barely touches the end of the tape.

The Square: The typical carpenter's framing square ranges in size from 4 × 5 to 8 × 12, 16 × 24, or 18 × 24 inches. The long arm of a square is called the *blade*, and the shorter arm is labeled as the *tongue*. The outside point of the square is the *heel*, and the top of the blade is called the *face*.

One of the best qualities of the combination square is that the head (the movable part) can be set at any desired point, then clamped into place by using the set screw inside the head. Another fine quality is that the combination square can be used as a depth gauge, height gauge, or scribing gauge. A level is also built into the square, and many have protractors built into them. (See Fig. 1-4.)

The Plumb Bob: The plumb bob is extremely simple to use. You hang the plumb bob from the desired point and when it is perfectly still, you can mark the target spot below the point for a pure vertical reading. This tool is helpful in positioning walls, studs, corner posts, and decorative posts in exact positions.

PROPERTIES OF INTERIOR AND EXTERIOR WALLS

Your home building project will involve two types of walls: the bearing and nonbearing wall. The *bearing wall* is one that helps to support the weight of all that is above it—ceiling joists, rafters, insulation, and roofing. The *nonbearing wall* supports only its own weight. This type of wall is used as a partition wall or curtain wall, and serves to divide one large room into two smaller ones.

Nonbearing walls are almost always interior walls. They are composed of a sole plate, top plate, common studs, and a top cap which serves to tie the wall to its adjacent wall or walls. Nonbearing walls are usually covered with plywood, paneling, plasterboard, wallboard, or gypsum board, wallpaper, and occasionally plaster. Many nonbearing walls have doors as well.

Bearing walls may be interior or exterior. Interior bearing walls are composed of the same materials as the nonbearing walls. Exterior bearing walls will have cripple studs, doors, windows, corner bracing, corner posts, insulation, sheathing, and exterior covering composed most frequently of bricks, lap siding, vinyl, asphalt, or aluminum siding, shingles or shakes, or one of the plywood products which is then covered with paint or stain.

Of the two walls, the bearing wall is more important. It is the link between the foundation of the house and the roof, or upper story rooms. The nonbearing wall should be sturdily built. It can be decorated as carefully as bearing walls, but you do not have to be concerned about the strength of the wall, other than its ability to support itself, and to resist any pressures put upon it in the normal life patterns of the inhabitants of the house. It might receive an occasional bump of shove, but little more.

The primary concerns involving both types of walls is whether the walls are *plumb* (perfectly vertical), whether they have square corners, whether studding is spaced properly, cross-bridging is installed accurately, corners are supported adequately, and the components of the walls are sound, strong lumber. You do not want to use green lumber or lumber that is defective in any significant way. These defects consist largely of decay or fungus growth, checking or splitting, weaknesses caused by knotholes or improper dressing, and warping.

You should not use green lumber for several reasons. One of the most important reasons is that green lumber still contains a great deal of sap and water. Decay, or fungus spores, thrive in moisture-laden wood. Fungus growth requires at least 20 percent moisture content in wood, and dried or cured lumber does not have sufficient moisture for the spores to grow.

Green or sap-laden lumber also is very *pliant*. This fact means that the lumber will bend, twist, or warp easily, and it will not hold its shape when installed under stress conditions. A ridgepole made of green lumber might be straight when it is installed, but a year later (or much less) it will be bowed and twisted. Other timbers attached to the ridgepole also will be forced out of position, and your building will be a shambles in a very short time.

Another major problem with green wood is that the fibers are soft and not as dense. If you have sawed green wood and then sawed cured wood, you have seen an amazing difference. Green oak saws readily, but, cured oak is incredibly hard. The same is true of other wood as well. Sappy pine is extremely soft, but cured heart pine is as hard as hickory in terms of sawing.

When a nail is driven into a piece of wood, the thrust of the nail shoves wood fibers apart vigorously. The fibers, reacting according to their nature, shove back and attempt to regain their previous space. This tightness, created by the resistance of the fibers, is what gives nails their holding power. Therefore, the larger the nail, the greater the holding power. In green wood, the fibers are loose, and the nail sinks into the wood easily. The wood fibers, because they are packed loosely, do not offer the resistance, and the tightness is lacking. The holding power is diminished greatly. Later, when twisting and bowing occurs, the nails will pull partially from the wood, and the building is weakened drastically.

Green wood, then, is one of the major causes of problems in walls. When your wood arrives, reject any that is heavier than it should be for that size of timber. Similarly, reject timbers that are soft, sticky with sap or resin, or bowed and twisted. This type of wood will not serve you well, and because it is your money, you are entitled to get proper value.

Other problems, likely to occur in the new wall construction, are studs that are spaced incorrectly or which have bent or bowed after installation, corners that are not square, and sagging or weak sole plates and top plates.

Whether you are redecorating an existing wall or building a totally new wall, you need to be aware of problems that can exist. If you can spot these difficulties and correct them in the early stages, you will benefit yourself greatly. You can make several easy tests. If the wall structure, as it stands, fails any of the tests, make needed corrections immediately.

Troubleshooting Early Problems

First, among the tests, is a visual inspection of the wall framing. If you are redoing an older wall, remove all of the wall covering, so that only the framing and insulation, if any, remain. Examine the wall frame with a highly critical eye. Look for knotholes that have weakened timbers. Watch for dark patches in the studs and sole plates, particularly in the lower areas of the studs and where the studs join the sole plates.

If you are not familiar with the components of a wall, keep in mind that the sole plate is the timber, almost always a 2 × 4 in residential buildings, that runs along the subflooring for the length of a wall. The studs are the 2 × 4s that stand vertically inside the wall and are nailed to the sole plate. At the end of the wall there is, or should be, a corner post that is the stabilizer of the wall, and the nailing surface to which joining walls can be nailed. Running along the top ends of the corner posts and studs is the top plate, also a 2 × 4. The timber that lies across the top plate is called the *top cap* or the *double plate*. Under windows, and sometimes over doors, there is a short 2 × 4 called a *cripple stud*. (See Fig. 1-5.)

On the inside of the rough window opening, there is, or should be, a pair of trimmer studs, one on each side. Each trimmer stud is made up of two pieces, one under the rough sill and the other above it. Over the window there should be a long assembly made up of 2 × 4s or 2 × 6s or 2 × 8s called a *header*. Headers should also be found over all doors.

The corners of each room should be braced with some type of material that is strong enough to keep them from warping or from moving out of square. This bracing consists of either strips of thin steel running diagonally, 2 × 4s nailed between studs and in a straight diagonal line from sole plate to corner post, or boards installed in shallow cutouts in a diagonal line from sole plate to corner post. At times, the corner bracing is composed of a panel of plywood nailed vertically on each side of the corner on the outside.

If you see dark areas on sole plates, lower parts of studs, or corner posts, use the blade of a pocketknife or screwdriver to test the area. If the wood is soft, you need to replace the timber before you start to cover the wall. The darkness, if present, is probably the result of water that has somehow leaked into the wall or condensed, because no vapor barrier was installed. The water seeped along the studding and collected where the stud and sole plate join.

If your visual inspection locates no problems, make another check. Studding should be installed at 16-inch, on-center locations or with 24-inch, on-center spacing. The reason for this spacing is so that sheets of paneling or plywood will fit properly. A good fit means

Fig. 1-5. A cripple stud is sometimes placed under windows and over doors.

that the edges of the panels should stop halfway across the studding so that you have a good nailing surface.

You can check your studding very easily and in a very short time by using a tape measure, a rule, or a board cut at the proper length. The easiest way is to set the tape at 16 inches, use a rule, or length of board, and simply measure the distance from the center of one stud to the center of the next stud. If you find that the studs are spaced properly, you can go on to other work. If the studs are improperly spaced, you should make the necessary corrections at this time, unless you are not going to use any panels of any sort on interior or exterior walls. What this fact means is that your studs might be spaced at 14 inches on center and you will have adequate strength, but, if you plan to use any kind of panels, nailed either vertically or horizontally, the edges will not come out at the right locations. If you are going to use lap siding on the exterior and diagonal tongue and groove lumber on the interior, you do not need to worry about the stud spacing.

The method of correction of faulty stud spacing depends to a great extent on your time, money, and energy. If the studs are 1 or 2 inches off center, and you wish to knock out the studs and renail them in their proper locations, you can do so with a rather modest expenditure of time. It takes 10 minutes or less to remove and reinstall a stud. The problem is that, in the removing of the stud, you might damage the ends of the studs and weaken them beyond safe and strong use. It might be cheaper, in the long run, to nail in new studs beside the old ones, unless your economy dictates otherwise.

You might find that while studs are spaced properly at the top and bottom, where they join the sole plate and the top plate, they might bend or bow and be out of alignment halfway down the stud. Correcting this problem might be fairly simple. You can start at the first true stud beside the swayed ones and cut a 15-inch length of 2 × 4. You should start nailing on the side where the arc or bow is closer to the next stud. In other words, the stud bow should extend toward the stud where you will be working, not away from it.

Install the 15-inch length of 2 × 4 by wedging it between the studs as tightly as you can, then tap the top edge of the stud with a hammer until you have forced it into a horizontal position halfway down the stud. At this point, the bent stud should have been forced into a straight or vertical position. Now nail in the blocking piece (the 15-inch 2 × 4) by sinking nails through the sides of the two studs. Repeat this pattern wherever the stud spacing is wrong. Such correction requires only a few minutes and can save you much time and worry in the immediate future.

If your windows do not have headers installed above them, you should remedy this deficiency at once. Keep in mind that the single longest unsupported space in your house might well be that of the window without a header. You can construct a header by using two lengths of 2 × 6 exactly the length of the distance between the trimmer studs in the window opening and a similar length of 2 × 4. Stand a 2 × 6 on edge and place the 2 × 4 atop it flat so that the outer edges are flush, then nail the two pieces together with 16d nails. Nail in the second 2 × 6 in the same fashion, then install the header, closed end down, atop the ends of the trimmer studs or two inches higher than the top of the upper window sash. Nail either at an angle through the sides of the header or, if you can, through the back side of the stud and into the header.

Check the sole plate to see that it is not weakened by decay or splitting. If the sole plate is defective, you must disassemble the entire wall frame, then replace the sole plate, and reassemble the wall frame. This process will involve a great deal of work, but it is better to do it now than to wait and have to rebuild the entire wall, (covering as well as the framing).

Make a visual inspection of the alignment of the edges of the studding and corner post, both inside and outside. If an edge protrudes further than the others, this edge will cause siding or wall covering to be irregular and ill-fitting. Correct the problem by using a hammer to knock the stud back into position, if you can. If you must, loosen the stud and renail it. If the stud is too wide for the sole plate and other studs, you must either replace it, take it out and plane it down to size, or use a circular saw and reduce it to size.

One easy way to check alignment is to find a long, straight board, or timber, and place it with its edge in contact with the studding, against the wall framing, horizontally. The timber should be in contact with every stud along the wall or, if not in actual contact, the discrepancy should be only $\frac{1}{16}$ inch or less. Make this check both inside and outside, and check at the top, midpoint, and bottom of the studding. It is possible that a stud will bow inward or outward, rather than from side to side, as a result of warping, if the stud was installed uncured.

Also check to see that window framing and door framing are flush with the wall line. If the framing is out of line, make the necessary adjustments.

You should check also to see if electrical switch boxes, plug installations, and pipes are aligned with the wall.

Do not neglect to use a square, the larger the better, to check corners for squareness. You can check both inside and outside to ensure that you have the needed accuracy.

You can use your level to ensure that walls are plumb. Use a tape measure to check the distance from the upper left corner to the lower right corner, then from the upper right corner to the lower left corner. The distance should be exactly the same or certainly within a fraction of an inch of being the same.

Use the tape measure to check distance from the outside of the corner post to the far end of the wall frame. Measure at the top, middle, and bottom. If a serious discrepancy exists in any of the readings, double check your measurements, and if the problem still exists, you need to make corrections, if it is possible to do so at this point in your construction.

If your wall frame is in excellent or correct shape, you can move on to Chapter 4: Installing Insulation. If any serious problems exist, see Chapter 2: Correcting Difficulties, for additional help.

2
Correcting Difficulties

IN THE PREVIOUS CHAPTER YOU WERE GIVEN SEVERAL PROBLEMS TO watch for in wall construction, along with brief suggestions for correcting the major difficulties. In this chapter, detailed step-by-step corrections will be suggested for installation of studding and sole plates, and suggestions will be made for removing and reinstalling studding. You also will be told how to shape studding that is dressed incorrectly, as well as how to modify improperly installed window and door framing.

First, if you need only to replace one or two studs that are out of alignment, you can do so with minimum damage to the studding or the sole plate, simply follow the directions and suggestions that are provided here.

Studding is installed in one of two ways—both difficult to correct or remove. In the first way, the wall frame is assembled while the components lie on the subflooring and then the entire assembly is raised as one unit. In the second way, the corner posts are installed on a sole plate that are already nailed in place, and the studs are toenailed to the sole plate. More efficient carpenters drive in two nails from one side and then two more from the other side.

The problem in this assembly is obvious. If the studs are nailed in through the sole plate and if you loosen the stud by driving it to one side or the other, you must bend the nails. Bent nails will cause damage to the end of the stud and, perhaps, will render it useless. If the studs are toenailed, you can drive the stud to one side only by forcing the nails on the opposite side through the edges of the wood. This action will also seriously damage the end of the stud. So, how can the stud be removed with little or no damage?

First, when nails are driven up through the sole plate, the best way to free the stud is to insert a hacksaw blade under the end of the stud and saw the nails in two. Nails are only lengths of shaped wire with a head on them. They saw very quickly and easily. You might have to saw through a small amount of wood if the stud is fitted extremely closely, but the hacksaw blade will move through the wood with ease. When you reach the first nail, saw by moving the blade with short, smooth strokes. You can feel the saw move through the nail. You should keep sawing until you reach and saw the second nail. When you have sawed both nails, you can swing the end of the stud free and then you can pull it from the two nails holding it at the top plate.

When you have freed the stud at the top plate, you will not be able to remove the nails because you would have to drive them upward and into the top cap—unless no top cap was installed. If the top cap is not installed, drive the nails upward and then pull them out by using a ladder and crowbar. If there is a top cap, you will need to use the hacksaw blade again and saw off the nails flush with the wood on the bottom edge of the top plate.

You might be able to make your work slightly easier by using a pair of good pliers to remove the nails. You can grasp the nail with the jaws of the pliers as closely to the wood as possible, and then bend the nail back and forth until the nail breaks. The nail usually will break within five or six bends, and damage will not occur to the top plate or the stud.

When you install the stud in its proper place, you will not be able to nail it as it was before. You will have to toenail it on both sides and on both ends—to the sole plate and to the top plate. Use two, 16d nails on each side.

Your job will be slightly more difficult if the stud was toenailed into the sole plate and top plate. Your best approach is to use your hammer and try to drive the stud ½ inch or so to one side or the other. Start at the sole plate and hit the stud about 6 inches above the nail heads. Do not drive the stud far enough that you damage the wood.

After you have moved the stud slightly, go to the other side and drive the stud back to its former position. When you do so, you will force the nails that are on the far side slightly from their seats. When you drive the stud back to its original position, you will find that the nail heads on the opposite side now stick out ¼ to ½ inch. You will now be able to get the claws of a crowbar on the nail head, and can then pull the nails out with little difficulty.

Now you can drive the stud in the opposite direction and free the remaining two nails, or you can use the same approach you used on the first nails and pull them from the wood by using a hammer or crowbar. You might even be able to get hammer claws or crowbar claws on the nail head without forcing the stud to either side, if the nails are not sunk fully. Consequently, you can remove the stud easily.

You probably will have to turn the hammer or crowbar so that it is parallel with the sole plate, or nearly parallel, in order to get the claws on the nail head. You might be able to use the blade of a large screwdriver behind the nail head to pry it out so that you can use the claws. One very old trick is to place the claws of one hammer at an angle so they will cut into the wood slightly. With the claws near the nail head, hit the face of the hammer with a second hammer and drive the claws onto the nail head. You can drive the claws of a crowbar over the nail head in the same fashion. (See Fig. 2-1.)

If you encounter problems with the previous method, you can always go back to the hacksaw blade to cut the nails and free the stud. When the sole plate end is free, you can work the stud back and forth and free it from the top plate. One effective way to free the stud at the top is to work the stud until the nails have pulled slightly out, and then slip the end of a crowbar between the stud and top plate and pry gently until the stud is fully freed.

When you install the stud again, do not use the same nail holes. You will get very little holding power if you do. Instead, move slightly to the side of the previous nail holes

Fig. 2-1. You will have to work the claws of the crowbar between the end of the stud and the sole plate. Then pry upward and outward at the same time.

and drive the nails back into the stud. This method will be sturdy and strong. Do not drive nails through the edges of the stud unless you can sink them so that they are fully flush with the wood. Otherwise, they will cause the wall covering to stick out slightly at that point. Also, you might hit the nails with new nails driven through the siding or wall covering panels.

It is possible that all of your studs are improperly spaced and you need to use wall covering panels, so it will be necessary to respace all the studding. Before you start, go to the corner post and measure from the outside edge of the post to a point 16 inches away. Mark the spot on the edge of the sole plate. Make the mark heavy enough to be seen clearly and easily. Then measure from that mark to another point, also 16 inches away. Keep repeating this process until you have marked the entire sole plate. Do the same with the top plate and then, to double check, drop a plumb line from the top plate to the sole plate. The two marks should line up almost perfectly. You now can install the studs.

When you come to the end of the wall frame and there is not enough room to install another stud on a 16-inch center and still have 16 inches between that stud and the corner post, go ahead and install the stud, even if it means that the stud is only a foot or so from the corner post. Your major concern is that you will have proper nailing surfaces for your wall covering.

It is probable that your wall, unless it was especially well planned, will not be the exact length to accommodate full widths of wall-covering panels. This difference in length is not a major problem. When you start putting up wall covering, start at the end from which you have measured for 16-inch on-center spacing, and continue nailing up panels until you reach the final full space. Then stand the final piece of siding in place and mark the piece along the outside edge of the corner post. Saw and nail the final portion of a panel into place. More details on this process will be provided in chapters 5, 6, and 7.

CORRECTING WALLS WITHOUT SOLE PLATES

Occasionally, you will find a wall erected years ago that has studding nailed directly to the subflooring, with no sole plates used. At times, this type of wall framing was installed by individuals working alone. They lacked the strength to lift an entire wall frame and decided to save a little money by not including a sole plate.

More likely is the possibility that the builder installed a sole plate but leakage and seepage of water and dampness created an ideal fungus growth environment, and the sole plate had fallen victim to decay. If this has occured, it must be replaced. This procedure is a very difficult one, and should be undertaken only when it is highly essential.

To install a sole plate under an existing wall, you must first realize that it is virtually impossible to install the plate in one piece, although it is recommended that the plate consist of one long timber. What you need to do first is start at one end and use the hacksaw blade or, in some way, free the sole plate ends of all studs in the first half of the wall. Do the same with the corner post, but do not take the post or the studs down at this time. If a sole plate was used but it must be replaced, cut through the sole plate at two or three places so that you can remove it from under the studs when you are ready.

Beside the sole plate, or studs, erect a 2-×-4 timber or, even better, a 4-×-4 timber, with a length of 2-×-4 doubled or a short length of 4-×-4 that will reach over a span of three or so rafters. Nail the short length, or lengths, of timbers in a T-shape on top of the 4 × 4 or 2 × 4, and fit this assembly tightly under the rafters. This procedure will ensure that the end of the wall frame will be well supported when you remove the sole plate.

Remember, this procedure is to be done only if there is no safe way of avoiding it. It is sometimes necessary, however. Therefore, we've included it in this chapter.

With the T-construction in place and ready to support the full weight of that end of the wall frame, gently remove the ends of enough studs so that you can remove the section of sole plate under the studs. Preferably, this should be one-third of the entire length of the wall frame.

Start at one end; install the new sole plate under the corner post and the first few studs. When the sole plate portion is in position, nail it to the subflooring. Then position the end of the corner post and nail it to the sole plate by toenailing through the lower edges of the corner post.

Next, nail the ends of the studs into place. When the entire portion of new sole plate is installed and all studs are again nailed securely, you can take down the T-support and move it to the next rafters. Install it again securely and repeat the entire process. Move the ends of the studding slightly to one side, remove the portion of sole plate, and install the new portion. Renail the studs to the sole plate, which has been nailed to the subflooring.

Finally, move the T-support to the final third of the wall and, again, repeat the process. When you are finished, you have a sole plate that, although not as efficient and strong as a single unit of timber would have been, is decidedly better than no sole plate or a decayed one.

One important point to remember: do not join the sole plate under a stud. Let the ends of the pieces meet between studs. You can cut a 15-inch section of 2 × 4, nail it between the studs to the sole plate, lapping the joint for maximum strength.

Why is the sole plate so important to the strength and the stability of a wall frame? As mentioned earlier, the sole plate is the link between the foundation, subflooring, the wall, and the roof. If the sole plate decays, it will slowly disintegrate and allow the wall to sink slightly, up to the 2-inch depth of the thickness of the sole plate. If sinking occurs, molding might be pulled loose from ceilings; wall coverings of all sorts (except bricks and other masonry products) might pull free or be poorly supported; and the entire wall will be ruined or severely damaged.

Also, if the sole plate decays, the decay is likely to spread to the ends of the studding and corner post. If these wall components fail to support the wall, it will be held in place only by the top capping, the tie-ins of the corner posts, partition wall studs, and similar nailing surfaces.

STUDS

When studs are bent and bowed so that you cannot straighten them by using blocking, you might need to remove them and replace them will better studding. If the studs are salvageable, though, you have several alternatives. First, if the studs are extremely bowed, they might be starting to pull the nails out of the sole plate and top plate. If you use the blocking procedure described in Chapter 1 you might succeed in straightening the studs, but you have done little to add strength to the wall because the nails have been extracted from the sole plate. Even if they are forced back into the sole plate, the wood fibers have been so worn by this time that little holding power is left.

No matter what type of interior wall covering you plan to use, solutions to the problem do exist. If you plan to use plywood or paneling, the solution is easy. It is even easier if you are planning to use horizontal, vertical, or diagonal tongue and groove boards.

Because the horizontal and diagonal boards cross several studs, you will not have to make any changes, as long as the deformed studding will not present a problem with the exterior wall covering. For instance, you can use bricks and other masonry products with little, if any, difficulty. So the blocking method already described will work well because you need to only bring the studs as vertical as possible and add a nail or so in each end of the studs to provide extra holding power.

Of the two types of wall sheathing, the horizontal does not provide quite as much strength as does the diagonal nailing. The main strength of the diagonal boards is that the boards reinforce in a side-to-side fashion, as well as an up-and-down manner.

Vertical wall covering, particularly boards, adds little to the strength of the wall, except by lending ceiling support and by reinforcing the studding. If the studding is weakened in the manner already described, even this support is lacking. You can, in a very simple way, add support and provide an excellent nailing surface for exterior wall covering by following a simple pattern.

First, you can nail in blocking to bring the studding back into conformity. Then you can select three long and very straight boards, either 4-inch or 5-inch lengths. Next, fasten one end of one board to the corner post and let the edge of the board rest against the subflooring. Drive two or three nails into the board and corner post for added strength, and then put a pair of nails through the board and into the sole plate, between the corner post and the first stud.

When you reach the first stud, start three nails into the board so that the nails are in line with the center of the stud. Use blocking to force the stud back to a straight position as far as you can get it. Then drive the nails into the stud. Follow this procedure the rest of the way across the wall.

Next, move to the first corner post and fasten the end of the second board to the corner post by driving in one nail halfway up the post. Go to the other corner post and lift the other end of the board until it is level. Use three nails to fasten the end to the corner post. Then return to the first corner post and add two more nails. The reason for using only one nail in the first post is that two or more nails make it very difficult for you to maneuver the other end of the board into position.

Both ends of the board are now well anchored. Your next step is to fasten the studs to the board. Before you do any nailing, pull or block the studs until they are as straight as you can get them. Then, sink three nails into the board and into the stud. Do the same with all the other studs.

Finally, nail up the third board at the top so that the board overlaps the top plate. Nail to the corner posts, to the studs, and to the top plate. You can complete nailing to the sole plate at the bottom, if you have not already done so.

When you are ready to nail up the vertical boards, you have three good nailing surfaces and the studs are also strengthened: You can add other boards between the three you have already installed if you want greater strength and better support for the vertical boards.

One of the major reasons for adding three or more boards is that you need them, with the sole plates and top plate, to support the vertical boards between studs. The boards will also give and bend when you push against them. Even if your studs are straight, you need to install nailers for the boards.

MODIFYING DOOR AND WINDOW OPENINGS

Some of the most difficult problems to correct in a wall frame are improperly framed door and window openings. Your job is much easier if the doors and windows have not yet been installed and if the door and window facing is not nailed in place. All you need to do is remove the side jambs and top jamb of the windows or door and use wedges or blocks for a proper fit. The jambs are the boards that actually make up the inside of the doorway or window opening.

If the facing is already installed, remove it gently by first prying the molding loose. Insert the blade of a large screwdriver under the molding and pry out in a slow, firm manner. Do not pry with too much force or you will break the molding. Start the screwdriver where you can see a tiny crack between the molding and the facing. When you have opened a small space, insert another screwdriver blade 3 or 4 inches from the first one. Continue in this fashion to loosen the molding all the way to the floor or to the top of the doorway. Remove the molding when you have loosened it all the way and then remove the top molding. You can now free and remove the molding from the other side of the doorway or window.

When you have removed all of the molding, you will have three door framing pieces to take off. Two of these pieces extend from the floor to the top of the doorway, and one piece crosses and fits to the top edge of the first two framing pieces.

Remove the side framing pieces first and then take off the top framing section. You probably will have to perform this same operation on both sides of the doorway.

After the framing is removed, you can adjust the door jambs. If the problem is with the top jamb, you will have to remove the entire jamb assembly. If the problem is with one side, you can make the necessary adjustments with the jambs in place, but, you might have to pry one side loose temporarily.

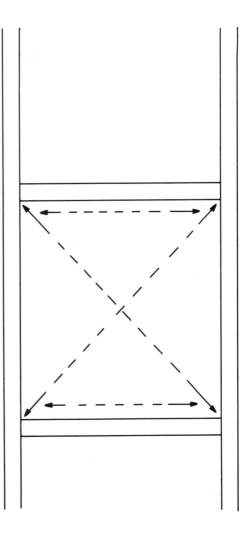

Fig. 2-2. Measure the window opening at four points to determine where the problem lies. You then will have to use shims or wedges or reframe the window.

Use your square and tape measure to determine where the problem is located. Measure first from floor to the bottom of the top jamb on both sides, and then compare distances. If the two are identical or very nearly the same, the problem lies in the side jambs. Measure across the doorway at the top, middle, and bottom. Again compare distances. If you have a considerable deviation, you know that the side jambs are installed incorrectly, but at this point you cannot determine which one is wrong. (See Fig. 2-2.)

Use your square in all four corners of the doorway to see which of the corners is out of square. If the two corners on one side are square, move to the other side and check those corners for squareness. Use a crowbar to pry the side jamb until the square shows that the corner is correct. When you correct one corner, you will, in all probability, correct the other at the same time, unless the difficulty lies in the subflooring. (See Fig. 2-3.)

With the jamb positioned so that the corners are square, you can look behind the jamb to see how much space there is between the jamb and the trimmer stud. A small distance or gap will probably exist near the top. The gap will widen as you move down the jamb. At the subflooring level, the gap will probably be widest.

Fig. 2-3. You can use a long square in window or door corners to see if the corner is square or, if not, how far off square it is.

You can correct the jamb difficulty by finding a block of wood 6 inches or so long, 4 inches wide, and just thick enough to fill the gap. You might have to use a block as thick as a 2 × 4, or a 1-inch board might be sufficient. As you move from the widest to the narrowest part of the gap, you will need a thinner block. You do not want a block thick enough to cause the jamb to stick out farther than is needed. (See Fig. 2-4.)

With the blocks in place, drive a finishing nail through the jamb, into the block, and then into the trimmer stud. Do not overnail, but, use enough nails to hold the block in place. When the jamb is correct, you can nail the molding and facing back into place. The problem should be solved.

Window problems are solved in basically the same way. Take off the molding and the facing. In many modern homes, the window sash itself will fit inside a track fastened

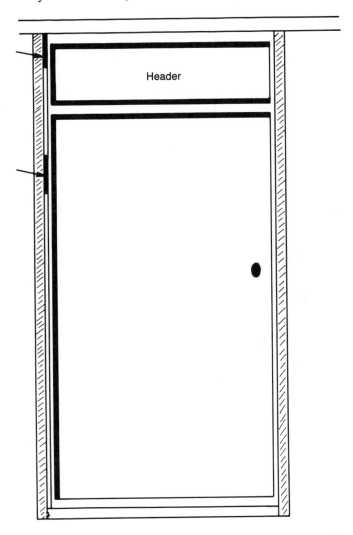

Fig. 2-4. Use thin wedges to bring door jambs back to a true vertical position. Use thick wedges at the worst positions and thinner ones in the closer points.

to the jamb by small nails. You should not have to disturb the sashes or tracks in order to correct the window problem.

Measure the window opening the same way you measured the doorway, and then use a square to determine which corner is the source of the problem. You can also pry the window jambs loose, as you did with the doorway. Then install blocks or wedges behind the jamb and reassemble the window framing and molding. You are then ready to move to the next work area. (See Fig. 2-5.)

One of the next tasks facing you is that of working around pipes and electrical switch boxes. In many states or municipalities very strict laws exist governing the installation

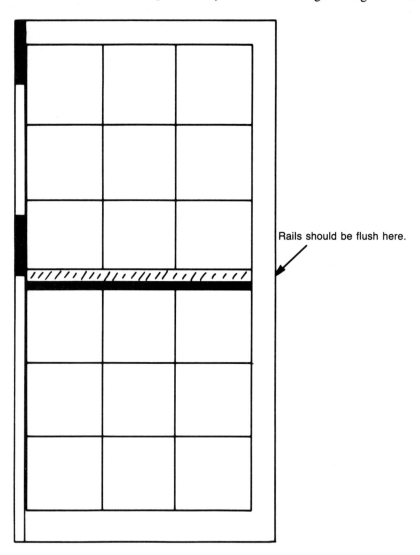

Rails should be flush here.

Fig. 2-5. Be sure that top and bottom rails are flush, then mark window positions and add wedges behind jambs.

of electrical wiring. Some of these laws state that only a licensed electrician can be hired to wire a house, or to do any wiring repair in a house.

Other laws state that any home owner may do the wiring in his own home; however, he must inform the building inspector, who can examine and approve the wiring. What this means is that you, even though you are not a licensed electrician, can wire your own home, as long as the wiring meets the building standards in your area. By the same token, a man who wires his own home and has had the wiring accepted by the building inspector cannot legally wire your house for you, even though his work is admittedly of an excellent nature, unless he is licensed as an electrician.

If you plan to change any wiring while you are working on the walls, be advised that the work must meet local inspection codes. You do not, however, have to modify wiring in any form to install insulation, sheathing, and other wall coverings around the switch boxes already installed in your house. Chapter 3 offers suggestions to prepare you for wiring and plumbing needs.

3
Preparing for Wiring and Plumbing Needs

EVEN THOUGH YOU MIGHT NOT BE QUALIFIED AS AN ELECTRICIAN OR plumber, and have no desire to do any of the plumbing or wiring in your house or added room, you can help prepare for the electrician and the plumber. You can also learn to deal with the pipes and wires that are inside the wall, when the electrician and the plumber leave and you take over.

First, the laws governing the electrical requirements for a house are a necessary and legal part of home construction for do-it-yourself home repair, and home improvement. In many areas of the country, the number of closets in a house determine the size, or capacity, of your septic tank. This example is just one instance of bureaucracy. Some laws and regulations maintain that any room that has a closet can be modified into a bedroom. The number of bedrooms in a house governs the number of people who might reside in that house and, by extension, use the bathroom. Bathroom usage, in turn, affects the size of the septic tank. Part of the consideration also revolves around the number of people who will have clothing which needs to be washed, and the amount of washing machine water that will empty into the septic tank. If you live in the city, and are on a city sewage hookup, you are not directly involved with the legal aspects and building requirements governing rural living.

Electrical codes also have their oddities; you must learn to accept these requirements. You will find, for instance, that in some localities the building code requires a wall receptacle or socket every 10 feet, or similar arbitrary distance.

Before you do any plumbing or call in the electrician, you can examine your own needs and be ready to offer the serviceman your ideas, notions, and needs. For instance, even though you must have a specific number of receptacles in a room, most building codes do not state where these receptacles must be installed. For unclear reasons, nearly everyone has receptacles installed along the baseboards in rooms. Then they move tables, television sets, and other furniture in front of the receptacles to conceal them from view.

People then experience considerable difficulties in unplugging the appliances that are connected to the baseboard receptacles. If you choose to do so, you can have your receptacles installed waist-high so that they are much easier to reach, as long as you don't find the appearance annoying. The point here is that you can make your decisions in light of your own needs, desires, and tastes.

When you have decided where you want the receptacles to be installed, consult with the electrician to see if the choice is feasible and complies with the building code. When you are satisfied, you can begin to get the wall framing ready for the work.

When you know the path the wiring must take, you can decide whether you want the wiring attached with clips and staples to the studding, or whether you want the studding notched so that the wiring is recessed. One advantage of recessed wiring is that there is less danger that the wiring will be damaged by settling of the house, or by rodents, such as mice and squirrels. These animals somehow manage to invade millions of houses and find some irresistible attraction in electrical wiring.

The electrician can tell you where the wiring will emerge from under the house and into the walls, and what path the wiring must take for the most efficient wiring scheme. Once you know the path, you can mark studs, and notch them shallowly so that the wiring can be inserted inside the notch and stabilized there.

Notching is very simple and easy. All you need to do is measure up the stud to the point where the wire will pass, and mark the stud. Then use a small saw, such as a keyhole saw or even the blade of a hacksaw, and saw into the stud for 1 inch. You should angle the cut upward at about a 45-degree angle. When that cut is made, move 1½ inches above it and start another cut that will slant downward and meet the first cut. The wedge of wood will then fall from the stud and can be discarded. (See Fig. 3-1.)

If angle cutting is difficult, you can saw directly across the grain of the stud making the cut 1 inch deep. Move up 1 inch and repeat the cut. Using a wood chisel, or the blade of a large screwdriver, place the blade at the back of the cut and hit the handle of the screwdriver or the chisel with a hammer. Tap lightly until the segment of wood is broken loose and removed.

You can notch all studs that will have wire going past them. If the wire simply passes across the stud, repeated pressures on the wall covering, such as paneling, might cause the wire covering to be damaged, leaving exposed wire.

Your choice of where to install switch boxes is somewhat limited. For convenience, you will probably want switches just inside doorways. This feature will enable you to reach inside a darkened room and flip on a light switch without having to enter the room; therefore, limiting accidental injuries in the dark.

The height of the wall switch is usually 4 feet from the floor. This fact means that the actual switch is 48 inches high but the switch plate starts 2 inches or so below that point, and extends a similar distance above it.

The location beside the door, and 4 feet off the floor, is a logical choice, but you need to decide how close to the door the switch actually will be. Remember, you have to leave room for the door framing and facing between the doorway and the switch. In most wall frames, there are usually double studs at doorways, one for the regular stud function and one trimmer stud. You can select the inside edge of the trimmer stud as the best place for the switch box. Mark the exact location before starting to install the box itself.

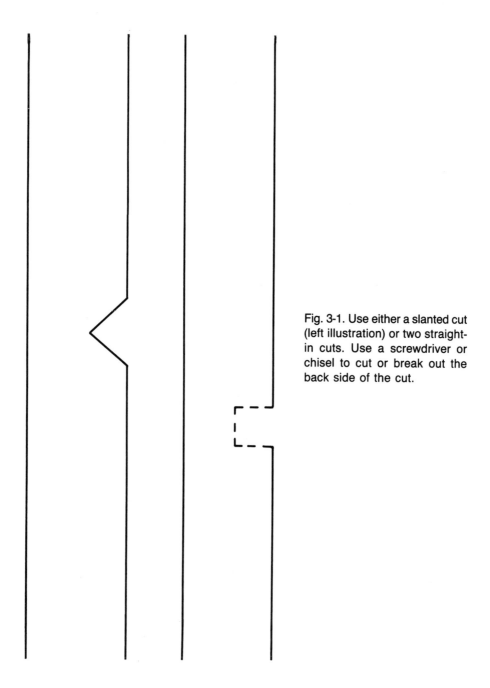

Fig. 3-1. Use either a slanted cut (left illustration) or two straight-in cuts. Use a screwdriver or chisel to cut or break out the back side of the cut.

You can install the box by using either long screws or nails. On the side of the box, you will see long holes extending in tubular shapes alongside the housing. The nail will slip easily through the hole, and you can then drive it into the wood of the stud. You can also use the elongated screws (often the screws come with the switch boxes). Slip the screws into the holes. Then tap the screw head lightly with a hammer to cause the point of the screw to penetrate the wood shallowly. Use a screwdriver to completely sink the screw, until the switch box is firmly and securely fastened to the stud. Do not leave any gaps or slack that would allow the switch box to move around on the stud. The movement could eventually wear away the protective covering on the wiring, or cause a screw, holding the wires in place, to come free.

Installing electrical receptacles is an easy task, but at times, the decision as to where to place them can be difficult. It has been estimated that at least 50 jobs in the typical home require good lighting. Good lighting, in this case, means sufficient artificial lighting is placed properly, and is of the correct intensity and has the correct glare factor.

In the ordinary home, the family will spend a great deal of time in the kitchen, family room or living room, bathroom, and bedroom. Home tasks, hobbies, and special interests include preparing meals, eating, extensive studying, reading, watching television, sewing, doing the laundry, cleaning, telephoning, personal grooming, dressing, caring for infants, keeping records, enjoying photography and similar avocations, and projects in maintaining the house. All of these efforts require adequate lighting. Before you decide where to install receptacles, you should consider where the family activities will be spent, predominantly.

Certainly, you should consider the major lighting needs that involve four central areas: living areas, work areas, private areas, and moving areas such as stairways, halls, entrances, garages, and driveways. Keep in mind, too, that light enhances the colors in your home. Walls, furniture, rugs and carpets, and appliances can look better, or worse, depending upon the quality of the lighting in the rooms. People's looks can also improve under good lighting.

Choose locations for receptacles that will offer the best lighting for the jobs, or interests, that will occupy a major portion of your family's leisure and task time. When you have made your decisions, you can begin installing many, if not all, of the receptacles for your house. You can install the receptacle box in much the same way as the switch box.

If you hold the receptacle box flat, with the plug facing you, you will see the long holes, mentioned earlier, near the front and back of the box. You install the box by using the same kind of long screws, or nails, that were used in the switch box. Nail the box to the side of the stud.

The electrician will install the actual plugs and switches, but you can have the boxes ready for him. By doing so, you will save him considerable time, and you will save yourself a serious amount of money.

When you are installing the switch boxes, 2-inch nails generally work well. One practice that is sound and safe is to mount the switch box between studs, but on a temporary basis, until the actual wall covering is installed. You can mount the boxes on temporary hangers and leave them there until you are ready to install wall covering, at which time you can free the box from the hangers and adjust them so that the front of the boxes will be flush with the completed wall surface.

If you do not take the time to do the temporary mounting, you might find that when you start to install the switch box cover plate, the screws will not reach the mounting holes, and the covers cannot be installed. You will be forced to take the box loose and remount it.

Metal hangers are available for easier installation if you wish to modernize from the traditional method of nailing the box to a stud. These hangers can be used for both switch boxes and receptacles, often called outlets. You can fasten the hangers between studs and then simply attach the boxes to the hangers.

You will find that the wiring you work with will probably be of two types: a nonmetallic-sheathed cable without a ground wire and a nonmetallic-sheathed cable with a ground wire. Some of the sheathing is black, some white. The color is immaterial.

If you do not wish to notch studs, you can use an electric drill or auger and drill holes in studs just large enough to let the wiring cables slip through. Some building experts feel that the holes drilled in studs weaken studding less than notched holes, and is also less time-consuming and energy-consuming. The actual wiring is usually brought into the house up through the sole plate or down through the top plate and top cap.

If you should decide to wire your own house, the procedure that is recommended is to bring the wiring, or cable, from the service panel at the outside meter location, through the sole plate, or top plate, and through the stud holes to the switch box, receptacle, or outlet box. Allow plenty of slack in the wire so that you will not have to pull the wire and place undue strain on it. Usually, anywhere from 18 inches up to 2 feet of wiring should be allowed for this application.

You can use a pocketknife to strip the outside covering from the wiring cable, but do not, at this time, strip the insulation from the wires. The box will have knockout plates in the metal, unless they have already been tapped out. Push the wires through the holes and then, with the wires in place, tighten the lock nut securely.

Do not, under any circumstances, work with live electric wires. If the wiring has already been installed, and you are changing a light fixture, turn off the power at the outside box. You will be told that if the wall switch is off, there can be no current reaching the light. This statement might be true; however, it is recommended that you take no chances.

If you are changing an outlet or receptacle, it is not a foolish precaution to turn off the electric power in the house. If you cannot do so without complications, then, by all means, take the following precautions. Switch on a lamp, radio, or similar small appliance, and be certain that it works. Then plug it into the outlet you are working on to see whether it works. If it does not, try it again in a live outlet. If it works before and after being plugged into the "dead" receptacle, it is fairly safe to assume that the outlet is not live.

The simplest way to change a switch, outlet, or light fixture is to remove the cover plate (with the power off to the outlet) and note how the defective switch, or receptacle, is installed. You can make your own drawings of the exact manner of installation. Note what wires are attached to what screws. Write down which colors are installed at which locations. Then, power still off, remove the faulty switch and replace it with the new one, following the exact procedure, except in reverse, that you used in removing the old switch.

Do the preceeding procedure with light fixtures. With the house power off, flip the light fixture switch several times to be sure that there is no possible way for the light to have current.

You will be told repeatedly that you are being overly cautious. We feel that when you are working with electricity, unless you are highly experienced, you cannot be too careful.

When you have brought the wiring to the described points, you can leave the work for the electrician to complete. Whoever does the final work, no matter how experienced he is, must still call the building inspector so that he can examine the wiring. He must pass the job before the power can be turned on permanently.

PLANNING FOR PLUMBING NEEDS

You have been told already of some of the plumbing codes that are in effect in various parts of the country. You might not be permitted by law to do any of the actual plumbing work for your house or special building project.

Some municipalities require that all plumbing be done only by licensed plumbers. Some small, rural communities have few, if any, county regulations. Check with local authorities before you make any real efforts to have plumbing installed.

No matter what laws govern the actual plumbing, you can still do some of the rough work preparatory to the plumbing itself. You will need many tools and equipment, so you will probably come out cheaper by hiring a licensed plumber.

Still, you can do some planning and roughing-in. You can also have a voice in what materials go into the walls. The plumber might wish to install galvanized pipes and you might prefer copper or plastic tubing.

You can also voice your opinions on where, and how, you would like fixtures to be located, and where you would like water lines installed. If you live in a cold area, water pipes installed up through outside walls have a much greater risk of freezing and breaking. Similarly, there will be more condensation and dripping on pipes in outside walls.

Any work or planning you do on roughing-in the plumbing should be done with several factors in mind. First, it is less expensive to stack plumbing or install back-to-back supply systems. Stack plumbing means that if you are adding an upstairs bathroom to your house, install the new bathroom over the downstairs bathroom, so that you can save money and labor by using many of the already installed pipes. If the new addition that requires plumbing is to be added to the ground floor, try to plan it so that you can install back-to-back pipes and thus save time, money, and energy. (See Fig. 3-2.)

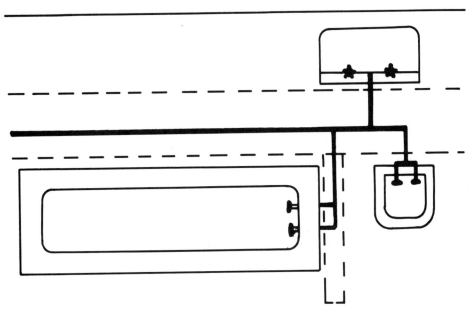

Fig. 3-2. If you can arrange your plumbing so that kitchen and bathroom are back-to-back, or so that two baths are back-to-back or one above the other, you will save money.

When you are planning your plumbing, it is wise to plan for the future, as well as for the present. For instance, if you think you might expand in the near future, it is much easier to install, or have the plumber install, extra T-joints with plugs, while he is working than it would be to cut into the existing plumbing system to make connections later. To add later, you would have to pay someone to open walls or floors. The inconvenience of having the debris and workers in your living area is considerable.

Plan, if you can do so feasibly, to have all of your bathroom fixtures located on the same wall. By doing so, you can save on pipe, space, money, and worry. Later, if you have trouble with the pipes, the plumber will have to open only that one wall, or he can do the work under the house.

If you choose the vertical or stacked arrangement, again try to keep the pipes all on one wall. You can imagine the problems you would encounter if you had plumbing difficulties, and the plumber had to open both walls upstairs and downstairs along the plumbing lines.

While the wall frames are still open, decide upon the exact height of lavatories, sinks, and other fixtures. The roughed-in plumbing will depend upon these heights, and it will be very difficult to change after you install the wall coverings.

Normal height for sinks and lavatories is 33 to 35 inches, but you might need to modify this height in terms of your own uses and needs. Very tall, or very short, people have difficulty in using sinks that are at an awkward height for them. You need to consider too, the extent to which children will be affected by the height of the sinks and lavatories.

Investigate the possibility of having the plumber hire you as an assistant. If he will permit you to help, you will save money and learn a great deal about plumbing.

You can, for instance, drill holes in the studs to admit the water lines. To do so, mark a spot halfway between the top and the bottom of the stud. Use an electric drill or a hand-operated auger. Never drill or bore a hole in a stud larger than ¼ the width of the stud. A hole any larger will weaken the stud excessively.

By the same token, you should not notch a stud more than ¼ of its width. If you must notch for wiring or pipe, the 1-inch suggestion, made earlier, should be observed. Try, also, to keep the notch within 4 to 6 inches of the end of the stud or joist. If a joist must be notched deeply, try to make the notch at the top and then run a length of 2 × 4, or at least a 1-inch board, along the joist, just under the cut, and for 3 or 4 feet total.

After the plumbing is installed, and you suddenly have a problem with your water lines or faucets, you can make several repairs without calling a plumber. Prevention, though, is better than repair. Following are a few ways you can prevent damage from freezing.

Two major ways exist to prevent freezing. The first is use of insulation, and the second is to keep the water moving. Generally speaking, insulation does not stop heat loss. It merely reduces the rate of loss. If a water line is insulated extremely well but the water remains motionless over a period of freezing weather, the water in the pipe will eventually be lowered to the freezing point. To prevent freezing, you need to have the water moving, at least slightly. A dripping faucet is often sufficient to prevent water from freezing.

You also need to keep the insulation dry on the pipes. Few materials are as warm when they are wet as they are when they are dry. Because of the moisture factor, it is difficult to insulate pipe laid in the ground. Your major protection is to lay the pipe below the frost or freeze line. In most areas of the country an 18-inch depth is recommended.

You can purchase electric heating cables for use on pipes in your home. These cables are also useful in thawing out pipes that have frozen.

One very important step you can perform is that of wrapping pipes with insulation before the wall coverings are added. The insulation especially is needed on the cold water pipes for two reasons: to cut down on condensation and to keep the water cool for drinking purposes. The wrapped pipe also should be wrapped in a good vapor barrier to prevent condensation from collecting over a period of time, inside the insulation.

If you install outside faucets, you can buy frost-proof varieties that will help prevent freezing. You can also see that an ample number of cutoffs for water are installed in the house at all crucial points. There should be a cutoff under each sink and lavatory, at each toilet, and in other critical areas. There should be a hydrant cutoff at each outside faucet, and in very cold weather, the hydrant cutoff should be used. You should open the faucet to drain the water and prevent freezing.

Before the walls are covered, insist that the plumbing system be given a rigorous test. Check for leaks at all fittings and joints. Check to see that there is satisfactory draining of all pipes carrying away waste water. Faucets should open and close satisfactorily.

Simple Plumbing Repairs

No matter how carefully you check, there will be times when you need to repair some simple elements of your plumbing. These problems range from leaking faucets to faulty toilet fixtures. You can do a large number of repair jobs if you will follow the simple steps described here. If you have a leaky faucet—one of the most common problems in the home—you can repair it in the following manner. First, turn off the water supply at the nearest cutoff. There should be one under the sink. Remove the handle to the faucet by unscrewing the holding screw in the top of the handle. Lift the handle off. Then remove the packing nut, the packing, and the faucet stem. If the stem is stubborn, set the handle back in place and use it to turn the stem so that you can remove it. You will find a screw holding a washer in place. Remove the screw, take out the washer, and replace it. An extremely large portion of leaking faucets are created by a worn or damaged washer.

If a faucet creates an unusually large amount of noise when the water is running, you can press down on the handle to stop most of the noise. If noise persists, you probably have a loose washer, which can be tightened or replaced if you will follow the steps outlined previously.

Sometimes water will spray erratically from a faucet, and, at times, the flow is diminished greatly. You can correct this problem in many cases by unscrewing the faucet strainer cap. Usually you can remove the cap with your fingers, but if you must use pliers or a wrench, be careful that you do not scratch or scar the cap. One way to use pliers safely is to wrap thick cloth around the faucet cap and then apply the pliers to the cloth. You can use sufficient force to loosen the cap in this way, and the cloth will keep you from damaging the fixture.

One very simple, but troublesome, problem is that of leaking connections under sinks and lavatories or toilets. The connecting pipes are usually copper, which is very soft. If you apply excessive force with a wrench, you can break the fitting. One very simple repair solution is to turn off the water supply and then loosen the fitting nut with a wrench. Turn it backward, one-half to three-quarters of a turn, then tighten it again.

It is a mystery why this simple technique works, but it does, in fact, work in a high percentage of cases. If leaking persists, loosen and retighten again, this time backing the fitting off a full turn or more before tightening again.

When a hard freeze splits a pipe, the pipe must be replaced. You cannot repair a large slit in the pipe. If the leak is a pinhole type, which is often the case with frozen pipes, you can make the simple repairs easily and quickly. Pinhole leaks occur very often because the freezing water is expanding and the expansion creates great pressure. As soon as one tiny rupture in the pipe occurs, the pressure is relieved, and the rupture, at this time, terminates, while the water sprays in a tiny jet through the opening.

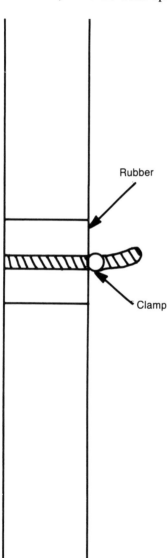

Rubber

Clamp

Fig. 3-3. If the pipe has only a pinhole break in it, a 1-inch square of rubber placed over the hole and a clamp tightened securely over the rubber will repair the hole effectively.

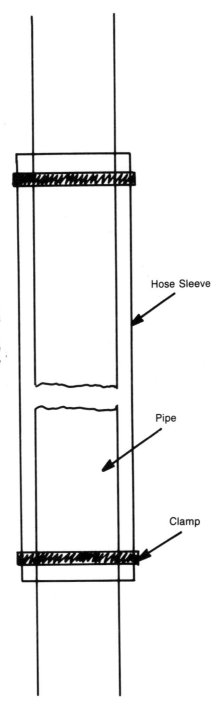

Hose Sleeve

Fig. 3-4. If the pipe is badly split, saw it in two, then slip both ends into a length of garden hose. Use clamps on both ends of the hose, and the leak is temporarily stopped.

Pipe

Clamp

You can buy small clamps with adjusting screws at any hardware store, and you can repair the leak with one of these clamps and a small strip of rubber or pliant plastic. Leave the water turned on until you locate the leak. Then turn off the water as soon as you have marked the leak. Unscrew the clamp until it can be opened, then slip it around the pipe and engage the screw that tightens the clamp. While the clamp is still loose, insert a small strip of rubber under the clamp and wrap the rubber around the pipe completely. Then, making sure that the rubber stays over the pinhole leak, tighten the screw so that the clamp closes very tightly over the leak. This simple solution will cure most of the small leaks. (See Fig. 3-3.)

Often freezing will break pipes at connections, resulting in leaking at the connection. This type of problem can be repaired usually if you will turn off the water and unscrew the connection and then apply some pipe joint compound. First, though, dry the connection thoroughly, then apply the compound and reconnect the joint. Allow the repair to set for 2 hours before using the water line again.

One emergency repair that is useful is the use of a length of rubber hose to repair a split pipe. As you were told earlier, long splits in a pipe cannot be repaired. You need to turn off the water and use a hacksaw to saw out the split portion of the pipe, which will usually be only 3 to 6 inches at the most.

Next, cut a length of plastic or rubber tubing that is at least 4 inches longer than the length of pipe you removed. The tubing must be large enough to slip over the ends of the pipe, but it should also fit as tightly as possible.

Before you install the tubing, you can coat the pipe with rubber cement or compound. Then slip the tubing over the pipes and use pipe clamps over the tubing and pipe. Tighten the clamp until there is no leakage. Such a repair should be seen only as an emergency repair and a plumber should be called as soon as you can do so. This repair will, however, last for weeks, even months, if the tubing is strong enough to withstand the water pressure inside the pipe. (See Fig. 3-4.)

One of the best methods of preventing freeze damage, other than keeping water flowing and using insulation, is to use pipe that will expand slightly, or stretch. Galvanized iron pipe will not expand appreciably at all. Copper tubing will stretch slightly, but it will not resume its original shape when the water thaws. Repeated freezings will cause the pipe to rupture. You can buy flexible tubing that will stretch considerably and will return to its original dimensions after the water thaws. Repeated freezings will, or course, cause eventual damage.

When all pipes and wires are installed, it is time to add the insulation in exterior walls. Chapter 4 deals with how to install insulation.

4
Installing Insulation

ONE OF THE BEST BARGAINS IN HOME CONSTRUCTION TODAY IS INSULA-
tion. This material serves to fireproof, moistureproof, and weatherproof, and, to an extent,
soundproof your home. In addition, it serves as a barrier to insect invasion and helps prevent
fungus growth and rot.

You have several choices when you select the type of insulation you want in your
home. The traditional rolls, or batts, of fiberglass insulation most often are used, or you
can choose the rock-wool insulation. In addition, you can choose between several types
of sheathing which, when installed properly, can take the place of the usual insulation
blankets.

You will want to insulate all exterior walls thoroughly, even if you live in a temperate
climate, because insulation keeps warm air, as well as hot air, outside, or inside, the house.
If this statement sounds confusing, remember, any insulation prevents the passage of air.
Air will carry warm air (heat) as well as cool air. If your house is well insulated and if
the weather is very cold outside, your insulation barrier will keep the heat that is inside
from passing through the walls. At the same time, it keeps cold, outside air from passing
through the walls, into the house.

Like many materials used in construction, however, how well the insulation works
depends greatly upon the methods and the thoroughness with which you install the insulation.
The success of the insulation also depends upon the type of structure that is being insulated.

A poorly constructed house with cracks, holes in the wallboard or plaster, poorly-
installed siding, and windows and doors that were not installed properly, cannot be helped
to any great extent by insulation. You need to install the insulation correctly, and you
need to have the house ready to utilize the maximum capabilities of the insulating materials.
(See Fig. 4-1.)

One mistake many do-it-yourself people make is to assume that wall insulation is the
total job. This belief is terribly incorrect, because ceilings and floors should be insulated,

Fig. 4-1. The siding has pulled loose from this house, and insulation alone will not weatherproof the structure. The wall must be renailed.

too. Heat rises, of course, and heated air will collect at the ceiling of a room, unless the room construction permits the heat to filter through the ceiling and escape into the attic.

One of the best places to start insulating is underneath the house. Before you start the job, crawl under the house and examine the joists and sills for signs of insect infestation, dampness, and other trouble signs. If you see a joist or sill that is thoroughly damp, you need to find the source of trouble and correct it before you install any insulation.

One of the likely causes of such dampness is leaking water connections. If the connection leaks only to the extent that a few drops per hour fall into the wall, in a period of several months there can be a surprisingly large accumulation of moisture in the wall and subflooring, as well as on the joists or sills underneath the leak.

Because a wall is usually cool and protected from sunlight, any water that falls into the enclosure will stay there for a long time, because there is no wind to help evaporate it. It will tend to run down the water pipes, fall to the sole plate where the pipe passes through the floor, eventually seep through the layer of subflooring, and finally emerge atop the sills or joists, where it will then fall to the ground underneath.

Insulation that is installed under the conditions described here, will serve to keep much air from entering into, or escaping through, the floor. It also will serve to trap the moisture that is accumulating there. The trapped moisture will saturate the wood and make it susceptible to decay.

It is possible that you will need to take siding off the exterior wall or the wall covering off the interior wall, in the vicinity of the leak, and correct the problem before you proceed with the insulation. You will find such leaks under sinks and bathrooms with regularity. They cause serious damage over a period of months or a year.

Dry joists and sills can mean only that your house is in good shape as far as leaks are concerned, and you are ready to start to insulate. As always, check first to see if any problems should be corrected, such as cross-bridging which has worked its way loose as the house settled, evidence of termite presence, or damaged electrical wiring. If you see wiring with the insulation stripped away, the evidence suggests that rats or mice have been working under your house.

CORRECTING MOISTURE PROBLEMS

Measure the distance between joists as you start working. They should be 16 inches on center, and also 15 inches should be between the joists. If the joists are installed correctly, you can start to insulate.

If you chose to use batts of insulation, spread a sheet of polyethylene on the ground before you open the roll of insulation and start to spread the blankets out. The thin plastic will keep the insulation, and you, partially protected from the dirt and from the moisture that is invariably present under such conditions.

Before you begin to work seriously, dress for the job. You will need to protect yourself from contact with fiberglass insulation as much as you can. This protection consists of wearing boots, a long-sleeved shirt, gloves, protective glasses, and a face mask.

Wearing protective clothing should be taken seriously. If fiberglass particles come into contact with your flesh, you can burn and itch for days, as a result.

When you have spread the batts on the polyethylene, have a staple gun handy, as well as a sharp knife or pair of scissors. Cut the batts, or blankets, at the desired length and locate the flange on the sides of the batts. Pull the flange out at the start of the batt and begin between the first joist and the sill. Lie on your back, if necessary, and push the insulation between the floor joists, starting at one end. Immediately staple both ends to the joists, using one staple every 6 to 8 inches. As you move down the joists, continue to push the insulation into the space between the joists and staple as you go. (See Figs. 4-2, 4-3.)

In this fashion, completely insulate the underside of the house or room. When you are finished, it is helpful to staple a sheet of polyethylene over (actually under, but covering) the insulation. This part of your job is now finished.

If you fear moisture might cause the flange part of the insulation batts to soften and rip, you can nail thin strips of wood at right angles across the joists to hold the insulation in place. (See Fig. 4-4.)

The next place to work is on the outside walls. It was earlier suggested that you space studs 16 inches apart on center. One of the reasons for this spacing is to make it easier for you to install insulation and wall coverings. If the studs are so spaced, you will find that insulation batts will fit snugly between the studs.

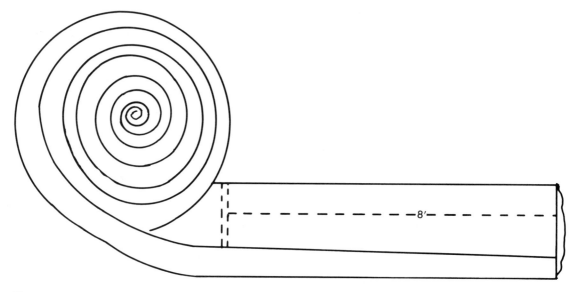

Fig. 4-2. The rolled insulation usually has perforations for easy tearing. You can also cut the insulation with scissors or a knife.

Install the insulation the same way you installed it under the house. Start at the top of the wall, spread the flanges, and staple to the studs. Work your way slowly down the wall, again using one staple on each side every 6 to 8 inches. Staple all the way to the sole plate.

It is good if the insulation blankets are slightly too wide for the stud spacing so that you will have to pack the batts into the space tightly. The better you pack, the greater the resistance to air passage.

You can buy insulation with a vapor, or moisture, barrier attached to the back. This barrier has a thick paper surface. When you insulate, the vapor barrier should be toward the heated side of the room. When you are installing the insulation, then, the vapor barrier should be against your body, and the raw part of the batt should be installed away from you.

Braces or blocks probably are nailed between the studs in your walls. If so, you will need to measure and cut insulation so that it will fit into the shorter, or smaller, spaces. Always cut the length a little longer than you need it for better packing and insulating qualities.

If *cut-in bracing* was used (2 × 4s angle cut and nailed between the studs in a diagonal line between corner post and sole plate), you will have to cut the batts at an angle. To do so, you can measure the distance from top to bottom of the space on the long side and then again on the short side. If the long side is 23 inches and the short side is 17 inches, go to your blanket and measure down 23 inches on one side and 17 inches on the other, draw a diagonal line connecting the two points. Cut along the diagonal line.

Save the angle-cut end of the batt. For the next angle cut, you can start to measure for the long side at the point of the angle, and measure for the short side on the short side of the angle. Cut the blanket straight across this time, and the fit will be nearly exact.

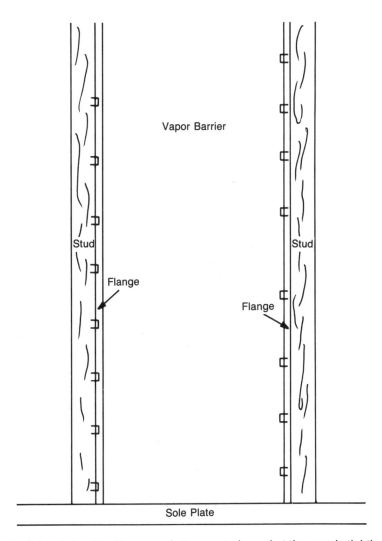

Fig. 4-3. Push insulation into the space between studs so that the area is tightly packed. Staple or nail the insulation in place, always with the vapor barrier to the warm side of the room.

Keep the pattern going. Angle cut for one length. Use the angle for the long and short sides of the next cut, and cut at right angles across the batt. Do this pattern as long as you have angles to cut for the bracing.

For insulating around blocking, you need only to measure and cut rectangular lengths shorter than the wall studs. When you come to the end of a roll, if a short piece is left over, or if you have a triangle left over from an angle cut, save these odd pieces to use later when you are doing the touch-up insulating.

Insulate all outside walls. When you are finished, take the pieces that are left over from odd cuts, find small places where these might fit, and pack the pieces into the wall.

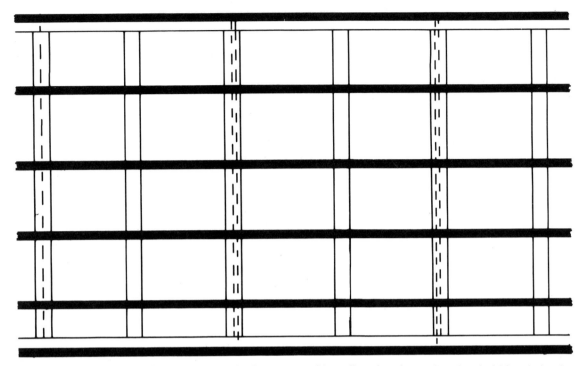

Fig. 4-4. Nail thin strips of wood over stud edges to provide nailers for plywood and to hold insulation in place.

When you are finished with a wall, the insulation should be fluffed out and even with the inside edges of the studding. (See Fig. 4-5.)

Do not leave the wall until you have insulated around every possible air passage. Pack insulation around switch boxes, between window frames and trimmers, between door jambs and headers, and between headers and top plates. You will be amazed at how much air can find its way through a tiny hole. (See Fig. 4-6.)

If pipes are in the wall you are insulating, wrap some insulation around them, with the vapor barrier to the outside. Do not neglect even the tiniest space on the surface of a pipe. Remember, moisture will collect when condensation occurs, and damp insulation loses a great deal of its effectiveness. (See Fig. 4-7.)

When you are finished with the exterior walls, you can start insulating the ceiling, because you lose a great deal of heat in this part of the house, too. The easiest way to handle this task is to climb to the attic and lay blankets or batts between the timbers until you have the attic completely insulated. You can get insulation in bags, so that you can pour the wool insulation in the places where batts or blankets cannot be laid.

You can combine insulation work and sheathing installation if you want to buy sheathing boards for the outside walls of your home or room. These boards come in 4- × -8 foot panels and you can nail them up just as you would nail up paneling or plasterboard.

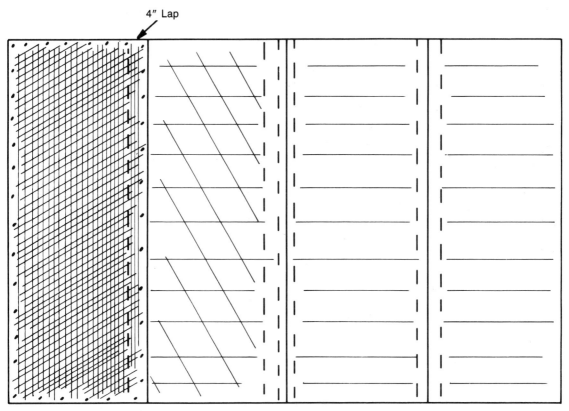

4″ Lap

Fig. 4-5. You can strengthen and insulate at the same time by using plywood panels at the corners of all walls.

INSTALLING INSULATING BOARDS

When you start to install insulating board, do not use it on corners. Instead, nail up 4-×-8 foot plywood sheathing. Plywood provides reasonably good insulation, and it also serves an even more important purpose—it reinforces corners as well as any composition material on the market today.

Plywood, because it is made of thin layers of pressed wood glued together at right angles, supports both sideways and up and down. Nailed to outside corners of your house or spare room that you are building, the plywood keeps the corners square and also prevents warping and shifting.

Start nailing up insulation board adjacent to the plywood panels. You should first examine the studding from outside to see if the wall framing is ready for sheathing. As suggested earlier (see Chapter 1), run a cord from the corner post to the first handy stopping place, such as a corner, doorway, or interruption of any kind in the wall line. Check to see whether any studs are too recessed or protrude too far for a good wall line. Correct any problems you encounter. (See Fig. 4-8.)

If the wall frame is ready, stand a panel of insulation board in place and check quickly to see if the panel will fit the stud spacing. If it does, nail it in place.

Fig. 4-6. Pack insulation in all cracks and crannies. Do not neglect space between window frames and jambs. (COURTESY OF BURSON-MARSETELLER AND OWENS-CORNING CORPORATION.)

If you have assistants, have one of them hold the panel while you nail it, or vice versa. If you are working alone, you can drive two nails partially into the crack between the sills and the foundation walls, and let the panel rest on the nails while you prepare to nail it. (See Figs. 4-9 and 4-10.)

When you have nailed up the first panel, pull out the nails between the sills and the foundation walls, and drive them in for the next panel. Repeat the first process. When you come to a window, nail the panel over the window as if the window were not there. Follow this procedure for all openings except doors. (See Fig. 4-11.)

Later, when the entire house is covered with insulation board, you can go back to the windows and push the point of a pocketknife through the insulation board, from the inside of the building, so that the blade is flush with the window opening. Run the knife

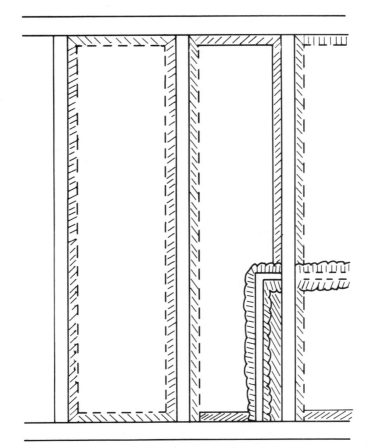

Fig. 4-7. If pipes are inside the wall, wrap the pipes with insulation to prevent damage from condensation.

Fig. 4-8. If you choose not to use plywood, nail the insulation boards tightly to the framing. Do not nail too hard or you might damage the panels. You can see slight damage to the panels shown here.

Fig. 4-9. Note the nail to the left and at the top of the sill. The worker is concealing another nail. These nails will help hold the plywood in place while you nail it.

blade all the way along the length of both sides of the window opening, and then cut along the top and bottom edges. The waste will fall from the opening and can be used later, if you need to sheath small areas.

The finished product is a fully sheathed house, with all exterior walls covered except for the plywood-supported corner areas. You are ready now to install siding.

Before you leave the insulation work, be sure to clean up the work area thoroughly. With your work uniform still on, sweep the entire floor thoroughly and use the broom to brush any random traces of fiberglass from the studding. Wear your face mask while you do this work. Breathing particles of insulation can cause many respiratory difficulties, including bronchitis.

Fig. 4-10. With the bottom of the plywood secured, nail the rest of the panel into position.

Several suggestions can be made as a review concerning insulation installation and nailing up insulation board. When you are working in the attic, lay down boards or plywood panels across the attic joists so that you will have a walking surface. Leave the insulation packaged until you are ready to use it. When you open the package, the blankets expand suddenly and greatly, taking up needed work space.

Let the insulation extend far enough to the edges of the attic that it covers the top plate and top cap. A great deal of air can enter through this area. But, do not cover any vents that are installed in the eaves. You need air circulation and ventilation in the attic, particularly in hot weather.

It is a good idea to start laying insulation batts at the eaves edge of attics, because you can shove the batts to the top plate area. Then you can work outward to where you have more room, as the attic rafters rise sharply. If you have wiring running through the attic joists, push the insulation under the wiring, if you can do so without pressing or compressing the insulation.

Wherever a batt ends and another begins, push the two ends as close together as you can. A gap, or loose fit, can allow much air to escape or enter.

You can buy unfaced insulation batts, if you wish. Faced insulation has the stapling flange on both sides, and the unfaced insulation has no vapor barrier. If you use unfaced insulation, which is often considerably cheaper, nail up a polyethylene vapor barrier on the warm-in-winter side of the room. Do not leave the polyethylene exposed. As soon as you have installed the insulation, you can install wall covering.

Fig. 4-11. You can install insulation panels over the window openings. Then use a knife to cut out for the window area.

You should not leave faced insulation exposed, because the facing will burn. It is made of heavy paper, and the insulation should be covered as soon as you are able to do so.

Basement walls should be insulated, too. Before you start to install insulation, you should check to see that the walls are sealed and that no dampness seeps through. Remember that dampness damages insulation badly and quickly.

You can stud a basement wall by laying out a sole plate and by nailing a top plate to the joists overhead. Then install studs between the sole plate and top plate by toe-nailing at both ends. Your basement wall provides all the support you need. The studs serve only as a boundary for the insulation. If you wish, you can nail furring strips to the wall instead of studs and install the insulation between the furring strips.

You can also place the studs 24 inches apart, rather than 16 inches on center if you elect to use studding. Again, support is not a vital concern, and you can be more relaxed and save a few dollars.

If you are adding insulation to an already insulated area, use unfaced insulation batts. If unfaced insulation is not available, you should cut rips in the facing of the batts and then install the insulation with the facing away from you—just the opposite of the way you would have done it normally. Do not let insulation rest less than 3 inches away from recessed light fixtures. Use a shielded light if you are using temporary lighting.

Some builders recommend that you use a sharp knife to cut the insulation blankets, others prefer to tear it. You will find that a pair of large scissors will work excellently. However you cut it, take care that your wrists do not come into contact with the fiberglass. Be sure to clean the cutting device thoroughly when you are finished.

You can cut the insulation board easily with a knife. At doorways, you can measure the amount to be used over the door opening. Mark that amount on a sheet of wallboard and cut it out on a good work surface. Do not try to use a knife while you are precariously balanced upon a stepladder.

If you have concerns about the insulating properties of the insulation board products, you can refer to the manufacturer's recommendations and get a good idea of how well the product works. The manufacturer of Thermax Insulation Board, for instance, states that it is "unsurpassed in insulating efficiency by any insulation board of glass fiber product." This claim is justifiable. Keep in mind, the claim is not that their product is unsurpassed, but that it is unsurpassed by any in the glass fiber line.

The manufacturers also provide a table of product thickness and R-value. The *R-value* simply indicates the degree to which a product insulates. The values are listed for all insulating board products manufactured by Celotex (Thermax) from ½ inch through 4¼ inches. When the average temperature is 40 degrees, the following R-values are given:

**Table 4-1. R-Values of Various
Thicknesses of Insulation at 40 °F Mean Temperature.**

INSULATION THICKNESS	R-VALUE
½ inch	4
⅝ inch	5
¾ inch	6
1 inch	8
1½ inch	12
2 inch	16
2½ inch	20
3 inch	24

Many tests have been made on glass fiber insulating board that has been installed for as long as five years, and the R-values have remained excellent. Some products, such as those manufactured by Celotex, service temperatures which range from -100 degrees Fahrenheit to 250 degrees Fahrenheit.

INSULATION THICKNESS	R-VALUE
½ inch	3.6
1 inch	7.2
1½ inch	10.8
2 inch	14.4
3 inch	21.6

Table 4-2. R-Values of Various Thicknesses of Insulation at 75 °F Mean Temperature.

You can buy insulating board in panels 4 feet wide and in a variety of lengths. The boards also have aluminum foil vapor retarders, so the product is not intended for use with other vapor barriers, such as faced insulation. It is not recommended that any other type of insulation be used with the insulating boards.

To fasten insulating boards, arrange to have the boards span three studs and secure with ⅜-inch-diameter, diamond-head-resistant fasteners that will penetrate the framing by at least 1 inch. When the boards are in place, you can tape all joints with aluminum foil tape. This tape is available at the dealers where you bought the insulating board.

The manufacturers recommend that you clean the work surface thoroughly for all taping work, so that the tape will bond well to the edges of the boards. Do not allow any grease, oil, moisture, or dust to remain. If you do not clean thoroughly, the adhesive properties of the tape will be lost after a short time.

It is also recommended that temperatures be above 50 degrees for installation of insulating board. Store the boards flat on pallets so that they will not be in contact with the floor or ground. Protect the stacked boards from rain and other types of moisture.

Keep the boards at room temperature before use. When you nail up the insulating boards, fit the edges as close together as you can without jamming the edges. The close fit is important to maintain the best adhesive qualities of the tape. When applying the tape, keep it flat and unwrinkled. Use a knife or scissors to cut it. You should not tear the tape.

If you do not use insulating board, you will probably want to use some other type of sheathing. Chapter 5 offers several suggestions concerning advantages and disadvantages of the various types of sheathing and how to install it.

The cost of insulating board is modest—$6.50 or less for a panel 4 feet wide and 8 feet high. Rolls of 3½-inch-thick, faced insulation containing 88 square feet sell for $12. Six-inch unfaced insulation, for use in attics, sells for $11 per roll. For the price, you get almost 50 square feet.

5
Sheathing

SHEATHING, USED GENERICALLY, CAN MEAN ANY OF SEVERAL TASKS
connected with home construction. Pronounced "sheeting," the term means an inner
covering of boards or waterproof material on the roof or outside wall of a frame house.
Sheathing does not necessarily consist of nailing boards to the rafters on a roof and then
nailing shingles on top of the boards, any more than it consists of nailing diagonal boards
to the studding of a house before installing the siding.

Some people like the idea of tongue and groove boards nailed to studding. It is still
one of the tried and true building practices. The major reasons for its diminishing popularity
are time, cost, and availability of materials.

Decades ago, every rural community had its sawmill, from which lumber could be
readily obtained at a very low price. You could buy a truckload of lumber to install on
the sides of a modest-sized house, and the total cost would be less than $25. Nails also
were extremely inexpensive. People had far more time than money, so the act of sheathing
a house provided employment for many people and was inexpensive for the home owner,
even considering the low incomes and high buying power of the dollar at that time.

In modern times, the towering trees that grew virtually everywhere are diminishing
rapidly, and, in many cases, are near total depletion. As a result, the cost of lumber has
also increased. Because one of the major expenses in building is the cost of the labor,
which generally amounts to one-half of the total cost of the finished house, home builders
today choose one of the many plywood products that can be nailed up in minutes, as opposed
to the lengthier process of installing board siding.

Builders also found that plywood siding worked well for them, because they could
weatherproof a house in a very short time. Each hour saved was $10 they did not have
to pay the employee. The strength of plywood was also a factor in the changeover. As
we stated previously, plywood supports in two directions rather than in only one.

Trees that are not suited for many building purposes are ideally suited for the production
of plywood. Small poplars that yield very little usable lumber can be converted into a

plywood panel quickly and inexpensively. In general, board sheathing was, and is, being phased out of construction.

Boards, however, are a good choice for sheathing if you wish to use them and if you can buy them at a reasonable price. In some parts of the country, you can buy rough-sawn sheathing boards for $40 per thousand feet. A delivery fee would be added to the initial cost.

If you know someone who operates a small sawmill, you might want to contact them to get a price quote. You will nail in the sheathing and then cover it with siding, so you do not need to worry about the appearance of the lumber. In fact, the rough-sawn lumber is not at all unattractive. Many people buy the lumber for use as wall covering in many modern and beautiful houses.

INSTALLING BOARD SHEATHING

Should you choose to sheath with boards, you have a choice of square-edged boards or tongue and groove boards. Of the two, the square-edged boards are much easier to install. The tongue and groove boards, however, provide much better windproofing, although neither will actually windproof a house without other materials installed behind it.

Using square-edged boards is very simple. When you buy the lumber, secure 5-inch boards if you can, and settle for 4-inch widths only if necessary. The reasoning is clear: with a 5-inch board you save the width of a 4-inch board every four boards. Each board you save is one less board to measure, saw, and nail in place. You also save on nails, because you will need nearly as many nails for 4-inch boards as you will for wider ones. Another factor to consider is the wind resistance obtained with the boards. Four-inch boards will create more cracks in a given wall than 5-inch boards. Each crack, no matter how tightly fitted, will admit some wind. The result using 4-inch boards will be a house that is less comfortable or more expensive and difficult to heat.

Tongue and groove lumber is more difficult to install; however, it is better in terms of wind resistance. Each board has one edge that has a tongue and another that has a groove. When you install these boards, the tongue of the previous board accommodates the groove of the next board. If the boards fit well, there is very little passage of wind possible, and heat loss is cut very appreciably.

When your lumber arrives, or if you pick it up at the lumber yard to save money on delivery fees, you should inspect each unit of lumber as you load it or as it is unloaded. If a tongue is crushed partially, you will have great difficulty in fitting the piece into the groove of the adjacent board. Damaged grooves also render the boards impossible to use. Feel free to reject any lumber that is damaged. Remember, each unit of wasted lumber raises the price of your building project by a dollar or two, perhaps more. If you damage tongues or grooves after you have paid for the lumber, you perhaps can make use of them as the first or last board in a wall.

The first and last boards will end on a sill or perhaps a top plate or top cap. There is little wind problem in these areas. You might also be able to use parts of the boards for shorter sheathing jobs, such as in alcoves or recesses.

You can install board sheathing by two methods. The first, and easier way, is to install it vertically. Then, when you nail siding at right angles to the sheathing, you get strength in two directions. The second way is to nail it up diagonally, which means more difficulty in measuring and angle-cutting. You also have to get started properly or encounter difficulties in getting the sheathing to work out properly at the other end of the wall. These problems, though, are relatively easy to work out.

Sheathing is considered a part of the framing of a house because it strengthens and braces walls. Siding, because it is not a part of the structural strength of the house, is part of the exterior finish of a house.

When you are using square-edged sheathing in a vertical fashion, nail one board in place so that the edge is flush with the edge of the corner post. Cut the board long enough so that it reaches to the top of the corner post. Cut and nail the next board so that it fits snugly against the first one, and so that it also reaches to the very top of the wall framing. Depending upon the style of house you are building, each unit of sheathing will be cut longer, and you will have to angle-cut the top end to conform with the slant of the roof. Some people prefer to nail up vertical sheathing only as high as the top plate or top cap (actually as high as one-half the thickness of the top cap). Later they will cut shorter boards to reach to the roof line. (See Fig. 5-1.)

Continue this nailing pattern all the way across the wall of the house. Use 16d nails with three nails in the ends of the boards and two nails at each point where a board crosses a stud or blocking timber.

If you have not yet nailed in blocking, do so before you try to install vertical sheathing. Remember, the blocking is short lengths of 2 × 4s cut to fit exactly between the studs and nailed in place one-third of the way to the top, then two-thirds the way to the top. In this fashion, you will have four backing supports for the sheathing boards: the sill, the two blocking timbers, and the top plate or top cap. If you want more backing support,

Fig. 5-1. Nail up plywood or other sheathing to the top of the studs. Then you can use shorter sections of sheathing from the studs to the peaks.

you can nail in three blocking timbers, spaced evenly between the top and the bottom of the studs and staggered from one stud space to the next.

Sheathing installed without adequate backing supports will not be satisfactory. You will have long expanses of boards with nothing to support them. These boards will give and, with each inch of bend or sway, air passages will be created. (See Fig. 5-2.)

When you reach the other end of the wall, cut the final board so that it will be flush with the outside edge of the corner post. As you start to turn the corner to sheath the next wall, nail the first board so that its outer edge is flush with the edge of the last piece of sheathing that you installed.

You can also nail up sheathing horizontally, if you wish. Start at the bottom with the first board flush with the bottom edge of the sill, and use three nails every 3 feet, if you are using 5-inch boards, and two nails (16d) every 3 feet, if you are using 4-inch sheathing. When you start to sheath up the studs, use three nails in the ends of each 5-inch board and two nails at every point where the sheathing board will cross a stud. When you are installing 4-inch sheathing, use two nails in each end and also two nails at every stud crossing.

The ends of all sheathing boards should be cut squarely and should be flush with the edge of the corner posts. When you reach the top of the corner post and start working toward the roof peak, you will need to angle-cut each board, so keep it flush with the rafter at the end of the roofline.

The major problem with horizontal sheathing, and the reason few people use it, is that you must install wall siding that is vertical. Otherwise, you simply will have boards nailed on top of one another and no weatherproofing, or strengthing, or bracing will occur.

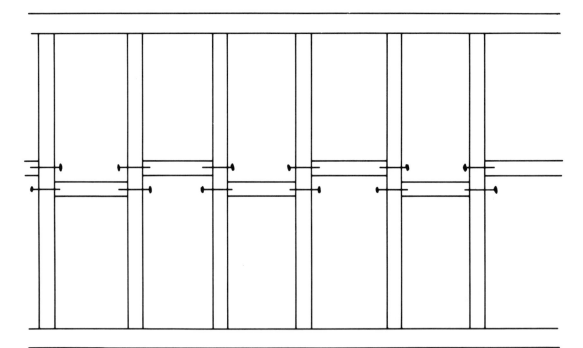

Fig. 5-2. You will need blocking, such as that shown here, for all vertically-installed sheathing.

To install diagonal sheathing, which is in many ways the best method and the most popular approach, you start in one corner and nail in a triangle cut from the end of a sheathing board. This triangle should fit so that one side is flush with the outside edge of the corner post, one side is flush with the bottom edge of the sills, and one edge faces the wall to be sheathed.

Cut the next board so that it fits against the first board neatly, and angle-cut the ends of the board so they will be flush with the bottom edge of the sill and the outside edge of the corner post. Continue this pattern until you have covered the entire wall.

When you reach the top of the corner post and start sheathing the peak, do not interrupt the line of your work. If you wish to speed up your work, you can take a few minutes to make a simple miter box to help you with your angle-cuts. To make the miter box, cut a length of sheathing board about 3 feet long (the exact length is not crucial) and lay it flat. Cut a second board the same length and lay it flat on the top of the first one. Then nail the two boards together for added thickness and strength. Use two nails at each end and two more in the middle. Turn the two boards over, bend the ends of the nails, and drive them flat against the wood so you will not risk scratching yourself as you move the completed miter box around.

Use one end of a sheathing board to get the proper angles. For diagonal sheathing, you can measure the width of a board and then measure that distance up the side of the board. If, for instance, your board is a full 4 inches wide, you should measure 4 inches up each side of the board, and then mark the board so that you have a perfect square. (You will recall that nominal width and actual width of a board will not be the same. This distance is given only for demonstration purposes.) Now mark the square diagonally from one corner to the other and saw along the line you have just marked.

Cut two more lengths of sheathing board, and nail these to the side, or edges, of the two pieces you have nailed together so that you have a squared U. Be sure to nail the side boards so that they are on the outside edge of the combined boards; otherwise, you will not have sufficient room inside your miter box to lay the units of sheathing boards to be cut.

Lay the triangle you have just cut on your miter box so that what had been the squared end of the board is flush with the end of the miter box, but on top of the side boards. The original straight edge of the sheathing board should now be flush with the edge of one of the upright boards. The long cut, which should be about 5¾ inches if you cut from corner to corner of a 4-inch board, will then stretch diagonally across the opening, or top, of the miter box. Mark along the edge of the diagonal cut, across the top edges of both of the side boards. (See Fig. 5-3.)

Complete the marking, then use a handsaw or circular saw and cut along the marks all the way to the top side of the two combined boards. Take care not to hit any nails you used earlier to join the two boards.

Lay a sheathing board inside the trough of the miter box so that the end of the board is flush with the end of the bottom boards. Hold the board steadily and lower the saw blade into the two slit cuts you made. Then saw the sheathing board so that you have the proper angle. That end of the board is now ready to nail.

Measure the length needed for the board, then turn it and cut the other end as you did the first one. Note that the two ends of the properly-cut board will not be parallel. You will not have a parallelogram but an isosceles trapezoid. If it will make it easier for

Fig. 5-3. A simple miter box can be made in a few minutes. Mark as shown here, and cut along the marks for proper angle positions.

you, mark the other end of the miter box so that all you need to do is cut the first end, then pull the board straight ahead, and cut the second end at the proper length.

You can use the same triangle to mark both ends of the miter box, but keep in mind that because the cuts are not parallel, you will have to turn the triangle over before making the marks.

Later, when you are having to angle-cut for the peak, you can make a third mark in the center of the miter box for that angle. The easiest way to secure the correct marking is to hold a board in place so that its bottom edge rests upon the top edge of the board under it, and the end sticks out slightly beyond the peak timbers. Mark the board by reaching behind, keeping the tip of the pencil against the outer side of the peak timber, and making the corresponding mark on the inside surface of the board. Cut the board along the mark. Then use the end of the board to make the miter box mark.

Hold the board so that the long side of the cut is flush with the edge of the upright board of the miter box, and mark along the edge. Mark both upright boards, and then make the slot cut down to the top edge of the bottom board.

This procedure might sound like a great deal of trouble, but you can make the miter box in only a few minutes. You also can save yourself considerable trouble by not having to mark each board before you cut it, and you will not ruin boards by cutting them improperly.

There is one shortcut you can make that will keep you from making the miter box, if you do not wish to use good boards for this purpose. You can cut the bottom end of each board by marking from one corner to a point up the board the same distance as the width of the board. You can do the same with the other end until you reach the peak slope.

Even for peak-slope angles, you can get by without a miter box and without having to hold each board to mark it. You can mark and cut the first board, but save the waste end and use that angle for marking subsequent boards. Be careful that you do not reverse the board and cut the angle in the wrong direction.

When you are measuring lengths of diagonal boards, measure for the top edge length of the next sheathing boards, because the top edge will be somewhat longer than the bottom edge. If you are using 4-inch boards, mark a point 4 inches above the last board at the top and bottom points on the wall frame. Then measure from point to point and cut your board accordingly.

When you are installing tongue and groove boards (at times called dressed-and-matched boards), start the first diagonal board so that the groove is away from the house and the tongue is turned toward the house. If you nail the boards so that the grooves are turned up, it is possible that moisture can accumulate.

Try not to damage either tongue or groove as you are nailing up the boards. If you should accidentally damage a groove, you can sometimes correct the damage by running a screwdriver blade, turned sideways, so that it will clean out the groove. You can also, at times, use a pocketknife to trim away splinters that have been knocked into the groove and are still attached. If a tongue is damaged, you can use a chisel and tap the handle lightly with a hammer, while you hold the blade at an acute angle against the damaged fibers. You might also have some success in trimming the damaged tongue with the blade of a sharp pocketknife.

Keep nailing up the diagonal siding until you have covered the entire wall, including the peak surfaces. You need to brace and strengthen, as well as insulate, attics.

It is always a good idea to nail building paper over the studding before you install any type of sheathing, unless you are using some of the synthetic materials. In these cases, you should follow the manufacturer's instructions.

The cost of dressed tongue and groove lumber can add rather significantly to the cost of your building project. A 5-inch board costs about 13.5 cents per linear foot, or if you want to buy your lumber in bulk, you will have to pay about $470 per 1000 feet of 5-inch boards. You can buy square-edged boards for considerably less—about $270 per 1000 feet. Four-inch boards are cheaper, but some lumber yards do not carry 4-inch sheathing boards as part of their inventory. You will have to special order the lumber. Be prepared to wait for the lumber to be cut. You also will have to pay slightly extra for the special size. It will be cheaper to pay for these special boards than to pay for the 5-inch boards. You do not necessarily have a bargain, however, because the smaller boards will not cover as much area as the 5-inch boards.

You can buy sheathing boards with three kinds of board ends: square edged, shiplapped, and tongue and groove. The *square edged*, as the name implies, are boards that simply abut with straight edges fitting snugly. The *shiplapped boards* are cut with squares half the width of a board sawed out of the ends. When you install these boards, one cutout fits into the square left on the other board. The *tongue and groove boards* have ends that are cut out or left protruding in a rounded fashion so that the protrusion on one board fits into the cutout in the next board.

When you are installing these boards, you use square-edged boards as you would use any other lumber siding. The shiplapped boards fit together like pieces of a jigsaw puzzle, as do the tongue and groove ends. There is very little advantage to the various ends. The most important aspect is to have ends meet on a stud. If you accomplish this aspect, the board ends will have adequate support, and if you use building paper, you will eliminate most of the wind entry and heat loss through cracks in the walls.

One slight advantage of shiplapped lumber is that the board with the male end is not only nailed to the stud, but is also partly supported by the female end of the abutted board. The same is true of tongue and groove board ends. These advantages do not really outweigh the increased cost of such lumber.

INSTALLING PLYWOOD SHEATHING

One of the great advantages of sheathing with plywood is that you can cover such a large space in a very short time. Most plywood panels come in 4-×-8 foot sheets. Therefore, if your house is 32 feet wide, you can cover it with eight panels of plywood. It would take many more boards to do the same job, since each board covers only 5 inches in width and up to 10 or 12 feet in length. You also must saw many board ends, and you must nail each board at each stud crossing.

If a sheathing board is 12 feet long and 6 inches wide (an unusually wide sheathing board), the board would cover about 6 feet of wall space, while a plywood panel would cover 32 feet of wall space. The sheathing board will span 11 studs, if you use long boards and consequently will require 24 nails, while the panel of plywood will probably require only 16 nails. Don't count only the cost of the nails as your savings, include the time it takes to drive each one. Also count the time needed to saw board ends, particularly if you are working without electricity and must use a handsaw.

These facts are not to say that plywood is unquestionably better than sheathing boards. It is saying only that, in terms of wall space covered in a set time period, you will get the job done faster with plywood panels. Advantages and disadvantages exist for the use of both boards and plywood panels. For example, the tongue and groove boards might seal a wall against air infiltration and dust better than plywood with square edges. If you have to saw the plywood panels with a handsaw, time and energy will be an expenditure.

You must make your decision of which type of sheathing to use in view of your own finances, physical needs, and desires. If you choose plywood, and many reasons exist for doing so, you can install it in the following manner.

First, you can install it vertically or horizontally. While most people nail the panels up vertically, there is no particular reason that you should do so. If you decide to nail it vertically, drive two or three nails between the foundation wall and the sill before you lift the paneling into position. The nails serve two purposes. The first purpose is to hold the sheathing in place while you nail it, which is particularly useful if you are working alone. The second purpose is to provide a small space between the concrete blocks and the wood. It is excellent if you have a sheet of plastic or thin gauge metal between the concrete and the wood, because concrete will cause wood to decay quickly. (See Fig. 5-4.)

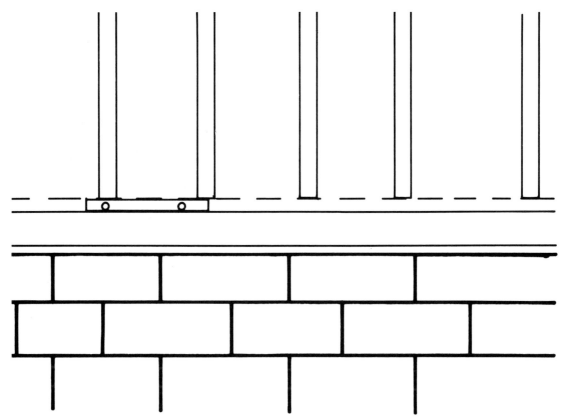

Fig. 5-4. You can install thin-gauge metal between sill and foundation wall. If you plan to brick walls, you can omit the metal if you prefer.

You need to begin installation at either corner post in a wall frame. With the panel in place and resting on the nails (which can be pulled out when the panel is installed), line up the edge of the panel flush with the outside edge of the corner post. Start to nail through the plywood, into the corner post. Drive two nails in far enough so that the plywood panel is help in place. Then check to see that the two edges are still flush. If they are not, pull the nails out far enough so that you can move the panel and start the nails again. Check again for correct positioning of the panel.

When you are satisfied, use your level to see that the panel is vertical. You also can make a visual check to see that the edge of the panel reaches halfway across the stud. If it does not reach exactly halfway, be certain that you have an adequate support to which you can nail the next panel. If you do not have adequate support, you will need to do one of three things: you can nail in another stud adjacent to the existing one, you can knock the stud loose and renail it in its correct space, or you can use blocking to force the stud into proper alignment. The last method is used particularly if the stud provides nailing surface at the top and bottom but not in the middle.

If the stud in the middle is too far under the panel, nail the blocking between the corner post and the stud. Use one length of blocking stock one-third of the way down the stud and another piece at the two-thirds point. If the stud curves away from the panel, use the blocking in the same locations but between the stud in use and the next one. In your efforts to align one stud be careful you do not create added problems with later nailing. If the first stud is out of line but subsequent studs will work adequately, correct the first one and leave the others as they are. It is better to spend a little time in correcting the one problem than it is to have to restud an entire wall. (See Fig. 5-5.)

When you are satisfied that the panel of plywood is flush with the corner post and seated halfway across the last nailing stud, nail it in place by using 16d nails spaced every

Fig. 5-5. Modify the on-center distance if necessary for the panels of plywood to fit perfectly over the stud edges.

foot across the top, sides, and bottom. Be sure to drive the nails through the plywood and into the middle stud.

You will repeat this pattern and process as you move across the entire wall, until you come to a window or doorway. When you reach a window opening, the easiest way to install the plywood sheathing around the window is to drive the nails between the sills and the foundation wall. Stand the panel in place and abut it against the last nailed panel. Start two nails in the side of the panel, against the last panel; start one nail just above the window opening and start another below the window opening. Drive the nails in only far enough to hold the panel so you can check and mark the plywood.

When you are sure that the panel is safely stationary, you should stop and check to see that the ends of the two panels are still abutted and that the other edge of the panel will fit well against the stud. You must also leave room for the next panel to have nailing support on the same stud. If the panel covers the window opening fully, you need to check the stud past the opening. If the panel reaches only partially across the window opening, check nailing surfaces on the cripple stud below the window opening and also above it, to be sure that you have a good nailing surface in both places. (See Fig. 5-6.)

Once you fit the panel and position it, go inside and use a pencil to mark the saw cut. Mark along the inside frame of the window on all three sides. Keep the point of the pencil tightly against the window frame.

Go back outside and take the panel down. Then saw along the lines and remove the unwanted material. If you are using a handsaw, you can saw in from both edges until you reach the line in the center of the panel. At this point, you will need to drill a small hole at some point on the center line. Drill the hole so that the edge of the circle barely laps over the line. It should be large enough to get the point of a keyhole saw through it. Use the keyhole saw until you have sawed a kerf that will permit the use of a handsaw

Fig. 5-6. Arrange cripples over and under windows so that you will have a perfect panel fit.

for the remainder of the cut. If you drilled the hole in the center, you can saw in one direction until you intersect with the cutline. Then you can saw in the other direction to the cutline intersection.

You can also drill the hole at either corner of where the cutlines intersect, and make the entire cut in one direction. Pause to blow the sawdust off the cutline frequently, so you will not let the saw drift from the line. When you near the end of the cut, use one hand to hold the loose portion of the panel so its weight will not cause it to fall abruptly and splinter the plywood. When the cuts are completed, the panel should fit perfectly over the window frame opening.

If you are working with an assistant, one of you can position and hold the panel while the other does the checking and marking. You can speed up the work considerably with an assistant, however, you can still use the nails to hold the plywood slightly off the cement wall foundation.

Use the same procedure when you come to door openings as you used on window openings. Mark and saw as you did before.

When you have electrical power, you can shorten sawing time greatly by using a circular saw. Start on the inside line near the center and lower the saw with the blade turning at cutting speed, to the cutline. Hold the saw firmly, but do not use excessive pressure or the saw will buck, or jump. Instead, let the blade barely touch the wood and cut its way through. When the blade is all the way through the plywood, let it move slowly forward until it reaches the end of the line. You will have to saw slightly past the cutline intersection in order to cut out the entire marked portion of the panel. The circular shape of the blade causes the larger part of the blade to cut slightly ahead of the center part of the blade, and, unless you let the top of the cut extend $\frac{1}{4}$ inch or so beyond the cutline, the cut will not be complete. Stop sawing and check your accuracy before sawing too far.

Turn the saw and cut in the other direction until you reach the cutlines intersection. When this cut is finished, cut along the other two lines. Each time you cut, cut slightly deeper than the line indicates so the cut will be complete.

When the cuts are completed, install the shaped and fitted panel as you did before. Before you sink nails fully, start two or three—enough to hold the panel in place—and double-check the fit. If all is well, complete the installation of the panel.

When switch boxes or outlets must be sheathed around, work as follows. Position the panel in its correct position, and start enough nails to hold the panel securely in place. Then go inside and use a sharp pencil to mark an outline around the switch box or outlet.

You will have some marks that open to the edge of a panel. If so, you can use a keyhole saw to cut around the outline. Often the outline will be square or rectangular, but you will also have some outlines that have octagonal shapes or diagonal corners. You might need to drill holes at each corner in order to get the best fit possible.

If the entire outline is inside the panel surface rather than on an edge, drill the holes needed at the corners and cut from one hole to another. Usually, you can drill only two holes, if the outline is square or rectangular. Make one hole in the upper left corner and another in the bottom right. When you saw, you can cut from the upper left in both directions, and do the same with the bottom right hole. Using this method, your fit probably will be better and your work easier.

At times, you will find that no matter how carefully you tried to frame your house or room, an unseen problem existed. It is possible that the corner post was not totally true or that the door frame is slightly out of square. If such a problem exists, when you start to install the first or last panel, you will find that one edge cannot be aligned properly.

If your corner post is not true but the rest of the wall is, you can handle the problem easily without having to reinstall the corner post, unless the problem is acute. You would have noticed by visual inspection a genuinely great discrepancy, so your problem might be that the edges of the panel and corner post are off by not more than an inch or fractional inch.

You still need to correct even a minor discrepancy. The easiest way to make the correction is to set the panel in the best position—so that it gives a true vertical reading, and so that you have good nailing surfaces on the studs—and start enough nails to hold the panel while you mark it.

The part of the panel that fits improperly will extend past the edge of the corner post, either at the top or at the bottom, and probably in a slightly slanted line. With the panel in place, mark a cutline along the corner post. Take down the panel, cut along the line, and then install the panel. The rest of the wall should be easily sheathed at this time. (See Fig. 5-7.)

Sometimes if you are reworking an older house, you will have settled walls or foundation piers that make an accurate fit for sheathing totally impossible. Even if you install blocking, the studs will not conform accurately, or perhaps the foundation has settled so that there is a slight *V* at the bottom of the panel fit line, although the panels fit acceptably at the top. Or the reverse might be true. One pier might have settled very little, if any, and the ones on either side might have settled more, which will leave you with panels that fit acceptably at the bottom and the *V* is at the top.

If the separation of the two panels extends beyond the stud edge, nail a short length of the studding to the existing stud so that the opening is covered. Then use a scrap piece of plywood, and cut a long triangular piece to nail into the gap between the panels. The best way to get an accurate cut is to trim a piece of cardboard so that it fits well into the gap. Then use the cardboard as a pattern for the plywood cut. Use two small nails to install the fitted piece.

Occasionally, settling will occur in a wall so that the plywood panels will overlap slightly from top to bottom, on a slanting line. When this overlap occurs, start nails in both panels and install them temporarily. Before you nail them up temporarily, mark a point on the foundation wall and top plate that indicates the exact center of the stud.

With the two panels tacked up, use a straightedge or chalk line and make a mark from the mark on the top plate, or top cap, to the one on the foundation wall. The chalk line, or mark, should be clearly visible down the edge of the plywood panel.

Take down the panel and cut along the marked line. Then put it back up with just enough nailing to hold it in place. Mark along the recently-cut edge to mark the other panel. Now take down both panels, cut the second one, and then nail both up in a permanent fashion. (See Fig. 5-8.)

When one wall is sheathed, go to the next wall and start with the corner post where you installed sheathing on one side. Position the first panel of plywood so that the edge is flush with the edge of the plywood panel that has been nailed flush with the corner post.

Remember, when you are sawing plywood with a circular saw, the upper surface will be splintered because the circular saw blade turns "backward," or counterclockwise. Turn the paneling when possible so that the upper surface is the one that will be turned inside

Fig. 5-7. If you have to make slight adjustments in the panels at the corners, you can do so without interrupting the alignment of other panels, and a slight fitting will not be apparent to the eye.

Fig. 5-8. Occasionally there will be slight deviations at the top or bottom of studs where panels are fitted poorly.

Fig. 5-9. Some fitting will be necessary for the panels to fit into the wall space remaining here. Measure, mark, and cut carefully in order not to waste a sheet of weatherproofing.

when installed. You can also run a sheet of coarse sandpaper over the cut edge of the plywood if you wish to smooth it slightly.

Complete the sheathing in the manner described previously. Make your choice of sheathing materials with your own needs in mind.

You have been provided with the approximate cost of sheathing boards. A panel of plywood sheathing with a regular 4-×-8 foot measurement and $^{15}/_{32}$ inch thickness can be bought for about $8, or slightly less. If your house is 32 feet wide and 48 feet long, you can sheathe it for about $320, plus nails. You can sheath a room with two outside walls, each 12 feet long, for $48 at the current cost of plywood sheathing.

If you can buy sheathing boards at a superior price, you might wish to sheathe with boards: If your time is very limited, you might find that plywood is more efficient.

It is a good practice to read the newspaper ads carefully in order to find the best bargains. Watch for salvage ads in the newspaper or in the telephone directory yellow pages. At times, you can buy plywood sheathing very economically through one of the many salvage outlets. It has been advertised as recently as 1987 for only $4 per panel.

If you can find a good buy, you can cut your material cost in half for many of the tasks connected with wall construction. Do not use any salvaged materials until you have checked with local building codes or inspectors. Once you have verified that you may use salvaged materials, you can often buy sheathing boards in excellent condition for one-tenth the cost of comparable materials at your building supply house.

When your house or spare room has been sheathed and the house is weatherproofed, you can arrange to have all electrical and plumbing work roughed in. When all inside-the-wall work is done, you can start to cover interior walls. Chapter 6 deals with covering walls with gypsum boards and various other materials used in interior wall covering.

6
Interior Wall Coverings

THE TWO MAJOR TYPES OF INTERIOR WALL COVERINGS ARE USUALLY classified as plaster and drywall. You would use *plaster*, which is a pasty mixture of lime, sand, and water, to coat ceilings, interior walls, and partitions.

Historically, plastered walls are one of the world's oldest building techniques. Primitive people plastered their crude living quarters with a mud mixture that helped to seal the dwelling against rain and wind.

Plaster is very durable. The pyramids of ancient Egypt contain plasterwork that is still very hard and durable after more than 4000 years. The best plasters often have been made of *gypsum*, a hydrate sulphate of calcium used in making plaster of paris. The use of lime as one of the central ingredients has made plaster easier to use. The lime-based plaster is excellent for stucco work. It receives and holds decorative designs very well. To start wall plastering, you must prepare a wall surface to receive and hold the plaster. This surface includes a base substance which is used to correct minor variations in the wall surface.

One of the most common base materials is a simple wood lath, or furring. *Furring* consists of strips of wood 2 or 3 inches wide and ¾ inch thick. A wire screen lath has been used in many forms of plasterwork as well. You use lath on concrete or masonry walls to prevent the plaster moisture from penetrating the pores in the masonry surface. If too much of the moisture seeps into the pores, the plaster has a tendency to dry too fast and crumble.

Nail furring strips across the studding in the wall frames, close enough to hold the plaster easily. Never permit the ends of furring strips to overlap. Also, do not permit abutments of furring strips to occur repeatedly on one stud. Stagger the joints for best results. Otherwise, you will possibly create a weak joint and the plaster will often crack here. For good results, let every tenth strip end on the same stud, if you can arrange for it to do so. (See Fig. 6-1.)

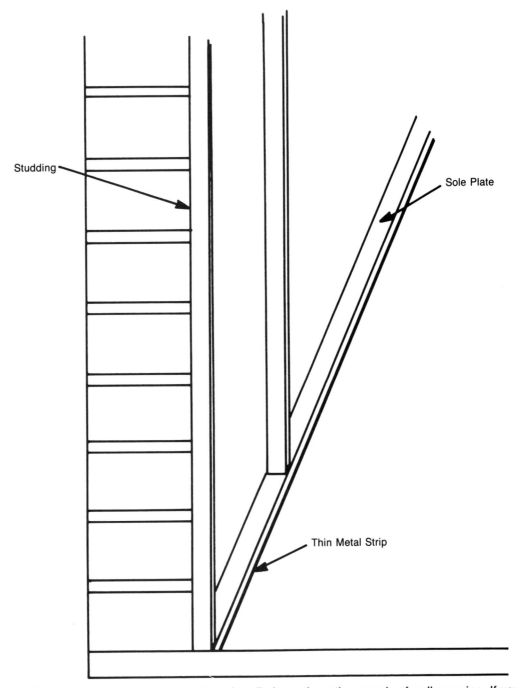

Studding

Sole Plate

Thin Metal Strip

Fig. 6-1. Furring strips make it much easier to install plywood or other panels of wall covering. If you are mounting the panels on a concrete base, use a thin metal strip between the wood and the concrete.

You can also use lath composed of gypsum, fiberboard, or metal (usually steel). Because of the fragility and expense, the wooden lath has been declining in use for years and rarely is used today.

Gypsum lath is generally composed of sheets of perforated or solid boards with square edges. The sheets are usually 16 inches × 48 inches. You install it horizontally to studs and at right angles to joists. Nail it to the studs or furring strips with nails that are flat-headed and 1⅛ inches long. You can buy special gypsum-lath nails, if you wish. Use five nails to each stud, or joist.

Fiberboard is a flexible, boardlike material composed of pressed fibers of wood. For plaster furring work, use strips of this material 16 inches × 48 inches. The fiberboard strips might be square-edged or shiplapped. Install these strips as you would install gypsum lath, except you should use 1¼ inch special fiberboard nails.

Metal lath is often composed of sheets of meshed or ribbed metal, 27 inches wide × 96 inches long. Nail these sheets horizontally to the studding. You can nail them to studs or to furring strips by using metal-lath staples or with 8d nails driven in partially and then bent to form a clamplike fastening.

Do not install lath before you have installed *plaster ground*, which consists of strips of wood the same thickness as that of the thickness of the lath and the plaster. Nail these grounds to the framing around the doors and the windows and along floor lines to serve as stops or guidelines for the plaster so that the plaster behind the door casings, window casings, and baseboards will be the same thickness.

These grounds must be level and plumb. The thickness of the grounds depends upon the number of coats of plaster you will be applying. If you plan to use metal lath and three coats of plaster, your grounds will need to be ¾ inch thick. If you use gypsum lath and two coats of plaster, the grounds will be the same. With wood lath and three coats of plaster a thickness of ⅞ inch is needed.

It is possible to buy metal lath composed of woven wire mesh that is 8 feet long × 24 inches wide. You also can find metal lath in wire mesh 100 feet long or more. This type of lath is fireproof and is extensively used, as a result. Wood lath is extremely flammable.

The actual plaster mix might include a cementing agent, an aggregate such as sand, and a binder. You can buy the materials, which at times includes jute fibers to hold the plaster mortar together. Lime or gypsum plaster usually is used for interior walls or ceilings.

Lime is obtained by heating limestone to such a temperature that its carbonic acid and water are removed. The finished product is called *quicklime*. To use quicklime, you must first slake it by mixing it with water, which causes considerable heat as the slaking process occurs. The lime swells to more than twice its bulk, starts to crumble, and then turns into a paste.

You can buy hydrated lime on the market. This product is the quicklime that already has been hydrated or slaked. You can get it in the form of mason's lime, which is grayish, or as finishing lime, which is pure white and has a smoother texture.

Gypsum plaster is made by mixing gypsum powder, which is derived by heating gypsum rock until it converts to a powder, and a retarder to prevent premature hardening and jute fiber. This product is water soluble and therefore cannot be used except on interior walls. Rain would dissolve it in a short time.

Apply the plaster to the walls in two or three coats, depending upon the type of lath used. If you use wood lath or metal lath you will need three coats; you will need only two coats if you use gypsum lath.

The first coat of plaster is called a *scratch coat*. It is usually about ¼ inch thick—just thick enough to have the needed strength to hold the subsequent coats. Start at the bottom and, using a steel trowel, spread the plaster mortar by pressing down hard enough to force it into the perforations in the lath or into the cracks in the lath strips. Work upward with an overlapping, sweeping motion and with overlapping, diagonal motions.

When you have covered the entire wall, let the mortar harden slightly and set up firmly. Then scratch or score the surface of the mortar thoroughly. This scratching gives the first coat its name. The purpose of the scratching is to provide a good bonding surface for the next coat or coats. A smooth surface provides very little bonding power for the next coat, and the mortar will break away as soon as it sets, sometimes earlier.

The second coat is called the *brown coat*. Mix the mortar so that you have one part gypsum to three parts sand. Mix these dry ingredients thoroughly and then add water and work the mixture into a paste. Apply this paste at least ¼ inch thick by working upward with overlapping strokes and diagonal strokes as you used earlier.

The third coat is called the *white coat*. This coat consists of a paste made of lime into which you work plaster of paris at the time of the application. Do not apply the plaster of paris until the brown coat is very nearly dry. Mix only small amounts of the third coat mixture, because it will set up very hard and very quickly. Apply the third coat in three stages. The first stage is a scratching-in process in which you use a steel trowel to spread a thin coat of mortar. The next coat is the doubling-up coat, which should bring the thickness of the plaster to its desired level. Apply the final coat with a steel trowel and damp brush. The purpose of this third coat is to correct any deviations on inequalities of thicknesses and to produce a smooth, polished surface.

The combined thickness of a plaster surface on a wall is about ⅝ inch. If you decide to use gypsum lath or fiberboard, you can get by with only two coats, because these two laths will provide the equivalent of the scratch coat.

For a very easy and workable scratch-coat and brown-coat plaster mortar, you can mix one part lime to two parts sand. You can vary the brown-coat mixture by using less lime or slightly more sand. The water amount depends upon how thick you want the paste. You can buy commercially-prepared cement which contains calcium sulphate instead of lime. You can also purchase marble dust to add to the mixture, if you wish.

You can mix a superior white-coat paste by using some of the commercial cements, four parts cement to one part lime putty. The directions on the container will guide you through the mixture and application of the plaster.

The previous information offers basic guides to plastering. You can however, find a fairly wide variety of materials with which to work. Some of these mixtures and processes might be more suitable to your needs than the material presented thus far. Following are some common possibilities.

PLASTER MIXTURES AND TOOLS

Plaster mixtures are similar to concrete mixtures. Both require a binder, an aggregate, and water. You must allow both to set up into a hard surface. You apply both in a plastic condition before they harden. Plaster and stucco are even more similar than plaster and concrete. The only distinction is that when a plastic mixture is used outdoors, it is called stucco; if it is used indoors, it is referred to as plaster.

Concrete and plaster differ greatly in their strength. You can use concrete in a load-bearing capacity. Plaster is never used as a structural support. Experiments are being conducted with the idea of developing a plaster that has the same load-bearing strength as concrete.

Concrete and plaster depend upon an activator for the cementitious dry ingredients. In both cases, water furnishes the hydration affect that causes the mixture to harden.

Another common quality is that Portland cement, gypsum, and lime are often used in plaster as a binder. Of the three, only gypsum plaster cannot be used in outdoor construction.

Keene's Cement, a form of gypsum plaster, is sold commercially. This product contains gypsum that has been crushed and heated until nearly all of the water has been vaporized. Adding alum offsets the unusually slow-drying or setting-up properties of this type of plaster. The following four types of gypsum plasters exist today:
☐ gypsum neat,
☐ gypsum ready-mixed,
☐ gypsum wood-fibered,
☐ gypsum bond.

The gypsum neat plaster contains only gypsum powder, no aggregate. You must add this powder, in the form of sand, at the worksite. The ready-mixed variety contains the crushed gypsum and a mineral aggregate. You need to add only water to the mixture at the jobsite. Wood-fibered gypsum contains less than 1% of nonstaining wood fibers and can be used with only water, as it comes from the package. You also can mix it with one part sand, for a very strong plaster. Gypsum bond is designed to bond or adhere to concrete walls. It contains a mixture of gypsum and up to 5% lime.

Several types of finish-coat plasters also are available. These plasters are:
☐ ready-mix,
☐ gypsum acoustical,
☐ gypsum gauging (including the quick-set, slow-set, and high-strength mixtures)
☐ gypsum molding,
☐ Keene's Cement named after the Englishman who discovered the practical use of adding the alum already mentioned.

The ready-mix gypsum plasters need only to have water added when you are ready to use them. Acoustical plasters are very useful in soundproofing rooms because they reduce most sound reverberations considerably. Gauging plasters contain lime putty which helps stabilize the plaster as it dries and also adds some degree of surface hardness. Molding plaster mixtures are used primarily in casting and ornamental work. Keene's Cement, mentioned previously, is highly resistant to fine cracking.

Lime plaster is very common. Made from crushed limestone, it is one of the types that you must slake. Slaking is done by adding the quicklime to the water, not the water to the quicklime. As you add the quicklime to the water, watch for steam to be produced. When you see the steam start to rise, mix the lime and water mixture. Continue to add more lime until the steaming stops.

If you are mixing medium-slaking and slow-slaking limes, add the water to the lime, just the reverse of the way you mixed the quicklime and water. Add the water slowly but steadily. If you add too much water, the mixture "drowns." If you add too little water, it burns. Either way, you waste the mixture.

One of the terrible qualities of quicklime, and one of the reasons you should use it only as an emergency measure, is that you must soak it for as long as 21 days before you can use it. A hydrated lime mixure is available which needs to be soaked for only 16 hours before use. One of the major uses of lime plaster in modern times is to add it to other plaster mixtures to increase hardening and to improve plasticity.

You can use Portland cement plaster indoors or outdoors. Its best qualities are water-resistance and extremely hard surface. Often the mixture contains only cement, sand, and water. For improved mixtures, you can add lime, or ground asbestos, to make the mixture more plastic.

The aggregate most often used in plaster is sand. Be careful not to permit any organic matter, such as decayed vegetation or soil, to mix with the sand. Another precaution is to keep any very coarse sand out of the mixture.

Other aggregates you can use are vermiculite and perlite. The first is a mineral subjected to intense heat, and you should use it only with gypsum plaster. *Perlite* is a volcanic glass which is heated and then crushed. Use perlite aggregate with Portland cement or gypsum.

Water, used in mixing plaster, should be clean and fresh. Do not use water that has been used previously to wash trowels and other tools because tiny portions of hardened plaster might be mixed with the new plaster which would prevent the plaster from setting up properly. Do not use water with organic impurities, such as stagnant water.

One of the most difficult tasks is to determine how much plaster to mix. You can obtain tables which will show you, for instance, that 100 pounds of gypsum will equal .69 cubic feet; one cubic foot of lime putty will equal .26 cubic feet; 100 pounds of hydrated lime will equal .64 cubic feet; 100 pounds of sand will equal .61 cubic feet; and, 94 pounds of Portland cement will equal .48 cubic feet.

You already know that one gallon of water equals .13 cubic feet. On the basis of eight gallons of water mixed with the plaster ingredients, you will have 3.25 cubic feet of plaster, if you use 100 pounds of gypsum, 250 pounds of sand, and the necessary water. How does this information help you to decide how much plaster mixture you will need? You need to figure how many square feet of wall space you will need to cover ⅝ inches thick. For a base coat, you will need about 230 pounds of gypsum, 575 pounds of sand, and enough water to give you a plastic mix, or about 22 gallons. Add the water in smaller amounts, not all at once, in the event the water proportion needs to be reduced or increased.

To mix plaster, dump the dry ingredients in a mortar pan and use a hoe to mix it thoroughly. You can purchase perforated hoes, but you also can use ordinary garden hoes. Mix the dry ingredients completely, then make a trough in the mixture and add enough water to mix well into the dry ingredients. Keep adding water until the consistency is that of a thick paste. Do not mix more than fifteen minutes. Increased agitation can cause premature hardening.

You can buy or rent electric mixers which will greatly reduce your work. If you use one of these machines, be sure to clean it thoroughly as soon as the plaster is removed. If you do not, the plaster will harden on the mixer blades and the mixer will not mix properly.

For proper plastering, you will need several tools, including a series of trowels (rectangular trowel, pointing trowel, angle trowel, and margin trowel), a hawk, and a wood flat, angle float, and sponge float. The rectangular trowel is the most important of these tools because it is the one that you use primarily to apply the plaster to the wall.

Use the pointing trowel in places where the rectangular trowel will not go. The margin trowel is smaller than the rectangular trowel. It is the one you can afford to do without, if you are trying to keep your expenses down. The angle trowel has a squared end and sides. It is used for corners and all other right-angle surfaces. (See Fig. 6-2.)

The *hawk* is a square or rectangular board or light sheet of metal with a handle extending from the center of the bottom of the board. Hold the hawk by the handle in one hand and load it with plaster. At the same time, use a trowel in your other hand to apply the plaster. The hawk has a surface 10 inches square or larger. (See Fig. 6-3.)

After you apply and smooth the plaster to the wall, use the floats to smooth it even more. Fill in any tiny cracks or crannies and level any uneven surfaces. The float also gives texture to the plaster surface.

You can buy cork floats, carpet floats, sponge floats, and other tools of a similar nature, which will help you produce the type of wall surface you want. You will not need all of these tools. Probably the cork, wood, and angle floats will provide all of the variety you need.

In addition, you can purchase or borrow rods, straightedges, featheredges, and darbies for your use. The rod and straightedge are made of wood or lightweight metals. They are 6 inches wide × 4 to 8 feet long. A handle fits into the blade. You would use this tool to straighten or level the plaster between the grounds.

The featheredge is made much like the rod. The blade tapers to a sharp edge. You would use it to cut in corners or to shape straight lines at corners or intersections.

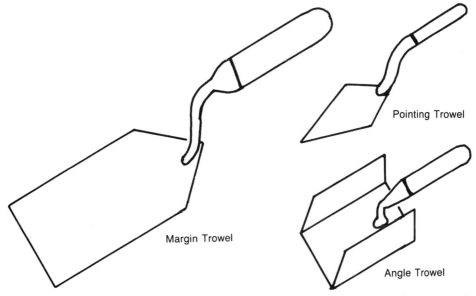

Pointing Trowel

Margin Trowel

Angle Trowel

Fig. 6-2. Shown here are three types of trowels used in plaster or other wet-wall coverings.

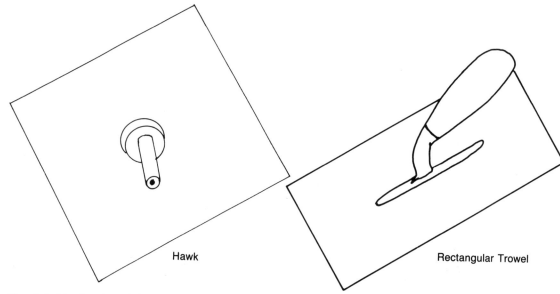

Hawk

Rectangular Trowel

Fig. 6-3. The hawk and the rectangular trowel are also necessary for plaster work.

The darby is like a float except that it has a wider blade (up to 4 feet) and a handle so that you can use both hands on it. It is used to straighten the wall even more, after it has been rodded. It is used in the same fashion as a razor blade except that the darby is inclined in the opposite direction. It is laid nearly flat and pulled along the surface of the wall for extra smoothness. (See Fig. 6-4.)

Proper plastering takes considerable practice. You might choose to hire the work done. If you decide against plaster on your walls, you might want to try one of the many other wall coverings that are available and do not require installation expertise.

One of these wall coverings is gypsum board. You have seen how gypsum is used in the preparation of plaster. The use of gypsum board gives you a similar wall covering in one respect—the same basic material is used, even though the application is vastly different.

Gypsum board comes in 4-×-8 foot dimensions. You buy it ready to install. If you have extra high ceilings, you can buy gypsum board in lengths up to 16 feet. Examine your room dimensions to see what lengths will best suit your needs.

Your room might have 8-foot ceilings, but if the room is 16 feet long, you might choose to buy the 16-foot lengths and nail them up horizontally. If the room is 20-feet long, you might choose to use a combination, such as one 16-foot board nailed up horizontally and one 4-foot width nailed vertically.

You can adapt many combinations to your room needs. Whatever combination you choose, try for combinations that will not require you to do a great deal of cutting, sawing, or piecing of shorter lengths.

Nail up the gypsum boards with 5d nails that are cement-coated, if the boards are ½ inch thick. If you use the ⅜-inch boards, use 4d, cement-coated nails. Space the nails 6 to 8 inches apart in all studs covered by the board. One 4-foot panel will cover three studs. Nail the stud surface at the edge of the board and the one concealed behind the board.

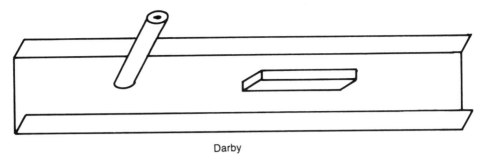

Darby

Fig. 6-4. The darby might range in length from 18 inches up to 4 feet. The handles enable you to maneuver it more smoothly across a wall surface.

Do not hit the nails extremely hard when the nail head is nearly flush with the board surface since the gypsum board will dent easily. You do want to make a small indentation when the nail is sunk. The purpose for the indentation is to drive the nail head below the actual surface of the board. Later, you will use a compound to cover the nail head. If you have a crowned or bell-head hammer, you can drive the nails more effectively. The rounded head of the hammer will make the slight indentation. A ball-peen hammer will give you the same results.

Notice that the edges of the gypsum board are slightly recessed. The surface slopes slightly so that when the two edges of panels are abutted, they will be perfectly even. You will later use the joint compound and the tape to seal the edges of the panels. The tape and compound will bring the slanted surface to the same level as the rest of the panel.

Before you start to nail, make a visual survey of the room to determine the best way to space the gypsum boards. Try to find ways to use as many whole pieces as possible. You might have to use one of the previously mentioned combinations of the horizontal and vertical nailing.

If you must cut a sheet of gypsum board, use a sharp knife with a thick blade and good point. Lay a straightedge over the surface of the panel, and position it along the cutline. Then place the knife against the straightedge and tilt the knife so that the point penetrates the paper covering and the actual board. Press down firmly—but not hard enough to break the knife blade. Pull the knife toward you, but be careful that it does not contact any part of your body if the blade slips.

Generally, the board will break almost cleanly at the point of the perforation. When you have finished with the knife, lay the board across a length of 2 × 4 so that the slit is on the outer edge of the timber. Press down firmly, and the board will break. You might need to use the knife to cut away any of the paper cover that clings to the back of the board.

After you have cut a board, position it so that the ragged edge will be in a corner or against a door facing or similar boundary. You don't want to have any edges, other than factory edges, abutting where they will have to be taped and compounded.

One of the easier ways to install gypsum board around doors and windows is to take off the facing of both. You can install the board where the facing had been—if you can do so without causing the window facing to fit poorly. In many instances, you can install gypsum board, paneling, and other wall coverings without creating difficulties.

By using the previous method, you eliminate the need to try to trim cut edges and then tape and compound them beside the windows and doors. Do the same thing around cabinets, cold air returns, bookcases, and other permanent fixtures in the room.

When you have installed all of the gypsum board, you can start the compounding work. For this phase of the work, all you need is two sheets of sandpaper—one medium and the other fine—and a putty knife.

It doesn't matter where you start—with the joints, or seams, or at the nail heads. You should complete all aspects of one stage of the work before going to the next stage.

The nail heads are easier than the joints to compound, so this might be the proper place to start, if you are not experienced in this type of work. Clean the surface area surrounding the nail head, making sure it is clean and free of all grit and other foreign substances.

Open the joint compound, or joint cement, and mix it well. During storage, the compound tends to separate slightly. If this separation occurs, mix it with a paint stirrer or putty knife. Dig the edge of the putty knife blade into the cement, turn the blade, and keep repeating this process until you have worked the ingredients back into one plastic mixture.

Dip out one-quarter bladeful of cement. Smear this over the nail head and indentation with a firm, downward pressure or sideways pressure. You should have the indentation completely filled with the compound. Use the square tip of the putty knife to scrape all excess cement from the area and return this surplus to the can. When you are finished, you should see a cemented area the size of a golf ball. It should be flush with the surface of the wall.

Apply compound to all nail indentations in the wall, and let the cement dry. While it is drying, you can start cementing and taping the joints. This work is a little harder than compounding the nail heads, and it requires considerable care and expertise if you are to keep the gypsum board joints from showing.

You can buy the joint compound in powder form. Mix the compound with water until it is the consistency of putty or other caulking compounds. When you are ready to apply the cement, use a wide-bladed putty knife, one that is at least 4 inches wide. You can use the same knife for all of the cementing work.

Be sure that the cement is not lumpy or too stiff. If it is, you will have irregularities in the joint seams or the cement will not stay on the wall properly.

When the cement is of the correct plasticity, dip out a generous bladeful, and spread it between the joint edges until all of the sloped area is filled with cement. Apply it from the floor to the ceiling. When the seam is filled, lay the putty knife blade nearly flat and pull it from top to bottom while you are exerting firm pressure. Smooth the entire seam until the cement is totally even in surface and texture. If you see any tiny lumps resulting from improperly mixed compound, stop and remove them. You can feel the lumps, even those tinier than a B-B. Dip them out with the corner of the putty knife blade.

At this point, the seam should look like a bead of butter or shortening that is perfectly uniform. Next, you should measure and cut a length of tape exactly long enough to reach from the top of the joint to the bottom.

Press the tape, starting at the top and working to the bottom, into the bed of cement. Use the putty knife to push the tape until it is embedded. Use enough pressure so that cement will start to seep through the holes in the tape.

With the tape embedded, use the putty knife again to spread more compound over the tape until it is totally hidden. Smooth the cement, as you did before, until there are no visible irregularities in the surface. Be sure that the surface is still even with the surface of the rest of the board or nearly even. If you still have a slight dip in the seam, the dip resulting from the pressure of the putty knife, do not be concerned.

Use the blade of the knife to scrape all excess compound from the gypsum board. Then let the joints dry until the cement hardens.

By this time, if the room is fairly warm, the cement over the nail heads should be dry. If it is, use the medium grade sandpaper to sand the surfaces of the cement lightly. Then use the finer sandpaper to smooth the surface even more. Nail heads should not be visible after the sanding. If any metal can be seen, apply more cement and allow it to dry.

One word of caution: it is very wise to wear a mask over your nose and mouth during the sanding stage of the work. Dust from the cement can be very irritating and damaging to lungs and membranes, and you should not be exposed for a prolonged time to the dust. It is also advisable to have plenty of fresh air coming into the room while you work.

When you have completed the sanding, you should be able to run your hand over the nail locations and not be able to detect any type of irregularity. You can also use the old plasterer's trick of standing in one corner, holding a flashlight against the wall, and shining the light across the room. If irregularities exist, they will be evident by the light and shadows.

The cement on the joints might be dry by this time. If it is, sand the joints just as you did the nail head areas. Wear the mask again to protect your respiratory tract. When you have completed the sanding, apply another thin coat of cement over the joints and nail heads to be certain that the joint or nail is covered fully. Let this cement dry and sand again. (See Fig. 6-5.)

One helpful trick is to feather the edges of the joint cement while the compound is still plastic. To feather, turn the putty knife blade sideways so that it is nearly parallel to the seams. With the blade leaning toward you slightly, pull the blade slightly down and away from the seam. As you move further from the seam, lighten the pressure gradually so that, by the time you are to the beginning of the sloped area, you are barely touching the cement. In this fashion, you thin the cement so that you blend it with the surface of the gypsum board.

When you have completed the sanding and the work is totally dry, inspect it once more to see that it is done to your satisfaction. If it is, you can clean the room by sweeping and then vacuuming the area, to eliminate all of the grit and fine cement that fell during the sanding.

Let the cement stand for a day or so. Check it again for any cracked or separated cement. You can now paint the walls as you would any other household surface.

INSTALLING INTERIOR PLYWOOD

We have previously discussed how plywood sheathing can be installed to the exterior studs and corner posts. Plywood wall covering is also easy to install on interior walls, and the finished look is rewarding and satisfying.

Like gypsum board, you can nail plywood panels vertically or horizontally. Also, like gypsum board, you can buy plywood in a variety of sizes. The most common size

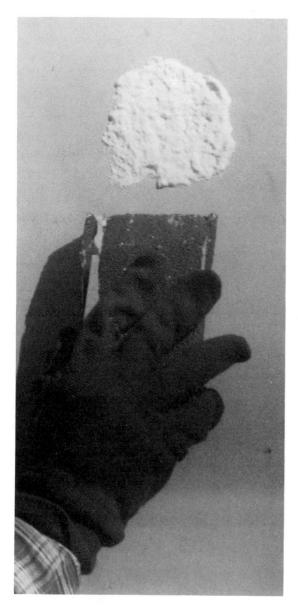

Fig. 6-5. Sand wall compound lightly until it is perfectly smooth and as thin as possible and still cover.

is the 4-×-8 foot panels. Many building supply houses stock only this one size, because most rooms have 8-foot walls.

Examine the room's measurements to see how you can best cover the wall with the plywood. Consider the smaller areas over doors and over and under windows. You will need sections of plywood about 1 foot high and 4 feet wide. Try to work out the installation plan so that you can use as many scrap pieces as possible and will not have to cut a whole panel in order to cover a small area. (See Fig. 6-6.)

Fig. 6-6. Use whole panels whenever possible. Use scraps or sections of panels for spaces around windows and doors. Here is the opposite side of a plywood-covered wall.

Always start installing plywood in a corner. Stand the panel in the corner as you want to install it and, with one edge of the panel abutted against the corner post, put a level on the other edge to see if the corner is truly square.

You must start with a square corner placement of the panel. If the room corner is not square, you will have to modify the panel so that the edge away from the corner is in a true vertical position.

You can determine where the problem is located by standing the panel in the corner, as before, with one edge abutted against the corner post and a level on the other edge. Hold the panel as steadily as you can by pushing it tightly against the studding. While holding it in this position, use a tape measure to see how far one corner is from contact with the corner post.

If, for instance, the top corner fails to touch the corner post, and if there is 1½ inches of space between the top corner of the panel and the corner post, take the panel down and mark a point on the bottom edge, 1½ inches from the corner that will fit against the corner post when the panel is installed.

Lay a straightedge on the panel so that it reaches from the mark you just made to a point on the very edge of the panel 4 feet up. Let the straightedge slant gently from the bottom mark to the corner edge of the panel. The 1½-inch-cutoff represents the distance from the top panel corner to the corner post. When this portion is cut off, the panel should then fit squarely into the corner so that the outside edge of the panel will be perfectly vertical. Now all subsequent panels should fit well and be vertical across the rest of the room.

If you do not make the out-of-square correction at the corner, you will find that the panels will not fit properly at any point across the rest of the wall. You will find that, in the far corner of that wall, you will have additional problems. Make the needed corrections while it is easy to do so.

Do not nail up the panel at this point. You first must decide what you will use for a wall support. If you nail the panel to the studs, you soon learn that the plywood does not provide very much wall support, and it will give considerably when pressure is applied away from the studs.

You can nail in blocking if you wish. Nail 2-×-4 blocks between the studs so that the blocks are spaced ⅓ and ⅔ of the way down. You can also use three blocks between studs if you wish. Just space these blocks evenly. (See Fig. 6-7.)

Another, and perhaps easier, way is to install nailers, or furring strips, across the studs, at right angles to them. These strips of wood can be 2 inches wide and 1 inch thick or slightly thinner if you prefer. Do not use strips thinner than ½ inch. Space these furring strips 15 inches apart from the top to the bottom of the studs.

When you are ready to install the panels of plywood, spread a coat of glue along the furring strips where the panels will fit. Set the panel in place, and then press it firmly into the glue. Hold it there for a minute or so, until the glue has had a chance to bond to the panel and to the furring strip. Nail the plywood to the furring strips for an even tighter bond. Use small nails designed especially for this purpose.

Use glue even if you decide to nail in blocking as support for the panels. In this event, you can install plywood panels in a better way. With the blocking even with the inner edges of the studs, you can spread a bead of glue on the blocking and on the stud edges as well.

Spread one bead of glue down the center of the stud. Make sure it is thick enough so that when you press the stud in place, a small bead of glue will emerge from under the panel and will remain there until the next panel is installed. Set the next panel in place, and press the edge tightly against the edge of the first panel. Then press the second panel toward the stud so that the bead of glue is pressed between the panels.

When the glue bead is dry, you can sand the glue down so that it is flush with the exposed surface of the panels. You can paint the panels when you wish. The glue will cover easily with paint.

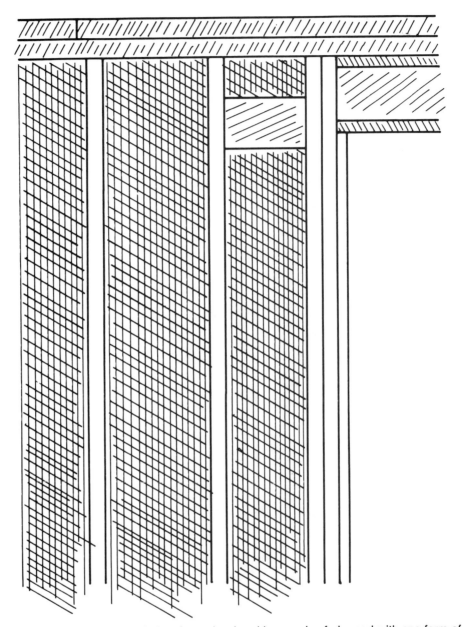

Fig. 6-7. Shown here is a window frame bordered by panels of plywood with one form of blocking.

If you have the equipment or access to it, you can bevel the edges of the plywood panels before you install the plywood. The result will be a smooth and attractive *V*. Some people enjoy the spline method of joining plywood panels. You can create this effect by cutting or buying thin strips of wood. After you have left a space between the panels, fill in the gap with the wood splines. You should glue the splines in place by applying a very thin bead of glue to the back of the spline and then pressing the spline into the gap between the panels. If you attempt to nail the splines in place, you might split the thin strips of wood.

Next, measure the distance between the last panel installed and the corner. If the distance is the same at both top and bottom, you can mark and cut your panel accordingly. If there is a serious discrepancy, you will have to cut the panel as you did when you installed the first panel. (See Fig. 6-8.)

Fig. 6-8. At corners and at windows and doors you occasionally must fit the panel to the existing edge.

Fig. 6-9. When you are installing plywood around an outside corner, you can hold the panel in place with a level against it and mark the edge of the corner. In this way, you can fit the corners well and retain the vertical trueness of the panel.

Measure the distance between the last installed panel and corner post at the top, middle, and bottom. Then measure off the same distances on the plywood, mark the locations, and connect the marks with a straight line along the complete length of the panel. (See Fig. 6-9.)

When you are ready for the adjacent wall, abut the first panel into the one that you have just installed. Check the corner for correct fit, then hold a level to the outside edge of the new panel. Make any corrections as you did with the first panel you installed.

When you have covered the entire room, you can install corner molding to conceal the edges of the panels in the corners. This molding is very inexpensive and you can nail it up in a few minutes with four or five finish nails.

Another wall-covering material available is fiberboard. This material usually comes in sections 2 feet wide × 8 feet long. Nail these up horizontally across the studding. Start at the bottom, or floor, and work your way up to the ceiling. You can join fiberboard easily, because the edges are either rabbeted or tongue and groove.

The only problem left is the installation of wall covering around wall plates and switches. We will discuss this problem in the following chapter, because the same methods are used in the installation of paneling. See Chapter 7: Installing Paneling, for more details.

After you have completed covering the studding, check for panels that might have broken their bond and have edges sticking out too far. Check also for nail heads that are visible or for joint tape that is coming loose. Correct any of these problems before leaving the job.

With gypsum board, plywood, or fiberboard in place, you can paint as you would any wood surface. You can also cover the panels with paneling or wallpaper, if you wish.

7
Installing Paneling

ONE OF THE MAJOR DIFFERENCES BETWEEN PANELING AND PLYWOOD, or gypsum board, is the thickness. Most paneling is only ¼ inch thick. Some types, however, are ³⁄₁₆ inch thick, ⁵⁄₃₂ inch thick, and ½ inch thick. The thicker the paneling, the more it costs.

Sizes range from the traditional 4-foot × 8-foot sheets to 10-foot lengths. Most of the time, anything longer than 8 feet will have to be a special-order product.

Because paneling is often very thin, you must have support behind it. You can use furring strips nailed over studs, or you can use studs and blocking, as you did with the plywood installation. See Chapter 6 for details.

Before you begin installation, you should consider the types of paneling available. Many times you can find paneling for sale at a reduced price, but beware of some bargains. At times, the reduced paneling is a closeout item, and no more will be available if you have miscalculated your needs or if you ruined a sheet. It is sometimes very difficult to make an accurate estimate on the quantity of paneling that will be needed for a particular job.

For example, let's look at a bedroom that is 16 feet wide and 18 feet long. You will need eight full sheets of paneling and several partial sheets, to fill in under windows and over windows and doors. The number of panels you will need depends upon the number of windows and doors in the room and the way the room is structured. In this example, there is a fairly large fireplace, a door leading to the bathroom, another door leading to the hallway, and one closet. Two windows exist on the fireplace wall and one window in the other exterior wall.

Paneling will be saved as a result of the three doors, three windows, and the fireplace, which has a full profile reaching from floor to ceiling between the windows. One full sheet will suffice for all of the spaces over and under windows and spaces over doors.

In an adjacent bathroom, which is 10 feet × 13 feet, more paneling was needed to cover the walls than is needed for the bedroom, even though the bedroom is more than twice as large as the bathroom. In the bathroom, you have the vanity area, which is separated

90

from the tub area, and the commode space is recessed. This fact means that the wall separating the vanity area from the tub area will require twice as much paneling because it must be covered on both sides. There is only one small window and two doors.

The commode recess requires nearly three whole sheets of paneling, while the fireplace wall of the bedroom needed only two large partial sheets and some smaller pieces above and below the windows.

It can be difficult to judge the amount of paneling you will need. The most obvious way to make the estimate is to use your rule, or tape measure, and record the exact distances across the spaces that will need paneling.

Take the bedroom example as evidence. On the north wall, from the corner to the window, it is 5 feet. From the window to the wall is another 5 feet. The east wall is, excluding doors, 10 feet long. The south wall has two 2-foot sections and a recess that is 4 feet wide and 2 feet 4 inches deep. The west wall has two 2½ foot sections.

The 5-foot sections require only one sheet of paneling and two small pieces from another sheet. The remainder of the sheet that had the two panels cut from it will be large enough to fit beside the closet on the south wall. In a similar fashion, you can use leftover sections to fill in smaller spaces. The result is that you will need much less paneling than you think.

The eight spaces above and below windows and above doors can be cut from one sheet of paneling. You can calculate your own needs in a similar fashion and find that you can save a great deal of paneling costs. Some supply houses will accept returns of unused building materials and give refunds; others will allow a price to be applied on other merchandise. Still others charge to deliver or pick up materials. You need to know how your dealer will react to the return or exchange of materials before you invest much money in something with such limited use as paneling.

You can use 2 × 4s or 4-inch boards in numerous projects around the house and yard, but paneling can have a very limited number of uses. Try to have an accurate estimate of paneling needs. Be sure you can purchase additional quantities, if necessary, or return unused paneling.

Start paneling in corners, just as you did plywood. Chapter 6 offers detailed suggestions for plywood installation. When you have the corner panel installed, proceed across the wall by abutting the next panel against the previous one.

Many manufacturers suggest that you use a dime, spaced between the panels, to allow for movement of the paneling during expansion or contraction caused by settling or weather changes. If you agree to do this, you should paint the stud edges where the paneling joints occur so there will not be a color contrast. When the joints separate slightly, the sight of bright white wood behind dark paneling is unattractive.

In our own home, we have never spaced the panels, and we have never encountered any difficulties. This statement is not to recommend that you not leave the dime's thickness between panels, but we, along with many others, have never left any space, and we haven't had any problems.

When you come to door and window frames, it is much easier and neater to take down the frame and install the paneling behind it than it is to try to cut the paneling to a perfect fit. You can use tape and cement to conceal plywood edges, but there is nothing but molding to hide paneling problems.

Cutting paneling can be tricky. When using a handsaw, you can mark the paneling for cutting on the back of the panel and cut without difficulty, if the edge is to be concealed by corner molding or under window framing.

You often need to cut down a panel seam. You cannot make this cut effectively without seeing the face of the paneling. If you use a circular saw, you will splinter the face of the panel, so you must use a handsaw. The smaller the kerf, the better, so use a saw that is thin or has many teeth to the inch. You can use a hacksaw blade for good results, if you can control the kerf line. Hacksaw blades are thin and easily bent. If you are not careful your cutline will be crooked.

Do not try to saw down the center of the joint seam. Instead, position the blade so that it is against the very side of the panel, so that the entire seam is left intact. (See Fig. 7-1.) You can saw the seam very easily, so use a slow, patient sawing motion and let the saw glide through the soft material.

You can also use a good pocketknife with a strong blade. One of the hawk-bladed knives works well if it is sharp. Lay the sheet of paneling on a hard, smooth work surface and place the hook of the knife blade against the panel. Press down hard enough to cause the blade to penetrate the soft wood and, with a straightedge held securely in place to

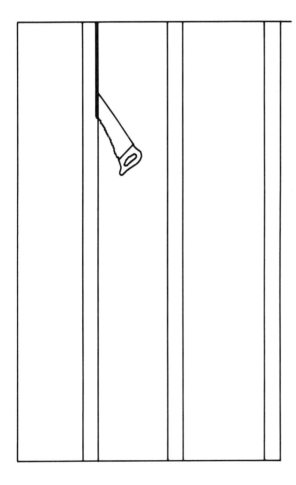

Fig. 7-1. When sawing paneling lengthwise, do not try to split the groove; instead, saw to the extreme side of the groove, and the next section will fit neatly against the cut edge.

guide the knife, draw the blade along the seam edge until you reach the end of the panel. You might have to return and draw the knife along the length of the paneling once or twice more. This method is very fast, and the knife blade does not create a kerf. Take care that the blade does not slip and scar the face of the panel.

When you are installing paneling, you can buy special nails that match the colors of your paneling. If you use such nails, they will be nearly invisible.

When you need to take down a sheet of paneling, do not attempt to use a claw hammer to extract the nails holding the paneling. Instead, slip the point, or blade, of a small crowbar or large screwdriver under the edge of the panel near a nail and lift, or pry, gently until the paneling slips over the tiny head of the nails. Go around the entire panel and do the same thing. Then the panel will lift out easily. (See Fig. 7-2.)

If you try to use a claw hammer, you will almost certainly scar the face of the panel or damage it beyond use. You should never use any edged tool or anything with an abrasive surface on the face of paneling, because the material is too fragile.

When you are installing paneling, the panel seams should be completely vertical. Stop occasionally, and use a level on the edge of a panel to be certain that you are not deviating from a plumb line. If you find that you have deviated, take down the panel and check the previous one. If it, too, is out of line, take down the next one, and continue until the problem has been solved.

You do not have to worry excessively, as long as you have installed the first panel squarely and if you have abutted all subsequent panels against the edge of the first or next panels. The only reason you might go awry is that you might have bought a panel that

Fig. 7-2. Instead of ripping down paneling, use a punch to force the nails all the way through the paneling. You can also use the punch to sink nails safely without damaging surfaces.

was manufactured incorrectly, but this is a very rare occurrence. Just be sure to install the first panel correctly.

When you reach the far corner, and when you have measured and cut the final panel, or partial panel, go to the next wall (the one that joins the one you have completed). Start the first panel as you did on the previous wall, making certain that it is vertical and that you have a good corner fit. Remember to stand the panel in place and then make a visual inspection of the fit. If you have a deviation at the top, measure it, and then measure and mark that same amount on the bottom. Then run a straightedge from the mark to the top corner of the panel. When you cut along the mark, your fit should be nearly perfect.

Any time you feel that there is not sufficient support behind the panels, stop and nail in blocking. A panel that is not well supported, in addition to being fragile, will allow a great deal of cold air to enter or conditioned air to escape.

As mentioned earlier, some people like to install paneling over gypsum board or plasterboard. Although it is rather expensive to do so, the double thickness of wall covering will give you improved insulation qualities, stronger walls, and some soundproofing qualities. Gypsum has the unique capacity to prevent reverberations from passing through it. You will be delighted with the results.

Should you decide to install paneling over gypsum board, nail up the gypsum board horizontally. Then nail up the paneling in a vertical fashion. Be sure that your studs are spaced properly if you choose this method of wall covering. If they are not spaced properly, they will not provide a nailing surface for the paneling. Only the gypsum board will receive the nails, and the gypsum board does not retain nails well at all. In a matter of a few days or weeks the paneling will pull loose and only the molding will be holding it in place.

If gypsum board is nailed in a vertical fashion, you cannot see the studding. You can see only the line of nails, and you must assume that there is an adequate nailing surface aligned with the nails.

If, for some reason, you cannot practically nail up the gypsum board horizontally, be sure that your panels lap when you install the paneling. You might find it necessary to cut one gypsum board panel lengthwise and install it in a corner and then abutt all subsequent boards against it. When you nail up paneling, each panel will lap the gypsum boards and provide a sturdier wall. The right-angle installation is still the best method, if it is at all possible and practical.

Earlier, it was suggested that you remove the facing on all windows and install the paneling under the window frame. Good reasons for doing so exist. You will find that if you do not do so, cold air will enter the room from under the facing and between the facing and the edge of the panels. (See Fig. 7-3.)

Secondly, the finished look will not be attractive if you do not follow this procedure. It will be necessary for you to cut panels, because it would be rare for a room to be designed that all windows would be 4 or 8 feet from a corner. If you cut paneling anywhere except along a seam, the cut will be visible from across the room.

If you plan to paint the window facing to blend aesthetically with the paneling, it is wise to paint the facing boards before they are installed. Otherwise, it is so easy to smear paint on the new paneling.

Another problem with window facing is that often window frames are not perfectly square and the facing is not perfectly vertical. If it is not, you will know it as soon as

Fig. 7-3. Here, the window frames had been removed and then replaced over the paneling, which was cut thick for a frontier look. Batten was used over grooves.

an edge of a panel is abutted against the facing. The paneling edge is a factory edge and is quite likely to be completely straight. Any discrepancy will be noticeable immediately.

INSTALLING PANELING IN RECESSES AND OTHER PROBLEM AREAS

In many rooms, there will be at least one irregular wall. It would be ideal for all rooms to be built square, with walls and doors and window spaces divisible by four, but this is not realistic. You must deal with the wall irregularities, if they exist.

In many instances, a closet is added to a large room. One of the usual ways of making the addition is to go to a wall that doesn't have any windows or doors and mark off the space for the closet. If the closet is to be large enough for you to hang suits or dresses without wrinkling or crowding them, it should be at least 28 inches deep.

The closet builder probably started in a corner and laid off a sole-plate line, 28 inches from the wall, and continued the line for the desirable length of the closet, (usually 6 feet).

Because it is not practical to run the closet directly to a window, there will probably be a recess between the end of the closet and the window. In other instances, a wall might be angled for a short distance in order to provide for suitable wiring installation, particularly if the room is undergoing the modification mentioned earlier. In such instances, it is often necessary to deal with problems in the most practical, if not the most desirable, manner.

If you have recesses or alcoves in a room that is being paneled, you can handle the difficulties very easily by using the following methods. First, be sure that you have sufficiently supported the closet or alcove walls, that you have properly placed the studs, and that you have installed any necessary blocking.

It is easier to install the back or deepest panel first. This piece, if it must be cut and fit, is the most difficult to adapt to a perfect size. Measure the back space at the top, the middle, and the bottom. Then select a panel and lay it on its unfaced side so that the face side is up. Measure and mark the needed panel size and saw carefully, using a handsaw or the blade of a hacksaw to keep the edges undamaged.

Slip this first panel into the existing space carefully. If the fit is good, you might have to maneuver it into position with considerable difficulty, particularly if the side walls of the alcove have any irregularities in them.

If the panel will not fit into the space, try to locate and mark the problem area. Trim this area slightly by using either a pocketknife or a plane. Be careful not to trim away much of the panel. After you have trimmed slightly, try the panel in the space again. Keep trimming and fitting until you have the panel the right size.

Nail in the panel in the normal fashion. Try to get the corner nail lines as close to the adjacent wall as possible. Nail the panel securely along the top and bottom as well as down both sides.

Install paneling on the inside wall of the alcove next. Here you must set a panel in place so that the edge abuts into the panel you have just installed. Hold the panel in place while you check to see if it fits good at the top and the bottom. If not, measure the distance from the wall to the trouble point. Mark the panel and cut as you did earlier.

When the panel fits perfectly or at least acceptably at the back, hold it firmly in place and mark the unfaced side where it passes the outer corner of the alcove. It might be necessary for you to secure the panel in place while you mark. If so, drive in one paneling nail at the top and bottom. Do not sink the nails. Drive them in only as far as necessary for them to hold the panel in place while you mark the unfaced side. (See Fig. 7-4.)

When the panel is firmly in place, go behind the edge that protrudes beyond the wall frame and make a mark as close to the corner of the wall frame as you possibly can.

Because the mark is on the back, you will need to saw the cutline with the face of the panel down. Circular saws splinter the top surface, so you will have the paneling in the proper position for sawing. If you use a handsaw, it will make no difference which side of the paneling is facing up. Saw the line as clean and as straight as possible, because when you install the panel, it will need to conform to the edge of the closet as closely as possible. You will nail another panel to the outside closet wall, letting the new edge cover the panel in the recess.

You can now nail up the paneling on the third and final wall of the recessed area, which will start you down the exterior wall. If the wall holds windows and fireplace, take down the window framing and try to fit the paneling against the fireplace with as much accuracy as possible.

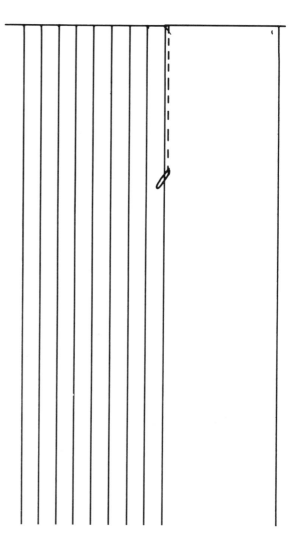

Fig. 7-4. With the new panel extending beyond the corner, mark the back side and cut along the line. Keep the pencil as snug against the corner as possible.

Some fireplaces stick out from the wall 6 inches or more, while others are flush with the wall. If the fireplace is flush with the wall, you can slightly lap the paneling over the bricks for a snug fit. A 2-×-4 stud will be beside the profile, but sometimes there is a slight space between stud and bricks. If this is the case, stuff as much insulation as you can get into the crevice.

Use your leftover pieces of scrap insulation in this crevice. Use a screwdriver to shove or poke the insulation into the opening. Keep cramming insulation in the opening until it is flush with the edge of the stud. When you nail the panel into place, no cold air will be able to enter the room between the stud and the fireplace profile.

After you have nailed the paneling in place, nail a strip, or batten, across the crack between the paneling and the fireplace profile for a neater appearance. The strip or the molding can slightly lap both panel and profile.

Install the insulation and paneling the same on both sides of the fireplace. Now turn your attention to the window and door frames and facing.

PANELING AROUND WINDOWS AND DOORS

You have already been advised to take down framing and facing before you attempt to install paneling around windows and doors. This task is not difficult or troublesome, and you can save yourself time and energy while improving the looks of the job.

To take down the door facing, you will first need to remove the molding or trim around the door. Use care and very little pressure. The trim work is composed of thin and fairly fragile wood which can be broken easily or scarred while you take it down. You need to be extremely careful where nails have already weakened the wood. You can break the molding or trim at these points very easily. (See Fig. 7-5.)

A reasonably safe place to start is at one of the top corners of the door. Choose a corner that will not show if you should scar the wood slightly. Use a small screwdriver, or similar instrument, and lightly tap the handle with a hammer until the blade of the screwdriver is forced between the top and side molding, which is mitered to fit around the door facing neatly.

Fig. 7-5. When using thick batten over grooves, use thin-shanked nails to keep from splitting fragile batten wood.

Work the blade up and down slightly until you have loosened the closest finishing nails in the top molding. When you have more working space, insert a small crowbar or larger screwdriver and pry the top molding loose or, after you have pried the piece up slightly, tap the top with a hammer and drive it back into its original position. The nails, which have been withdrawn from the fiber pressure, will sometimes not reseat. Instead they will remain a quarter-inch or so extended from the wood. You can pull them out with a claw hammer.

Keep working across the top until you can lift the top molding off. Then work the blade of a small crowbar or large screwdriver between the door framing and the molding. Insert the blade of the tool so that it will not break the outside edge of the molding but will still provide leverage.

Pry the molding loose at the top of the side molding and gently insert the screwdriver deeper until there is room for you to use a larger crowbar. Do not exert great pressure. The larger crowbar, or construction bar, provides powerful leverage. Even a weak person can damage molding severely without being aware of the force being exerted.

If you are not careful, you can damage the edge of the molding that laps over the front of the door frame. The crowbar will be in direct contact with the molding edge as as you pry. One way to avoid the damage is to try to pull out the nails once you have loosened the molding slightly. Another way is to slip a thin strip of wood (1 × 1) behind the molding, and work the wood wedge down the side of the door, loosening the molding.

You will not have a problem with molding if the wall is newly constructed. The material offered here is for rooms that were finished earlier.

When you have removed the molding from both sides of the door, you can use a crowbar to remove the facing. Facing boards are usually strong 1 × 4's which you are not likely to damage, if you use the leverage gradually. It is usually easier to pry the top facing loose first by inserting the blade or point of the crowbar behind the end of the facing and using the trimmer stud or common stud as your leverage point.

Next, take down the side facing boards in the same manner. Lay them aside so they will not be damaged. Be careful to drive out the finishing nails so there is no danger that a worker will step on a nail and injure his foot severely.

You can remove window molding and facing in basically the same way as door molding and facing. If the window or door is on an exterior wall, you might need to install the paneling around each door or window as you finish removing the molding and facing. If the weather is cold, a great deal of heat loss can result from the openings. If the weather is hot, you will have insect and heat entry.

While the facing is off windows and doors on exterior walls, pack insulation anywhere it was not installed properly when the wall was constructed. Use the same method as before: use scrap insulation, and pack it by using the point of a screwdriver until the insulation is flush with the inside edges of the studding and window or door framing.

Nail up the paneling by working from a corner and then moving toward the window or door. Set the final panel in place to see if it will fit against the window frame. Keep the panel whole if you can. Any cuts you make in the paneling will mostly be covered by facing, but above doors and above and below windows, the exposed cut can be seen.

It is a good idea to stand the panels against the wall from corner to window to get an idea how many panels will be needed. If you must cut one panel so that you will have a proper fit at the window frame, cut the panel that will fit in the corner. The cut edge will not show in the corner because another panel edge will be covering the cut edge of the panel on the window side of the wall. Even if this does not occur, you can use corner molding to cover the cut.

You might have windows and doorways that are 4 feet across. If so, you are fortunate, because the panel will not have to be cut vertically. If the window is not 4 feet across, you will still have to cut the panel vertically. Make your cut along a seam or groove and keep your saw at the extreme edge of the groove.

Install the section of paneling over the window or door first and then abut the full-length panels against it. Install the segment under the window and drop a perpendicular line from the edge of the top segment to the edge of the bottom segment to see if the two sections are properly aligned. If the edges do not align properly, hold a level against the two edges to learn which segment is not vertical. Make the necessary corrections, and then finish installing the two segments. It is always a good idea to fasten a panel with only four nails—one in each corner and in the proper locations—before you complete the installation. Do not drive the first four nails all the way in. You want just enough hold to keep the panel in place while you inspect it. When you are satisfied that the panel is positioned properly, complete the installation by driving the four nails in the rest of the way and then adding all other necessary nails.

Nail in the panels on both sides of the window next. Check to see that the fit is correct. If your window and door frames are square, your work will be much easier. If the openings are not square, you will have to tailor the panels and segments of panels in order to get a good fit.

When you have installed the panels on both sides of the window or door, you can replace the facing and molding. Use the same nail holes in both facing and molding, and try to hit the same holes in the framing. These pieces of facing and molding do not have any bearing capacity; their only purpose is decorative.

Move to the next window or door and repeat the process. You will find that, if you install the paneling under the frames, the results will have a professional and attractive appearance.

PANELING AROUND WALL SWITCHES AND OUTLETS

If you are working on a finished room, your wall outlets and switch plates will already be installed. You will need to take the covers off before you can remove the old wall covering (if it is paneling or similar covering). If you plan to panel around these wall switches and outlets, you will also have to remove the covers.

This task is quite easy to do. Most wall switch covers have two screws holding them in place—one at the top and another at the bottom. Outlet covers usually have one screw holding them. It is between the two plugs or outlets. All you need to do is use a small or medium-sized screwdriver to loosen the screws and remove them. You can then remove the cover plate readily.

While these cover plates are off, be very careful while you work if there is electrical power to the switches and outlets. It is never a bad idea to turn off the power to a circuit if you are working near exposed wiring or connections. If you must have the electrical power in order to operate your saw and other tools requiring electricity, work away from the outlets when possible.

If you are covering new walls, your job is much easier than covering older walls, especially if the adjacent wall has no wall covering on it. All walls will eventually be covered, though, and sooner or later, you must cover a wall that has no adjoining uncovered wall.

Two basic ways of paneling around wall outlets and switches can be used. The difficult way is to install all panels up to the point where the outlet or switch is located. Measure from all points to the top, bottom, and edges of the switch or outlet, and then mark your panel accordingly.

For example, assume that the outlet box is located near the middle of the panel you are installing. You will need to measure from the floor to the bottom and then to the top of the outlet box. Then measure from the edge of the last panel to the near edge of the outlet box and then to the far edge of the outlet box. Write down all measurements; then measure off the distances on the back of the panel you are ready to install. If your measurements and markings are accurate, you can mark off the perimeter of the switch or outlet box.

Mark the top and bottom, as well as both sides, of the outline of the wall boxes. You can use a strong, sharp knife blade to cut out the rectangle if the paneling is thin. Otherwise, you will need a saw.

When using a knife to cut the panel for the wall boxes, lay the panel facedown on a smooth, clean surface. Do not lay it on any surface that might scratch or deface the panel. With the panel in place, hold a straightedge firmly along one vertical line and sink the point of the knife at the top of the line. Holding the knife firmly (a hawkbill knife works well here), pull the knife toward you and exert enough pressure for the blade to cut $\frac{1}{16}$ inch into the paneling. Lift the knife and repeat the stroke until the knife blade penetrates the paneling fully. Then cut along the other vertical line in the same way.

When both vertical lines are cut, you can cut the horizontal lines. You will find that it will be more difficult to make these cuts, so do not put great pressure on the knife blade. Instead, make several shallow cuts until the blade penetrates the paneling across the length of the line.

Finish the cut by repeating the process along the bottom horizontal line. When the two horizontal lines meet the two vertical lines, the rectangle should fall free. Now hold the panel in position to see if the cutout fits over the wall box as it should.

An easier way to make the cutout is to mark the rectangle as before. Then use a hand drill to bore a small hole at one corner of the rectangle so that the perimeter of the hole barely touches the lines of the rectangle corner. Make one hole in the top left and bottom right of the rectangle.

When the tip of the drill barely penetrates the paneling, go to the next hole site and drill again until the point penetrates. Turn the panel, and complete the drilling from the other side so you will not splinter the panel face.

When you have drilled the two holes, insert a hacksaw blade in one hole and line the blade up with one line of the rectangle. Saw along the line until you reach the corner. Start again at the hole and saw to the other corner.

At this point, move to the second hole, and saw in both directions until all four directional cuts meet. Take the rectangle of wood out and discard it. You are ready to nail up the panel, once you try it to see that it fits well.

An easier way to mark the paneling for wall boxes is to remove the cover and simply rub chalk around the edges of the box. Stand the panel in place carefully so that you do not smear the chalk around the back of the panel. Press the panel firmly against the wall box. When you take the panel down, you should have a perfect outline of the wall box, in the exact location for the cutout to give you a perfect fit.

You can handle a switch box in a similar manner. While you cannot chalk the edges of the box because the switch will hit the panel and keep it from touching the box edges, you can apply the chalk to the switch itself. Take care that the switch is not flipped from the on position to off while you are marking. You will have a point of chalk on the back of the panel. Now measure from the switch (in the position it was in when you made the chalk mark) to the sides of the box and to the top and bottom. Measure and mark the outline on the back of the panel accordingly. Bore the holes, and saw out the rectangle as you did before. Then position the panel and nail it in place.

If your cutout did not work properly, the panel is not totally ruined. You can use it for filling spaces over and under windows and over doors. If the cutout is slightly incorrect, you can make slight modifications, because the switch and outlet plates will cover a slight discrepancy.

One of the most troublesome parts of a room is the space between the doors and the corners. Often the space is too small for a full board's width of paneling. You will have to cut a section of paneling vertically where there is no groove. When you nail up the narrow section, the cut edge will be visible, and you will not be able to use batten or molding to cover all of it.

Fig. 7-6. Here extra-thick wall covering is being installed. You will need extra-long screws for switch boxes and outlets.

Fig. 7-7. Here is a sample of homemade paneling, which was sawed from fallen trees with a chainsaw. You can use thin batten over the grooves or leave them as they are, if you install building paper behind the paneling.

The best way out of this problem is to measure the space between the door and the corner carefully at the top and the bottom. If the two distances are the same, you can mark the proper segment of the paneling accordingly. If they are not the same, you will need to tailor the piece to fit.

You will cover part of the cut edge with door facing and trim, but the part that extends above the door will be visible and unsightly. Cut the panel along a groove so that the entirety of the groove is left on the section you will use. Then trim off the surplus material from the corner side of the piece so that you will have a full groove to fit against the paneling segment to be installed above the door.

You can cut down the middle of one of the paneling board's sections. Then turn the piece upside down, using the exterior edge against the short segment above the door. When you nail in the segment, the cut will not show because the corner will be covered with molding.

Sometimes, a wall will not be perfectly flat. You might have short sections of slanted walls that will also have to be paneled. You can avoid the sight of raw edges by measuring and cutting the paneling so that grooves are abutted against the flat surface of the rest of the wall. If you have slight discrepancies at the top of the wall or along the floor, you can cover the problem with a baseboard or molding. The fit does not have to be perfect.

When you have completed these problem areas, the wall should be perfectly covered. All that remains is to put the covers back on the wall switches and outlets.

If the paneling is extra thick, the covers might not fit well on the outlet and switch boxes. You might have to use longer screws to secure the covers. You might need to turn off the power, then free the switch or outlet box by releasing the screws that hold it in place and moving the boxes slightly forward. See Figs. 7-6 and 7-7.

Chapter 8 offers some suggestions on installing wood siding to the exterior walls of your house.

8
Wood Siding

FOR CENTURIES WOOD WAS ONE OF THE MOST IMPORTANT SIDING MA-terials in America, and in post-World War II, brick building practices started to outdistance wood use in siding. Other important siding materials that emerged in prominence were stone, asbestos-cement shingles, wood shingles or shakes, aluminum siding, and, more recently, vinyl siding.

After all these years, though, wood has made a strong comeback. It is again a highly desirable siding for people of all income levels throughout the country.

Several reasons exist for the renewed popularity of wood as siding material. First, the cost, while not cheap, is not prohibitively expensive. Second, wood siding creates a beautiful exterior for many styles of houses. Third, few tools are needed for wood construction. You need a good saw, hammer, level, square, and a few other inexpensive tools, such as a plumb bob and a good tape measure.

Another reason for the popularity of wood is that the do-it-yourselfer does not have to possess a great deal of expertise or experience in order to do a very creditable job with wood siding. Bricklaying for many, if not most people, is a different matter. If you do not understand the work, it is very easy to create a catastrophe.

With wood siding you work with one piece of timber or lumber at a time, and you can measure, fit, cut, nail, and paint the completed work with a minimum of expertise. All you need do is follow a few basic suggestions and guidelines.

As with many areas of construction work around the house, first you must inspect the work surface carefully. You can do this visually first and later with some simple physical elements.

To make the visual inspection, all you need to do is look at the wall surface where the siding will be installed to check for any signs of bad wood or future problems. What you are looking for particularly are signs of decay or insect or rodent damage.

One clear sign of decay is fungus growth or dark patches of wood at the bottom of studding, along the sole plate, or on the sills. Such decay is caused by two major forces:

moisture inside the walls for prolonged periods, or the use of green lumber in the original construction. As you know, decay spores are constantly in the air in all habitable environments. These spores, which are fungus cells, can cause decay as they grow and spread around the timbers of any wood construction.

The key to controlling fungus growth is keeping the wood as dry as possible. Fungi need at least a 20 percent moisture content in the wood for them to survive. Water inside walls can provide this moisture content. The water comes from three primary sources. First, the house leaks badly enough for the rain or snowfall to find its way into the walls. The wall itself might not leak, but the water can enter through a defective roof, run down rafters, and then drip into the wall cavity. Or, the rain might blow behind the window frame and seep downward until it collects in the wall on top of the sole plate.

A second source of water is condensation from pipes. This condensation occurs primarily when temperatures fluctuate several degrees in a short period of time. The water in the pipes might come from a well or from a holding tank under the house. It might come through underground pipes. Any of these sources will cause the water temperature to be much lower than the temperature inside the wall.

Water from a well or holding tank might be 60-65 degrees, while the temperature inside the wall might be in the upper eighties or even higher. Water pipes carrying the water to bathrooms or to the kitchen or darkroom will cause the pipes to sweat. The drops of water will fall to the subflooring and remain there to provide moisture for the ever-present decay spores.

A third major source of water in a wall comes from the fact that green lumber was used. The sap in green lumber is primarily water. When you install the lumber in a closed-in wall, the water will remain in the lumber for years and years and present an invitation to decay spores and to certain types of insects.

Another source of water in walls is leaking pipes. The pipes might have a slightly loose connection that permits only one drop of water every few seconds, but over a period of time, a large amount of water can accumulate, particularly since little or no air or light is inside the wall to encourage evaporation.

You can also get water inside walls if the floor joists and sills are too close to the ground. Whatever the reasons for the presence of water, if you detect, by visual inspection, that water is in the walls, you need to make the necessary corrections before you do any other repair work to the wall.

The first step in correcting the problem is to cut off the source of water. If the roof is leaking, you should repair it quickly. You can locate the leak generally if you will climb into the attic during a rain or after a snowfall starts to melt. Look for moisture or patches of dark wood on the underside of rafters or the top side of exposed ceiling lumber. You can spot dampness in insulation between ceiling joists.

You can control water pipe condensation by wrapping the pipes with insulation and a vapor barrier. You can correct green wood problems only by replacing the green wood. If you are working in an older house, the wood has perhaps dried by this time, but you might need to replace defective studs.

If the house was originally built too close to the ground, one of the few steps you can take is to spread sheets of polyethylene on the ground under the house to keep water in the dirt from eventually collecting in the wood. You can also establish proper drainage of rainfall from the base of the foundation wall. This drainage can consist of better guttering and downspouts that will divert the rainfall into drain pipes buried underground that will carry the water a safe distance from the house. It is also important to landscape so that water does not gravitate toward the house. A truckload or two of topsoil is generally sufficient to handle the problem.

When you are installing siding, you can also help correct the problem by including properly constructed drip caps on walls to keep the water from running down the foundation walls. This water can seep through concrete and keep the underside of the house damp virtually all the time.

One final correction that involves relatively little is the establishment of some type of venting system, if there is none at the present. Such venting can be accomplished by removing one concrete block and replacing it with a vent that can be bought at any building supply house.

Your visual inspection should also include looking for signs of insect or rodent damage. Check first for presence of termites or other wood-damaging pests. Termites, like decay spores, must have a constant source of water, and if the house is wet inside walls or if the ground under the house stays wet, you can control the insects by contolling the water. (See Fig. 8-1.)

Fig. 8-1. Walls composed of defective siding create many subsequent problems. Here you can see masonite (at bottom) and old siding, both painted at the same time.

As termites emerge from the soil, they can enter the house by climbing up the foundation wall. They destroy the wood wherever they thrive. In a few months, studding can be little more than thin sheets of paperlike material. Because these studs support the weight of much of the house, you cannot afford to allow stud damage to occur. One method of preventing termite entry is to install thin, metal termite shields between the foundation wall and the sills.

You also can discourage termites by removing all scraps of wood left under the house by the builders. Wherever wood fibers and moisture exists, there will likely be termites.

While you are inspecting the walls, check for insect or rodent damage to wiring. Mice, rats, and squirrels have a tendency to gnaw the insulation from electrical wiring. Exposed wiring can lead to tragic consequences, such as a house fire.

Once you are satisfied that, from a physical standpoint, the walls are in good shape, it is time to make a more specific and equally important inspection. You need to see that all studs are securely nailed to sole plates and top plates. If the contractor used uncured lumber in the wall framing, it is possible that the wood fibers in the studding dried and, consequently, loosened their pressure on the nails and allowed them to slip or become loose. If you find such evidence of loose nails, drive additional nails into the problem areas so that the studs are again securely attached.

Use a tape measure to check the stud spacing across the wall on which you wish to install siding. Start at the corner post and, if you are working alone, hook the end of the tape over a nail tapped lightly into the edge of the post. Then as you proceed to stretch the tape measure across the wall frame, note how far the studs are spaced from the outside of the corner post. It should be 16 inches from the outside of the corner post to the center of the first stud, and each succeeding stud should be spaced so that it will be 16 inches to the center of all of the studs in the wall.

When you have checked the distances at the bottom of the wall, climb a ladder and check at the top to see if the same spacing is true. Or you can use a level and check each stud to see if it is a true vertical.

Even if you are not using 4-foot wide wall covering material, you will still want your studs spaced properly. If not, your butt joints will be staggered and unattractive.

NAILING UP CORNER BOARDS

If all is ready, you can begin to nail up your corner covering or corner boards. These corner boards are vertical boards nailed on each side of the corner posts. The purpose of the corner boards is to provide a butt point for the siding. If you do not use the corner boards, you will have a large gap, created by the lapping of siding, at the end of each siding piece. (See Fig. 8-2.)

These gaps will allow great amounts of cold air, as well as insects and moisture, to penetrate your walls. When you install corner boards, the gaps will be closed by the thickness of the corner boards. (See Fig. 8-3.)

These boards should have a nominal thickness of 1 inch, which means that the board will be ⅝ inch thick usually. Select boards that are long, straight, and of a uniform thickness. You will need one board that is 1 inch wider than the other. A good pair of corner boards is one 4-inch board and one 5-inch board, both long enough to reach from the top of the foundation wall to the top of the framed wall.

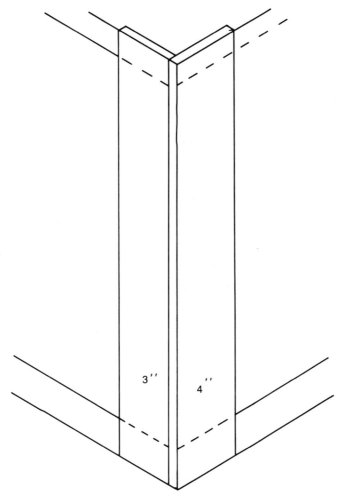

Fig. 8-2. Use corner boards at each corner. One board should be an inch wider than the other.

If you do not have boards long enough to reach the top of the wall, you will have to join boards. Join these boards one-third of the way on one side of the corner and two-thirds of the way to the top of the second board. Do not permit two joints to occur at the same height. If possible, keep joints at least 3 feet apart.

To nail up corner boards, place one board on the floor or other work surface, and start two nails into the board 1½ inches from the edge of the board and about 2 feet apart, starting one-third of the way up the board. Drive the nails in only enough that the points will barely penetrate the board.

If you are working with a helper, one of you can hold the board while the other drives the nails. If you are working alone, you can install the boards easily in the following manner. Start with the narrower board first and place it, nails already started in it, so that the outside edge of the board is perfectly flush with the outside edge of the corner post. Hit the nails

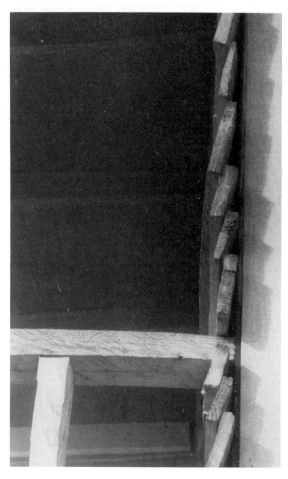

Fig. 8-3. The wide cracks that occur when corner boards are omitted allow cold air, moisture, and insects to enter the wall.

two or three times, enough to sink them about 1 inch into the corner post. Step back and check to see if the board is still flush with the edge of the corner post. If it is not, make corrections. If it is, drive the nails the rest of the way into the post. Use 16d nails and sink them in pairs, each about 1½ inches from the edge. Start 4 inches from the bottom and space the pairs of nails 18 inches apart the rest of the way up the board. The final nails should be 4 inches from the top of the board.

The board should reach all the way to the top of the wall. If not, when you nail in the first one, measure and cut the second part of the narrow board. Nail the new piece in so that the one side of the corner has boards all the way to the top.

If you must butt join boards, square the ends of both of the boards carefully so that you will have a neat, tight fit. With the first boards in place, start two nails in the wider board as you did earlier with the first board. Then position the board so that the outside edge of the new board covers the edge of the first corner board and is flush with the outside edge.

Drive the two nails partly in. Then check to see that your edges remained flush. If they did, drive the nails the rest of the way in, and then complete the nailing as you did before. If not, make the necessary corrections.

If you have to butt join boards again, do not let the joint occur where the first one did. You might wish to find a longer board or cut and install the top board first. Then measure and cut the bottom part of the board. In this way, the joints will not be even.

Install coverings on all corners. When this part of the job is done, you are ready to start nailing up siding. One of the first steps is installing a water table and drip cap.

STARTING THE SIDING

The water table is a way of causing the bottom of the first board to protrude from the wall about 1 inch. As you lap each succeeding board over the top of the first board, the water table will continue in effect.

The easiest way to install a water table is to cut 1 inch from a 1-inch board so that you have a 1-×-1 unit that can be nailed against the bottom edge of the sill, parallel to it the entire length of the wall. When you nail up your first siding board, the bottom of the board will lap over the 1 × 1. (See Fig. 8-4.)

Fig. 8-4. Cut an inch-thick board and nail it to the sill. Then lap the first board over the inch-thick board and all other boards over the top of the previous board.

Another way to install a water table is to nail a 1-×-4 board flat against the sill so that the edge of the board is flush with the edge of the sill. On top of the installed board, nail in a 2-inch-wide, beveled strip of wood, long enough to reach along the entire wall. The strip should be about 1 inch thick. Nail the strip so that it slants downward at about a 45-degree angle. Nail the next board so that the bottom laps the top third of the beveled strip, which serves to divert the water and cause it to drop to the ground rather than run down the foundation wall.

You can also buy strips of molded drip caps. These strips sit flatly on top of the first 1-×-4 board you nailed to the sill. Use 8d nails to fasten the drip cap to the bottom board and to the sheathing behind it. If you use wood sheathing, the 8d nails will be long enough. If you use a polystyrene foam or other similar types of sheathing, use longer nails so they can reach the studding and hold the drip cap in place.

You should also have all window frames, cornices, and door frames nailed in place before you start to nail up the siding. If you plan to use building paper, now is the time to install it.

You can use nails with short shanks and large heads, much like roofing nails, if you have access to them. You also can use a staple gun to fasten the building paper in place. Start beside the corner boards and measure the distance from the bottom of the sill to the top of the wall. If the wall is on a peaked side of the house, measure first to the top of the wall at the corner board. Then measure the extra distance from that point to the eave at a distance equal to the width of the building paper.

When you cut the paper, add 2 extra inches or even 3, so there will be a slight lap at the bottom. Let this lap extend over the foundation wall slightly, but not so much that the first siding board will not cover it. When you cut the paper, remember to angle cut the top to allow for the incline in the roof.

You can climb a ladder, hold the paper in one hand, and have a staple gun in your pocket. While you lean against the wall to steady yourself, position the paper and hold one corner in place until you can drive one staple (or nail, if you prefer) into the corner post to hold the paper in place.

Next, reach higher and hold the longer end of the paper in one hand while you staple or nail the end to the sheathing. Work your way down, using a nail or staple every foot or so along both edges of the paper.

When you have fastened the first strip, cut another strip. This strip will be the same length on the short side as the long side of the first strip. It will also be longer on the other side, to allow for the roof slant. When you start to fasten it, lap the first strip by at least 3 or 4 inches.

As you move across the wall, keep cutting each strip longer in relation to the roof slant. Lap each new strip over the edge of the previous strip. When you reach the peak, the strips will become correspondingly shorter. Fasten the building paper up to the edge of the corner post on the far end of the wall.

With the building paper installed, you can nail in the water table if you have not yet done so. You can also nail the metal flashing in place, if you wish.

The flashing is a strip of thin-gauge metal that is fastened against the wall and laps over the drip cap. It is then nailed to the edge of the drip cap. You can actually line up the metal with the drip cap edge, fasten it, and then nail the metal against the cant board above the drip cap.

Do not neglect the flashing. It will prevent water from soaking into the wood and causing decay. It also will protect the drip cap from alternating moisture and sunlight, a combination which can easily ruin a fragile piece of wood in a short time. You will need one nail (with a large head, again like a roofing nail) at each end of the flashing and one nail every foot along the rest of the length of the wall.

MAKING AND USING A STORY POLE

A story pole is a very simple and extremely useful item to help you keep the siding courses or boards even. You can make it yourself by sawing a 1-×-4 board in half lengthwise so that you will have two 1-×-2 boards.

You mark the story pole to show you where the top of every board should be nailed. If you are using 1-×-5 siding boards, you will lap each board 1 inch over the previous board. Each board you nail up will actually reach 4 inches above the earlier one. Mark your story pole in gradations of 4 inches. You can use a one story pole at each end of the wall or you can make only one and use it by carrying it from end to end.

Do not mark the story pole until you have stood it on end beside the foundation wall. Mark on the pole the point where the foundation wall reaches. Then mark in 4-inch gradations the remainder of the way to the top of the pole.

If it will help make your job easier, you can drive a pair of small nails (8d or smaller) into the story pole so that the points of the nails barely penetrate the board. Then place the pole against the corner boards with the end of the board even with the top of the foundation wall. Nail the board in place. Then mark the 4-inch gradations.

You should nail the story pole as close to the inside edge of the corner board as possible so you can see at a glance where the top of each siding board should reach.

Nail up a story pole on each corner board on that side of the wall and you have your board locations determined on both ends of the wall. If you do not want to take the time to make and mark a story pole, other alternatives can be used.

One alternative is to use a chalk line, a ruler, and a pencil, if you are working with a helper. If you are working alone, you can add a small nail to your list of equipment.

With the water table, flashing, and building paper already put up, start at the bottom of the corner board and make a light pencil mark 4 inches from the bottom. Make another mark on the edge of the corner board 4 inches above the first mark. Continue to mark the top levels of the siding boards until you reach the top of the wall. Do this on both ends of the wall.

Drive a small nail a quarter inch or so into the corner board where you made the first mark. Loop the end of a chalk line over the nail and pull the line taut as you move to the other end of the wall. Snap the chalk line briskly so that you have a chalked mark across the building paper at the precise height of the top edge of the first siding board.

Move up 4 inches and chalk another mark. Continue this pattern until you have reached the top of the wall. If you prefer, you can chalk one line, nail up the siding, chalk another mark, and nail the next siding board. Proceed on a one-board-at-a-time basis until you reach the top of the wall.

How you mark and install the siding boards is not nearly as important as keeping the siding perfectly level. If you do not do so, you will find that you have too little lap on one end of the wall and too much on another. The result is unattractive and, worse, ineffective in protecting your wall from the elements.

Before you nail up any siding boards, check the ends of each board for squareness. Most lumberyard-milled ends are square, but it is better to take a few seconds to be sure. When you are sure the ends are satisfactory, you can nail up the first siding board.

Place the board in position, and hold it in place while you start the first nail. You will find that it is extremely difficult to hold a long board level while you nail, but you can use a sawhorse or similar implement to hold one end while you secure the other.

One very simple method is to use a homemade siding holder. You can make one by choosing a board 3 or 4 feet long. A foot from one end, nail in a short length of board (4 or 5 inches) across the board you are preparing. Place another length of board (this one about 10 inches long and from the same stock as the longer length) so that the new piece covers the first segment nailed in place and crosses it at right angles. The new piece should reach beyond the first nailed-on piece by at least 6 inches. The finished product will be a holder for the siding ends.

When you use the siding holder, you can drive two nails into the long part of the lumber so that the nails are a foot apart. Then when you need the holder, you can drive the nails slightly into a corner board or stud to hold the siding holder in place. Place the free end of the siding inside the holder, which should be fastened at the height that the siding board will be nailed.

You can use the studs regularly, because nail holes in them will not show. It is better not to have the very end of the siding board in the siding holder. You need the holder 6 to 10 feet from you, at a maximum. Let the longer end of the siding board reach as far beyond the holder as necessary.

When you have nailed one end of the siding board, you can remove the siding holder and set it aside while you nail the second end. Because you drove the nails in only slightly, you can pull the siding holder loose with your hands. If you will drive nails in the end of the siding board and into the corner post, then drive two more nails through the siding and into the first two or three studs. The free end of the siding board will then remain in place while you complete the nailing.

Remember, use the level on the siding boards to be certain that you are remaining true with your installation. If you use a chalk line, which is a very effective method of installing siding, you can compare the top edge of the siding board with the chalk line as you proceed across the wall area. If you see a problem, make the needed adjustments at that time.

You can nail the first siding boards to the sill. Attach the next ones to the studs and corner posts. When you must butt join siding in midwall, be careful that all ends of boards are square. Try not to have butt joints occur at the same stud in succession. Vary joints for best looks and strength.

Before you are close to the top of the wall, measure and make an estimate of the number of siding boards you will need to reach the top. Determine if you will have too much or too little space for the last board. If you can see that the final board will lack 2 inches or so to reach the top of the wall, try either to decrease the lap in the lower boards just enough so that you can make up the deficit, or lap more than usual so that one extra full board will fit into the space.

In lapping extra, do not increase the lap by more than half an inch. If you need to make up 2 inches, lap the final eight boards an extra quarter inch, or lap the final four boards by half an inch.

When decreasing the lap, do so only by one-fourth inch. Decrease the lap in eight boards to make up the deficit. If you are not careful you might lap too little and air passage space will exist between the boards. See Fig. 8-5.

INSTALLING DIAGONAL SIDING

One of the most attractive wall arrangements is diagonal siding installation. You can slant all of the siding in the same direction, or you can mix slant angles for variety and for appearance. Use your own judgment in making the decision. You can use diagonal, horizontal, and vertical all in the same wall, particularly if the wall holds doors, windows, alcoves or other recesses, or if you have angled wall surfaces.

For simple, one-directional, diagonal installation, you can choose to use the perfect-half type of slant, or you can start with an equilateral triangle beginning. For perfect-half diagonal siding, you need to measure the distance from one top corner to the opposite bottom corner.

Make a chalk line from corner to corner across the building paper. Measure off and mark the rest of the first half of the wall in gradations equal to the width of the boards being installed. Use full-board measures, because you will not be lapping. It is much better

Fig. 8-5. When you reach windows or eaves, you might need to adjust the amount of lap in order for the boards to fit well. Note the greater lap at windows.

to use tongue and groove lumber for diagonal siding. You can use square-edged boards if you can get a snug joint and if you use building paper properly installed.

You might find that the most attractive method of perfect-half siding installation is found in walls that are very nearly square. A radical rectangle will mean that the final boards must slant too much to be attractive.

When you reach the corner of the first half, hold up a siding board so that it is parallel to the chalk line and mark it by using the bottom of the sill and the corner board as guides. Mark the siding board by holding a straightedge against the board, perfectly in line with the inside edge of the corner board and bottom edge of the sill. Saw the siding board along the lines, being careful to saw on the outside of the mark. When the board is ready, nail it in place, using 16d nails.

Hold the next board so that one edge is a good fit against the first board. Mark the angle for the corner board and for the sill. You can also measure and cut. Measure from the high side of the first board and get the exact distance from the sill to the corner board.

You can set up a miter box with slots that will give you the proper angles for all future siding cuts. All you will need to do is measure for the length along the lower edge of the new siding board. To get the angles for a miter box, use the ends of the first board before you nail the board in place, or use the waste ends you cut off. Be sure you do not cut the new board so that it is a parallelogram. You do not want the angle cuts ever to be parallel.

When you reach the halfway mark, start to shorten the boards slightly. At this point, you can measure for the long side of each succeeding board. When you need to butt join the boards, cut the ends according to the slant needed for the studs. You will want the ends to meet over a stud. Let each end cover half the thickness of the stud.

Continue your progression until you reach the other diagonal corner of the wall. At the end of the wall, you will be cutting very short boards. Use some of the shorter boards that could not be effectively used in longer areas.

You will find that the equilateral triangle method of nailing up diagonal siding will work for most walls. To get a proper start, cut an end of a board exactly as long as the board is wide so you will have a perfect square. If you are using 4-inch boards, measure up 4 inches and mark the board. Then mark and cut the board segment diagonally from one corner to the other. Nail up the triangle so that you have one side matching the edge of the corner board and another side flush with the bottom of the sill.

Proceed as previously detailed and measure, cut, and nail up longer and longer boards until you reach the halfway mark. Your halfway mark will not be the perfect diagonal center of the wall unless the wall is square.

When you reach window openings, mark the chalk line as though the window were solid. Measure, cut, and install boards so that they are perfectly aligned as if the window were not there.

INSTALLING VERTICAL SIDING

Vertical siding is easy to install. You can use tongue and groove or square-edged boards with batten. As a rule, the wider the boards, the better they look when installed vertically. You can use whatever widths you wish, however, depending upon your own tastes and availability of siding boards.

To install vertical boards, you must first nail in blocking between the studs. You will want the blocking to fit as snugly as possible. If the blocking is too short, it will not provide the needed support for the siding. If the blocking is too long, it will shove the studs out of their vertical position.

Measure for blocking length and cut the blocking out of 2-×-4 stock. If your studs are perfectly spaced, you can cut all of the blocking the same length. Do not trust the spacing. Cut one length to fit, and then try it between other pairs of studs. Try it at the bottom, middle, and top. If it works everywhere, then cut several of the blocking pieces and proceed to nail them in place. Nail in one blocking unit one-third of the way from the top and another two-thirds of the way to the bottom, or use three blocking pieces spaced one-fourth, middle, and three-fourths of the way down the studding. You will need to block all the studding in the wall for adequate support for the vertical siding.

Measure and cut the first vertical siding. Position it so that the edge is flush with the inside edge of the corner board and the bottom is flush with the bottom of the sill. Depending upon the thickness of the board, use 16d or 20d nails. Two-inch vertical siding boards are expensive, but they work magnificently when installed and battened.

If your boards are 6 inches wide, use three nails in a row across the board at the top, bottom, and on every blocking unit in the wall. Abut the next board snugly against the first one and nail it in place. Continue across the wall. If you need to butt join two boards, do so over a blocking piece.

You can cut boards so they will reach only to the top plate, or you can cut them to extend to the peak slant. If you stop them at the top plate, later you will want to butt join shorter boards of the same length and width, as if the boards have not been cut. Use a strip of batten over the butt joints.

If you extend boards to the slant line of the peak, you will also want to nail up batten, unless you are using the tongue-and-groove lumber. Batten is only strips of thin wood nailed across the cracks between boards to help weatherproof the building.

Before you reach the windows or the doors, you need to start making arrangements to have boards end at the proper place or to fit them around the frames of wall openings. When you reach the window frames, you can measure the distance between the last board and the frame and cut the siding board lengthwise so that it will be a perfect fit between the frame and last board. You can also cut out part of the board so that it will fit around the door or window frame.

When you saw the board to reduce it to fit beside the window, you will want to make chalk lines across the window frame and then match the boards above and under the window so that they give the impression of being one continued board. Use the same width boards over and under the window as well.

When you are cutting out a board to fit around the window frame corners, you can hold a full-sized board in place and mark it with a pencil at the level of the top and bottom edges of the window frame. Then measure the distance between the frame and the last board installed. Measure and mark the new board accordingly so that it is ready to saw.

To saw the cutout, you can use a circular saw. Start near the center and let the blade touch the line after you start the blade. Gently lower the blade until it makes light contact, then cut all the way through the board. When the blade has cut through the board, slowly saw along the line until the blade touches the line drawn in from the side of the board. If you try to saw too far, the circular shape of the saw will cause the teeth to cut part

Fig. 8-6. You will need to angle-cut siding boards to allow for the eaves slope.

of the way into the board. If you stop as soon as the teeth reach the line, you can then use a handsaw to cut in from the outside edge until the saw reaches the back line. Use the handsaw to cut the remainder of the line started by the circular saw.

Use the previous procedure at the other end of the cutout lines. When you have completed the cut, try the board for fit around the window frame. If the fit is good, nail up the board. If not, take it down and make the necessary corrections.

You can use the same procedure at door frames. The only difference is that you will need to cut only two lines instead of three, because the board will reach all the way to the sill. You can cut a small piece of board to fit horizontally under the door, if necessary.

When you end boards at the top plate, fit the boards from the peak line to butt join with the ones just installed. Try to use boards of the same width so that the butt joints will be even and attractive. Nail a batten strip horizontally from one corner to the other. Then nail up batten from the peak line down to the first batten strip. Let the vertical strips butt into the horizontal strip at right angles. Use the batten above and under the horizontal batten.

Cut the boards used up to the peak line 2 inches short. When you nail them in place, you can nail in a 2-inch strip that will fit where the wall and eave lines join. (See Fig. 8-6.)

Your choice of vertical siding includes the 2-×-6 boards, 1-×-4s, 1-×-5s, and 1-×-6s or even wider. Keep in mind that the wider boards are more expensive, but they also cover much more space and require fewer nails.

For horizontal siding, you can buy boards that have the rough-cut appearance as well as the traditional siding boards. Diagonal boards can consist of any boards that are used vertically or horizontally.

CHAINSAWING SIDING BOARDS

You can buy siding boards for about $4.30 each for boards 2 × 6. Or you can use your chainsaw and cut the boards for approximately ten cents per board. The chainsawed boards will have the rough-cut appearance and will not have surfaces that are as smooth as milled lumber.

Chainsawing siding boards can be extremely hard and rather meticulous work; but, the finished product can be extremely attractive and unique, in addition to being very inexpensive. A chainsaw can be a very dangerous tool, one that should be used with great caution. Observe all the rules of safe handling, and be satisfied that your physical condition permits you to use the saw safely.

You should also have access to trees from which to saw the lumber. After you cut the siding boards, allow them to season for at least a month before using them in a wall.

To chainsaw siding boards, choose trees with trunks at least a foot or more in diameter. The trunks should be as straight as possible and preferably free of knots and large limbs, although the knotty lumber can also be highly attractive when used as siding.

Start by sawing the log into lengths that are proper for the wall you are siding. If the wall is 8 feet high from the bottom of the sills to the top plate, cut the logs at least 8 feet 6 inches long, to allow for squaring of ends.

After you cut the log, lift the log on top of blocks or chunks of wood so that the log will be at least a foot off the ground. When the log is in place, trim off all small limbs and radically irregular surface areas such as growths on the sides of the log.

Make a chalk line the length of the log, exactly in the center. When this is done, start the chainsaw and cut a groove 1 or 2 inches deep along the chalked line. (See Fig. 8-7.)

Return to the starting point. Lower the bar and chain into the groove and lower the tip of the saw so that it is pointing sharply downward. Pull the saw slowly through the log. Keep the butt of the bar in the groove. When you complete this cut you will have one flat surface on each log half. (See Figs. 8-8 and 8-9.)

Use the chalk line to mark the outside slab cuts on each half. The mark should be as near the edge as possible; however, be sure you can get boards 2 inches thick when the slab edge is cut off. Mark one side of the log, then measure from the mark to a point 6 inches across the log (or as far as you can and still be able to get boards 2 inches thick).

Mark the log half on both sides and make the chalk lines. Then cut grooves along both chalk lines and later saw the slab edge completely off. You will now have three flat sides on each log half.

At this point, stand the log half on edge and measure over 2 inches from the tall edge. Do this at both ends. Then chalk a line between the two points. (See Fig. 8-10.)

Cut the traditional groove along the chalk line. Next, return to the starting point and lower the saw bar into the groove. Cut the entire thickness of the log section this time or cut only 2 or 3 inches deep and, with a later cut, complete sawing through the section. (See Fig. 8-11.)

As you are sawing, try to hold the saw in a vertical position. If you lean the saw significantly in either direction, you will have a board that is too thick or too thin on one edge.

Fig. 8-7. Your first step is to chalk the line along the log, and then you need to cut a one-inch deep groove.

Fig. 8-8. Cut the log all the way through the end and pull the saw slowly through the entire log.

Fig. 8-9. When the cut is finished, you will have two log halves with flat surfaces.

Fig. 8-10. With the log standing on edge, mark the saw line, and then prepare to cut off the siding board.

When you have cut the board, lay it flat on a pair of 2 × 4s spaced properly or on some other surface that will keep the board from contacting the soil. Let the board start to cure as you return to saw off another board.

You can get two or three boards from each log half. You might have to chalk another line down the length of the log. Then saw off more of the edge in order to get a full 2-inch thickness for the boards.

You can also have boards of various widths. The first board might be 8 inches wide, while the second might be only 7 inches wide. The final boards might be only 4½ or 5 inches wide, or less. The log will yield four to six or even eight boards, depending upon the original size of the log. When the log section becomes very thin, prop it with blocks of wood nailed to the sawing blocks. One method is to fasten one block permanently and nail the other only enough to hold the log section in place as you saw. With each cut, you will have to reposition the second block in order for you to hold the log steady.

After the boards are cured, you can nail them in place, or you can sand them briefly to make the surface slightly smoother and to eliminate any fibers still clinging to the boards. You will be pleasantly surprised at how smoothly a chainsaw can saw a board. You might conclude that you do not need to sand at all.

If you do not want to install board siding, you might wish to look at shingles and shakes as a nice alternative. Chapter 9 discusses this type of siding.

Fig. 8-11. Such a board as the one shown here can be cut in about two minutes at a cost of less than five cents per board, as opposed to nearly four dollars each at a lumber yard.

9
Shakes and Shingles

FOR MANY YEARS PRIOR TO WORLD WAR II ONE OF THE POPULAR WALL coverings for many houses was asbestos-cement shingles. These very hard and often very brittle (particularly during abrupt weather changes) wall coverings proved rather unattractive, difficult to install, hard to maintain, and even more difficult to cut and handle without incident.

The chief advantages of such a wall covering were that it was relatively inexpensive, it could be installed rapidly, and it could withstand rain and hail without corroding or fading. Such shingles can still be seen, decades later, as evidence of their ability to endure.

Endurance was not what people wanted exclusively, as tastes proved, when better wall-covering materials appeared on the market. One such product was the cedar shake, or shingle. This shingle is a wood product that is expensive to buy and difficult to install, but it is beautiful enough to convert rather plain houses to homes of striking physical appearance. Cost of cedar shakes is about $100 per square, or $1 per square foot. You can figure if a wall is 20 feet long and 10 feet high, plus a peak, you will have about 230 square feet to cover, and it will cost you about $230 for the shakes. If you must pay to have them installed, the cost becomes considerably greater.

You do not need to hire someone to install the shingles or shakes if you are at all handy with a hammer and saw. If you are a complete novice, you will want to take your time doing the work, which might progress very slowly until you get the knack of nailing them up.

You have a wide choice of selections in terms of sizes of shakes. You can buy individual shakes in packages called squares. Each square will cover 100 square feet of wall or a 10-×-10-foot area. One type of shake comes in 8-foot strips, and the shakes are mounted on sheathing boards which are ⅜ inch thick.

The 8-foot strips are the fastest and the easiest way to install shingles. Other sizes and thicknesses can be bought readily, ranging from 1 foot wide to 24 inches wide. Lengths also vary. You can find shakes that are 2 feet long, but most are shorter.

As with nearly all wall coverings, you must have your studding installed properly and the wall must not have waves or other distinct irregularities. Shakes cannot conceal the fact that the wall is not a true vertical or that the corners are not a true square. When you install shakes on a wavy wall, you can stand at one corner and look straight down the wall and see the waves, as they stand out clearly.

CORRECTING IRREGULAR WALLS

If the walls are not correct, and if you want to cover the walls with shakes, you need to make the needed corrections immediately. Do not start any part of the wall covering until you straighten the wall problems.

To see the complete extent of the wall problem, use your chalk line stretched from corner to corner. Drive a nail partly into the corner post about a foot above the sole plate. Loop the metal ring of the chalk line over the nail and walk toward the opposite corner as you pull the chalk line taut. At the other corner tap a nail in far enough that you can wrap the chalk line around it so it will hold. When the line is tight, you can walk along the wall to see which stud sticks out most and how far out of line the stud is.

Don't be content with merely seeing the irregularity. Use a ruler to measure the deviation. When you find a stud that the chalk line does not touch, measure the distance from the chalk line to the outside edge of the stud. If you find that the protruding stud is in the center, and studs to the left and right of it diminish in their distance from the chalk line as you move toward the corners, you can assume that the middle stud is the major problem.

Deviations of less than an inch or two can be left as they are, but anything more than this amount should be corrected. You can handle problems rather easily if the wall frame is one with no interior wall covering. If you have plaster on the interior wall, or some other material that cracks easily, you cannot make the correction in the studding. If the interior wall has paneling or gypsum board on it, you can probably correct the studding with little difficulty.

Before you start, use the chalk line halfway up the wall and then again close to the top to see if the deviations remain in a constant pattern. They probably will, unless one stud was nailed in while it was green and has since bowed.

Use your level on the studs that present problems. It is possible that the studs were installed out of vertical position. You can correct the difficulty by knocking the stud loose and nailing it in place.

If interior wall covering has been installed, don't bang on the problem stud excessively. Instead, run a hacksaw blade under the stud and saw the nails at the bottom. If there are nails from interior wall covering in the inside edge of the stud, saw these too, rather than try to pry the nails loose. Such force can cause severe damage to interior walls.

When no interior nails attach the stud, you can pull it free at the bottom and work it back and forth until the top nails are freed. You will need to saw these top nails as well, because they were installed through the top of the top plate, and the top cap was installed over the nail heads. You cannot drive the nails back out unless you wish to remove the top cap.

Usually your problem will be only that of a bent or bowed stud. You obviously cannot move the entire sole plate and studs without dismantling the entire wall frame. Your job is to find and remove the faulty studs and correct them with properly nailed-in studs. Usually, only one or two studs present a problem. These can be corrected fairly quickly.

Where interior wall units have been connected to studs, you will have to do one of two things. You can, after the faulty stud has been removed, go inside and again nail the plywood or other covering to the stud. After the nail head has sunk until it is slightly below the surface of the gypsum board or plywood, cover the nail with wall compound, let it dry, then sand it until the surface again blends.

The simpler way is to reattach the wall unit from the outside. When the stud is back in place and has been nailed in, use corner braces (no more than 2 inches per side) and some medium-sized screws. Attach one angle of the brace to the wall unit and the other to the stud. Use one brace on each side of the stud (a total of three pairs). Place one a foot from the bottom, one in the center, and one a foot from the top.

Occasionally, you will find that a wall line is recessed or that it bows toward the inside. Use the chalk line to see where the bow starts and how deep it is. Then nail panels of plywood, starting where the bow begins and stopping where the wall reverts to normal alignment.

On walls already covered with sheathing, your only method of correction, other than removing the sheathing and starting anew, is to use double sheathing where the problem is greatest.

You must use sheathing behind shakes. The best types to use are board sheathing or plywood. The insulation boards will not support the shakes and provide ample backing strength unless you use strong nailers. These nailers will be necessary no matter what type of sheathing you use.

PREPARING FOR INSTALLING SHAKES

Before you nail up any shakes, you need to do four basic preparatory tasks: install a starting board, nail in the nailer boards, plan your number of courses, and establish the drip cap in accordance with the methods described in Chapter 8. All of these steps are fast and easy to accomplish.

The drip cap can be a beveled strip of wood or it can be a square-edged strip. In both instances, you should nail the drip cap to the top edge of the starter board, which is nailed to the sill so that it laps the joint of the sill and the foundation wall.

The starter strip is only a 3-inch board that runs along the bottom of the sill and provides a slant or tilt to the first course of shingles or shakes to produce a watershed effect. Use any pine board long enough to reach from corner to corner, or you can join two or more shorter boards. This strip will not be seen after you start shingling, and it serves only the purposes of providing slant and a nailing surface for the water table.

The course planning and installation of nailer boards are the important phases. First, plan your courses of shingles by deciding what size shingles you will use and how much lap will be necessary. Then measure and mark course lines. You can also use the story pole described in Chapter 8.

If the shakes you are using are 24 inches long, you will need to deduct the amount of lap from the space one course will cover. For instance, if you lap one-half of the shingle, a 24-inch shake will give you only a 12-inch coverage. Most shakes will come with complete information concerning the lap necessary.

When you have determined the amount of lap and deducted that distance from the total coverage, you can arrive at a figure for each course and mark the wall accordingly. Use the chalk line to mark the first course, and mark it so that the top of the shake or shingle will stop at the line. In this fashion, when you are nailing up shakes, you can see that you are in line with the courses. Rows of shakes that sag or rise in the middle of ends are unattractive and suggest careless workmanship.

You can mark one course at a time if you wish, but you will need to know how well the last course will fit at the juncture of the wall and eave. If you have 12 inches of coverage, measure the wall height in inches, and divide the total number of inches by 12 to get the number of complete courses you will have. If the answer comes out in a fraction, you will need to lap more or less in order to make up the deficit or surplus.

Start by tapping a nail into the corner board or beside it at the appropriate height, in this case 2 feet, because the first course will not be lapped at this point. Go to the other corner and start a nail at the same height. Stretch the chalk line so that it is taut between the two nails and snap the line sharply to give your first course mark. Then move the nail up 1 foot on both corners and snap the line again. Keep doing this until you have marked the entire wall.

When you reach the top, if there is a problem, you can usually handle it by making minor adjustments in the final three or four courses. Suppose that the last entire course stops 4 inches short of the top of the wall. You will need to either shorten the lap of four courses by 1 inch, increase the lap of the final eight courses by 1 inch, or cut a shingle to length.

Because cut shingles have their appearances marred, you might prefer to lap eight courses an extra inch. This extra lap will not be noticeable in an entire wall. One other possibility is to use a molding board at the top of the wall. The board would take up the needed space.

When you have planned the courses, start nailing up the strips which will support the shakes. Remember that the 8-foot strips of shakes already have the nailer provided. Individual shingles will not have nailers with them. Fasten the first nailer so that the top edge of the nailer board aligns with the chalk line you made earlier. Fasten the nailer to the wall by nailing it to the studding and to the corner posts. The nailer boards should not be as thick as the starting board or the watershed property of the wall will be lost. If you need to do so, double the thickness of the starter board.

You will need to continue this pattern to the top of the wall, but you can stop at this point if you wish and nail up one course of shingles to see how the work goes. Use the size nail specified by the manufacturer. If no size is indicated, choose nails that will penetrate the nailer sufficiently to hold the shingles in place permanently.

NAILING UP SHAKES

Place the first shake or shingle so that the top is flush with the nailer and the bottom extends past the starter board only slightly. The starter board should not be thick enough to create a cap between the shingle, but it should cause the bottom to extend slightly more than the top.

Usually one nail in each top corner will hold the shake in place. Use the special markings for nails, if the shingles have them. If not, be sure that the nails are not too close to the edges. Move in at least 1 inch in both directions.

When you have installed the first shingle, nail up the next one by abutting it tightly against the first but not snugly enough to cause warping during weather changes. Use the traditional one-cent coin between shakes.

Try to have the course end with a full shingle. If this technique is not possible, then have the shingle as close to full size as you can, even if this means trimming two or three shakes. In other words, do not let the final shingle be only 3 or 4 inches wide. End with at least half a shingle.

Do the same at windows and doors. If you trim carefully, you will have a straight cut with little to suggest that the shake had been modified, particularly if you do not trim any one shingle an excessive amount.

At windows and doors, leave the framing installed and install shingles against the framing. At all corners be sure that the gap created by tilting the shingles for watershed does not create a space that will admit bugs and moisture.

When you have completed the first course, start the second by lapping the shingle so that there is no exposure to weather. In some types of shingle installation, you need to install a second course over the top of the first course, but you should lap all joints or cracks between shingles. (See Fig. 9-1.) The second true course will then lap over the top layer of the second course and will similarly lap all cracks or joints.

Each succeeding course will follow the same basic pattern. Each new shingle will lap the joint of the two below it. For this reason, you start every odd-numbered course with a whole shake and every even-numbered course with a half-shingle.

At recesses or alcoves, you will have no trouble, because the corner boards will be installed and you abut shingles against the corner boards for alcoves as you would for

Fig. 9-1. You must stagger the shingles by having each new shingle lap the crack between two shingles on the row under it. You also need to lap each shingle half the length of the ones in the previous row.

any other corner. You will need to measure the alcove dimensions carefully, though, because you will need to prevent small shingle cuts in interior corners.

Use corner boards for inside corners as well as for outside corners. If you shingle under windows, you will need to plan course lines carefully or have to cut shingles to allow them to fit under the window framing.

In the planning stages of the shingle installation, as you are marking course heights, note where the course line strikes or meets the window framing. If the course line is high enough on the framing that you cannot use the extra-lapping method, you will have to cut shingles to conform to the course line and to fit under the framing snugly.

At times, the course line will be only an inch or so higher than the bottom of the window framing. In such cases, you can overlap and the shingles will fit acceptably. Do not lap less than you need to in order to make a shingle fit. It is better to go ahead and cut a shingle rather than to risk allowing dampness to enter the wall.

If you want a really rustic look (and if you want to save a great deal of money at the same time), you can cut your own shakes or shingles. As with other cut-your-own projects, the work is rather slow and tiring, but if economy is highly important to you, you might want to try to cut a few shingles to see how well you get along.

These suggestions are made for one primary reason: the cost of building materials is at times near exorbitant levels. Most people who want to do the work themselves have money-savings as one of their top priorities. As an example, a home owner in a small New England town recently added a large room to his house at a cost of slightly over $30,000 for the one room. We added two small rooms to our house (a total of over 600 square feet for the two rooms) for under $500. We did all of the work ourselves, and we used as many money-saving devices as we could devise.

CUTTING SHINGLES WITH A FROE

If you have ever seen a roof or siding composed of shingles cut with a froe, you were probably amazed at the skill and beauty of the work. To make shingles the old-fashioned way, you will need a *froe* (which is a bladed instrument with a handle). The blade is sharp on the bottom edge and blunt on the top edge so you can hit it with a maul or mallet. (See Fig. 9-2.)

You will also need a maul or mallet, usually a long club-like piece of heavy wood, some wedges, and patience. You will need a large log of hardwood, such as oak. Cut the log into 2-foot lengths first, then split it down the center with the maul and several wedges.

Split each half into several pie-shaped pieces, and then use the wedges to cut off the final 3 or 4 inches near the heart of the log chunk. With the heart removed, split the sections again into several pieces as nearly the same thickness as possible. (See Fig. 9-3.)

Next, take each section, stand it on end atop a hard block surface, and place the blade of the froe in the center of the top of the section. Hit the top of the froe blade with the maul and, when the section starts to split, twist the froe handle to the inside with downward directions, and the shingle will split free of the rest of the section. (See Fig. 9-4.)

As you cut the shingles, stack them neatly on blocks so that they are never in contact with the ground. Lay them at right angles to each other and leave air spaces in between so they can dry faster.

Fig. 9-2. Here is an old-fashioned froe. You can make your own with a foot-long length of sharpened, thick metal, such as an old lawnmower blade cut half its original length.

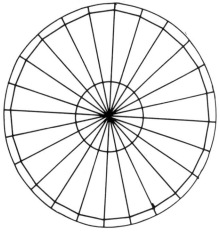

Fig. 9-3. With the log section standing upright, split it into quarters, then into eighths, and then split off the bark and heart surfaces. Finally, split the eighths into proper thicknesses for shingles.

This process is more difficult than it seems. You can learn quickly, however, and shortly your work will speed up considerably as you gain expertise. It is possible for an experienced shingle maker to turn out one thousand shingles in a single day.

The total cost of the shingles, other than your time, is negligible, unless you have to buy the tools. Older shingle makers used several devices, but you can get by easily with the equipment described here.

When you install the 2-foot shingles, double the first course so there are no joint cracks not lapped and then lap each course afterwards by 1 foot.

Fig. 9-4. Use the maul (foreground) to drive the froe blade into the shingle wood. When the wood starts to split, twist the handle toward you to pop the shingle free. In two or three hours you can make $200 or more worth of shingles.

CUTTING SHINGLES WITH A CHAINSAW

You can cut shingles or shakes with a chainsaw also, but the progress is somewhat slow until you catch on to the best way to work. You can cut the shingles in several ways, but the easiest way is to square a log and then cut off 1-inch squares (or you can have rectangles, if the log is such that squaring it is not practical).

Start with the log on blocks, as you did before. Cut both ends of the log so that you have a straight end. Hold a level to one end of the log and to one side as far as you can and still stay in good wood. While holding the level as it shows a perfect vertical, mark along the level from top to bottom of the log end.

Move to the other side of the log and then make another mark like the first. Do the same at the top and bottom so that when you have finished you have a perfect square on the end of the log.

Go to the other end of the log and mark another perfect square by using the level. The purpose for the level is to help you keep the square a perfect vertical so that later you can connect the square lines on both ends.

When both squares are completed, use the chalk line to make the connecting lines between square corners. Drive a nail lightly into one top corner of the squares on each end. Be sure to use the corresponding corners on both squares. Hook the chalk line over one nail, pull it to the other nail, and, holding it taut, snap the line. You should now have a straight line connecting the two corners.

Do the same with the other two corners. Use the chainsaw to saw a 2-inch deep groove along the line, and then return and saw the slab off. Saw the slab off the other side so that you have two flat sides to the log.

Fig. 9-5. An alternative method of cutting shingles.

Turn the log on one flat side and use the chalk line to connect the other corners. Then saw off the slabs as you did before. At this point you have a squared log, ready for shingle cutting.

You can cut the shingles in two easy ways. The first way is to mark and cut 1-inch shingles off the end of the squared log. You can mark the log with the chalk line. Mark the top and the sides, so you can see that you are staying true with the cut.

You can cut a large number of shakes off one squared log. If the log is 8 feet long and you can get nine shingles per foot, you will have 72 shingles from the single log. Assuming that each shingle is 1 foot square, you can cover about 50 square feet of wall space, or half a square. Instead of costing you $50, your cost will be less than $1.

Another way to cut shingles is to leave the log on the blocks and saw 12-inch boards, then cut the boards into the desired lengths for shingles. If the log is 8 feet long, you might wish to cut 2-foot shingles. You will get four shingles per board and probably ten boards from the log, depending upon the width of your saw kerf. If you get forty shingles, you can cover, again, 48 to 50 square feet at a cost of $.10 per foot instead of $1.00 per square foot. (See Fig. 9-5.)

To make your sawing easier, you can use smaller logs and saw only 6-inch boards instead of the 12-inch ones. While 6-inch boards do not cover as much as the wider ones, you will actually save time because you can saw so much faster.

When the shingles are complete, you can stack and cure them, or you can sand them with coarse paper before you cure them. When they are cured, nail them up as you would any other shingle and then stain or paint them or leave them natural.

10
Installing Plywood Siding

ONE OF THE MOST DELIGHTFUL BUILDING MATERIALS TO EMERGE IN recent years is plywood, particularly plywood siding. By using this superb material, you can cover an immense amount of space in a very short time, and the finished project looks comparable to far more expensive siding.

Many people, when they think of plywood, remember primarily the insipid sheets of dull brown that were manufactured decades ago. One of the prominent memories is that of peeling veneers and crumbling interiors.

The modern plywoods only vaguely resemble the earlier efforts in looks and durability. You can buy several kinds of plywoods and plywood siding. These come in a variety of thicknesses and exterior treatment.

Plywood is, by definition, a construction material made of layers of wood, placed with grains at right angles and then glued and pressed together. The same product, by extension, is a strong, attractive, and reasonably economical product that can be used for interior or exterior wall covering.

Two major types of plywood exterior wall coverings exist: plywood siding and hardboard siding. A third, and less-known wall covering, is called duraply siding.

Hardboard sidings are available in both smooth and textured surfaces. The nominal thicknesses of hardboard siding material are $7/16$ and $1/2$ inches. Most boards are either 8 inches or 12 inches wide, with some $73/4$ inches wide. You can buy hardboard sidings in single lap, beaded lap, double lap, and triple lap styles.

Among the attractive surfaces of these hardboard sidings are woodgrain and smooth finishes. Some look like weathered planks; others look like freshly-milled boards; some are primed for either painting or staining; others are prepainted.

One of the best qualities of hardboard sidings is that the boards or panels are manufactured so that few, if any, of the surface defects present in nearly all wood boards exist. You will not see any knotholes or knots, for instance, to create sawing or nailing difficulties.

Unlike real boards, hardboards do not have weak points, and they do not have areas where the boards are thicker or thinner than the usual expectancy. Most importantly, no decay or soft areas exist that can make the material weak at crucial points. (See Fig. 10-1.)

Because it is made of wood fibers bonded with resin under heat, there is no grain, which means that the siding boards are equally strong in all directions. Because there is no grain, there are no cracks or checking areas produced by counterstress. Some wood boards, notably poplar and pines cut out of season and cured improperly, are noted for their tendency to split or check. The hardboard sidings cannot do this. They are not as susceptible to dampness or prolonged exposure to weather as natural wood boards are.

Unlike aluminum, the hardboard sidings are not easily dented, and the boards cannot rust or corrode. Neither are they conductors of electricity. Because of this quality, you do not have any problems with exterior electrical outlets, fallen power lines, or lightning storms, other than the problems invariably associated with the near presence of lightning or the danger of touching exposed power lines.

You can saw hardboards with ordinary carpentry tools. A handsaw or circular saw will saw easily, rapidly, and smoothly. Splintering does not occur on the back side during circular saw cutting.

Fig. 10-1. Knotholes or weak grain areas do not exist in the manufactured hardboard and plywood sidings. These products are excellent for exterior siding.

You can install hardboards over sheathing, if desired, or you can use some types without sheathing. If you choose to leave off the sheathing, you can save a large amount of money. You do have to use building paper, but the paper is much cheaper than sheathing. (See Fig. 10-2.)

You can also buy panels of hardboard which are 4 feet wide, $\frac{7}{16}$ inch thick, and either 7, 8, or 9 feet long. The lap siding individual boards are available in 16-foot lengths.

If you use hardboard sidings, you can eliminate the use of starter boards or strips, but you will still need to use the 1-inch corner boards. The cost of installing hardboards is estimated to be $.64 per square foot, which is somewhat less expensive than natural woods.

You can also nail hardboard sidings as easily as you can install wood boards. In fact, hardboard, because of its uniform density, is often easier than nailing thoroughly cured natural wood boards.

Fig. 10-2. The hardboard and plywood products resist weather and will not buckle significantly when used as exterior siding.

Some manufacturers of hardboard sidings offer a limited warranty that includes a 20-year guarantee of the product against checking, splitting, cracking, chipping, delamination, and hail damage. The warranty usually does not cover the cost of installation but does cover the total original cost of the product. While this warranty sounds superb, you should consider several points before you buy the product.

The first consideration is if you buy a sufficient quantity of hardboard siding to cover a wall or an entire house, you might pay a hypothetical cost of between $200 and $2000. If, in 20 years, you need to replace the siding, the $200 or $2000 you will be paid by the manufacturer will not begin to pay the cost of additional siding to cover the same areas. If you can find a guarantee that will not pay, but will replace, the siding, you should choose it. The second guarantee will be an affective hedge against inflation.

The second consideration is if you are 45 years old now and in excellent health, in 20 years you will be 65 years old and perhaps not able physically to replace the siding. The limited warranty specifically states that no cost of installation is included in the guarantee.

In all fairness, if you install wood siding, you will probably receive no warranty at all, and the costs will be comparable. In future years, inflation will affect natural wood as much as, if not more than, it will affect hardboard sidings.

Hardboards are also guaranteed not to buckle. The warranty of at least one manufacturer states that the ½-inch-boards will be free of any buckling. *Buckling* is defined in the warranty as warping of siding exceeding ¼ inch out of plane as measured between the adjacent studs.

You should examine the warranty with a critical eye. If there are 20 studs in a wall and the buckling between any two of them is ¼ inch, there could possibly be a total buckling warp of 5 feet or so in the entire wall, and the warranty would not apply.

The guarantee is probably as good as any you are likely to find in any hardboard product, and the products are excellent in many ways. The finished work is attractive and durable. You can transform an old house into a new-looking one in a short time.

One fine quality of hardboard sidings is that the boards are self-aligning, which means that you can discard the story pole and chalk line, once you have made an accurate start. Once you have installed the first board, the other boards will align themselves well to the first. (See Fig. 10-3.)

The second type of plywood product that is making strong gains in popularity is plywood siding. This product resembles the natural wood surface and has all of the inherent strengths of plywood. According to manufacturer's claims, the $^{11}/_{32}$-inch plywood siding panels, when nailed to the studs without insulating boards between them, will provide twice the rigidity and nearly three times the strength of 1-×-8 lumber sheathing nailed horizontally across the studs. The claim is a good one, although horizontal sheathing is not very strong, and few builders employ this style of sheathing.

The best part of the claim is that some of the plywood sidings have greater strength against racking than 1-×-8 lumber nailed diagonally. This fact is the important part, because diagonal sheathing is very strong.

Plywood is excellent for corner bracing, and siding composed of plywood is amazingly strong. You can strengthen a house remarkably by using plywood siding.

Fig. 10-3. Many of the plywood products are self-aligning. When the shiplap edges are fitted together, the panel is perfectly aligned with the previous panel.

Because the plywood siding, like other plywoods, is made up of thin layers of wood with crossed grains, the product is very strong in all directions. Plywood is undoubtedly one of the best products you can put in a house. (See Fig. 10-4.)

The best qualities of plywood are that it will not shrink or expand more than two tenths of one percent; you can saw and nail it with ordinary carpentry tools; you can nail it as close as $3\!/\!8$ inch from the edge without splitting or cracking it; and you can install panels directly over studs, without adding insulation boards.

You can buy panels of plywood siding that are 4 feet wide and 8, 9, or 10 feet long. Most panels come in thicknesses of $11\!/\!32$ inch or $19\!/\!32$ inch. Surfaces are fir, red cedar, or Southern pine.

These siding panels are not simply sheets of plywood. They are beautifully designed, sturdily manufactured, and engineered to look like natural wood boards installed vertically.

The duraply panels are 4 feet wide, 8, 9, or 10 feet long, and range in thickness from $5\!/\!16$ inch to $3\!/\!8$ inch, $1\!/\!2$ inch, $5\!/\!8$ inch, or $3\!/\!4$ inch. You must paint these panels after installation, and they might require two coats for total smooth coverage.

To install hardboard sidings in a horizontal fashion, you need to prepare the wall first by installing a vapor or moisture barrier of building paper. If you use one of the foil-backed types of vapor barriers, such as polyethylene, you should install it so that the barrier is on the warm side of the wall. Staple the tabs to the studs, rather than on the inside edges of the studs.

If you staple the tabs on the inside edges of the studs, an air space will exist between the staples and a true vapor barrier will not exist. When stapling on the inner edges of studs, space the staples so that the polyethylene cannot gap or stand loose from the stud edge.

Fig. 10-4. Used on corners, plywood siding strengthens and insulates well. Although most people install these sidings in a vertical manner, they can be used horizontally or diagonally.

You can install foam-plastic sheathing over studs if you wish, but you must follow some basic precautions. First, have all edges butt join on the outside edge of a stud. Never let edges meet between studs. Second, you can use a special tape to seal horizontal and vertical edges. Many builders do not use the tape, but you can virtually air-proof the wall by doing so.

Before applying the tape, clean the surface where the tape will be placed so that there is no dust, grease, dirt, or any foreign particles under the tape. Watch for tiny particles of sawdust that might find their way between the tape and the insulation. If sawdust is present, the tape will not adhere permanently to the surface. You might as well not apply it because it will pull loose within a few days or weeks.

Third, you will not be able to nail plywood or hardboard sidings as tightly as you might wish. The foam-plastic sheathing can be crushed because of its low-density structure.

If the foam plastic is not crushed, it might be compressed so tightly that the air passages are constricted, and the insulating properties are severely retarded.

Install corner boards before starting to nail up the horizontal hardboard. When you are ready, because you will need no starter strip or board, you can nail the first hardboards to the sill so the siding will slightly lap over the gap between the sill and the foundation wall. Install any termite shields before you nail in the first boards.

To install the first board, drive a couple of nails into the top edge of the siding, just enough to penetrate the thickness of the board. Hold the board so that one end abuts evenly and snugly into the corner board. Hold the siding firmly while you drive one nail into the sill deep enough so it will hold. If the fit against the corner board is good, tap the other nail enough that it will extend through the siding and into the sill an inch or so.

Check the fit against the corner board again. If the fit is incorrect, remove the nails and refit the siding. If the fit is good, drive the nails the rest of the way, and complete the entire nailing. To make the preliminary check, you need to see that the end of the siding board is square against the corner post and that the entire board is level. (See Fig. 10-5.)

With two nails holding the siding, place the level on the top edge of the board and check the bubble position. You might find that you will have to adjust one end so that part of the sill is exposed in order to make the siding board level. If this situation is the case, take the board loose, lower the entire board, and then make the corrections.

If you are siding an older house, you might have an entire wall out of level, and there might not be any way you can have a level reading or a square fit at the corner board. In this case, you need to decide whether you want to cut the siding board or leave a poor fit and caulk the gap with a waterproof compound.

Cutting hardboard is not difficult, if you choose to create a perfect fit. Leave the two nails in the top edge free from the sill. Slide the siding forward only slightly so that both corners of the end are past the inside edge of the corner boards. Tap the nails lightly,

Fig. 10-5. When you are installing heavy panels, you can lightly tap a turnbutton, shown here, to hold the panel in place while you nail it. Do not use large nails.

just enough to hold. Use a pencil to mark the point where the corner board and the siding should join.

You can also use a straightedge aligned with the edge of the corner board and mark along the edge. Take the siding down, saw along the mark, and you are ready to install the first board. You will probably need to cut every piece before you install it as you move up the wall.

The easy way to install the siding is to keep the square fit and simply lower the siding until you get a level reading. The siding board might not be perfectly parallel with the sill. This discrepancy will not be visible and will not materially affect the structure of the wall as long as the other end of the siding boards fits well against the corner boards.

When you have installed the first board or section of siding, the work is virtually resolved. The hardboard siding units are self-aligning, so when you have made an accurate start, the hard part of the job is completed.

Leave window and door frames intact for this type of work. You will abut the ends or edges of siding against the frames and then caulk any discernible crevices or cracks between the siding and the framing.

You can install most hardboard siding either horizontally or vertically. Horizontal appearance is generally better. Before you try vertical installation, stand several pieces against the wall to get some idea of how it will look. You can get some very interesting effects from diagonal installation as well.

INSTALLING PLYWOOD SIDING

Plywood siding differs from hardboard in a few basic respects. First, plywood is made of wood veneers, while hardboard is composed of wood fibers. Plywood has cross-grained construction while hardboard is basically nondirectional. You can saw the hardboard units much as you would saw any Masonite or similar material. With plywood you are, in a sense, ripping and chipping at the same time.

The hardboard surface saws rather smoothly, almost without splintering or chipping at all. The plywood tends to chip and split if you do not saw carefully. For this reason, you should saw plywood face down, if you are using a circular saw.

You will need to install the plywood siding panels in a vertical fashion. To start, position one panel so that the edge is flush with the outside edge of the corner post. You will not need corner boards for this type of wall covering. Before you put the panel in place, either sink a pair of nails in the edge of the panel on the corner-post side and have a C-clamp and a cushioning material handy. This material can be a cloth folded several times or a scrap piece of paneling or hardboard six inches square or even smaller.

When you have the panel in place, drive the nails you started earlier slightly into the corner post, just enough to hold the panel in place. Go to the other edge of the panel, fit the cushioning material against the surface of the panel and the C-clamp over the panel edge and stud. The clamp will prevent the panel from slipping or being swayed by the wind and damaging the panel.

Check the edges carefully. The panel edge and the corner-post edge should be perfectly flush. If they are, use your level on the inner edge of the panel to see that the edge is perfectly vertical. Make any necessary adjustments. When you are certain that all is correct, you can nail the panel in place. Space the nails 14 inches apart down the corner post and down the two studs that are spanned by the panel.

Pause here to make an estimate of how many panels or partial panels you will need for the rest of the wall. Measure to window frames and door frames. Because the panels are mildly expensive (about $20 per panel), you do not want to ruin one or waste any more than necessary.

If possible, have the last panel before a window fit snugly against the window frame. Such fitting is unlikely. You will probably have to cut a panel or cut out for the window frame.

If you opt to cut around window frames, you will need to measure carefully. Measure at least twice to be sure that you got the correct reading the first time.

One safeguard against improper measurement is to place the panel in position and mark the edges for height. Be sure that the panel is exactly where you want to nail it. While the panel is held in place by a temporary nail, C-clamp, or turnbutton, mark the exact points where the panel strikes against the window frame. Mark both top and bottom. You can use a straightedge aligned with the top and bottom edges of the window framing for good results.

Next, measure from the window frame to the edge of the last panel installed. Measure at top, middle, and bottom. It is possible that the window frame is not installed on a perfect vertical.

Using the straightedge, continue the marks representing the top and bottom of the window frame into the panel for the same distance as that from the edge of the last panel to the window frame.

Cut out the rectangle not needed in the same way that you cut paneling. Bore a small hole at each corner so that the arcs of the circle barely touch the lines of the corner to be cut out. Use a hacksaw blade inserted into the hole and cut along the line for 4 or 5 inches in both directions. Saw out the corner so it is square.

At this point, you can use a handsaw or circular saw. You are far enough away from the corner that you will not damage the rest of the panel. You will have a neater cut, when you use a circular saw, if you will mark the back of the panel and turn it face down while you saw.

If, at any time, the edges of the panel do not stop over the edges of a stud, you must either remove the stud and reposition it in the proper place, or nail in another stud at the point where the panel stops. Nail the panel in place, using the common studs, cripples, and trimmers as nailing backgrounds.

At doorways, measure in the same way. Do not take down the frame of doors or windows, because the thickness of the plywood siding will leave windows recessed too much.

When you have completed the wall and you are ready to install siding on the adjacent walls, place the first panel so that the outside edge is flush with the outside edge of the first panel installed. Fasten it temporarily, and then check for perfect vertical lines. Make necessary adjustments and nail the panel in place.

On higher walls, if the peaks or eaves are higher than the length of the plywood, you might be able to buy longer panels. If sufficiently long panels are not available, you will have to nail in partial panels over the lower ones.

When nailing in partial or complete panels over the ones already installed, position the second panel precisely over the first one so that vertical edges match perfectly. The horizontal edges also should match as closely as possible. Measure from the top edge of

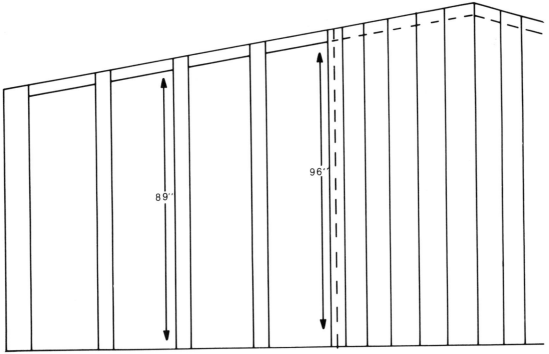

Fig. 10-6. When measuring for slanted eaves installation, you must measure on both sides of the panel location, and then cut the panel to allow for eaves slant.

the lower panels to the eaves. Because of the slant of the eaves or peak, you will need to measure carefully from both edges of the lower panels. Mark and cut the angled sections to fit the slant. (See Fig. 10-6.)

Measure, mark, and cut all subsequent panels until you have covered the space above the first panels. Nail in the partials in the same manner that you installed the whole panels.

You can save money by eliminating waste, if you are going to install the same type of siding on the other side of the house. When you are measuring for the eaves slant, remember that the other side of the house will have the same needs. You can mark one panel and cut it so that the remnant will fit correspondingly on the other eaves section of the house.

If the first partial cut is 3 feet long on its short side and 4 feet long on its high side, you should be able to take the leftover segment and fit it into the first partial space on the opposite side of the house. If the first cuts are even shorter, you might be able to use the remnants of two panels on the other side. By doing so, you save the cost of two entire panels.

On any walls with angled protrusions, such as bay windows with partial window surfaces, you can nail up siding on the parts not covered by glass or window framing. You will need to bevel the edges of panels where they meet at angles. One way to get the bevel cut is to adjust your circular saw to the proper angle (in most cases a 45-degree angle) and set the guide. Then cut the edge of the panel and the bevel cut will allow you to have a smooth joint where the panels meet.

Some plywood siding is manufactured with shiplap long edges. If you buy this type, you will not need to nail up batten strips. Otherwise, you will need to do so over all joints.

FINISHING UP PLYWOOD SIDING WALLS

When you have nailed all of your siding in place, you will need to complete the job by adding any batten, caulk, compound, or other finishing touches. For most plywood or hardboard siding, you can buy batten designed especially for use with each type. Use the recommended batten because it will fit and adhere better to the siding and it will look better. (See Fig. 10-7.)

You can also buy nails specifically recommended to match the colors in the batten or molding. These nails are engineered for the proper shank thickness and length to reach the studs or corner posts for maximum holding ability.

If your supplier does not have the specified types of molding, you can buy stock molding and install and paint it to your own tastes. The dealer can also help you to match the paint or stain colors.

Unless you are an experienced painter, you might find it easier to paint the siding before you install any molding. You can then paint the molding on a good work surface and install it later. If you try to paint it in place, you might smear paint on the siding while painting the molding. The resulting problem can be difficult to clean.

Fig. 10-7. When you have installed the panels, you can nail up molding, batten, or other trim to create a neater appearance.

You will have nail heads that are not the same color as the molding; but, you can touch the heads with a brush after the molding is installed. You will have only half a dozen nails in each batten and you might elect to leave them their manufactured color.

The batten, or strips covering the seams or joints in siding, might be only an inch wide. It can also be prestained or painted, if you buy the manufacturer's recommended batten.

Many of the styles of siding are already preprimed for either painting or staining. It is good to check with the dealer for specific paints or stains to be used with the particular sidings. You can cover plywood with semitransparent, oil-based, penetrating stains, solid-color stains, or latex paints. You can also use water-repellent preservatives. You should not cover duraply siding with one coat of primer and one coat of acrylic latex paint. You should not use oil-based or semitransparent stains on duraply materials.

When you have completed the installation of the siding, check for any possible holes that could admit insects, and plug these holes with compound or caulk that is waterproof. While the siding comes from the manufacturer usually in good condition, it might be damaged through improper handling or nailing. Even a tiny hole can become a haven for small insects which, in turn, are much desired by many types of woodpeckers. These birds can cause considerable damage to any wood product.

When you have sealed all nail holes and the siding is painted, you will find that the wall covering will last you for many years with a virtually maintenance-free endurance. You will also find that the plywood siding is an excellent insulation. Some builders insist that one panel of plywood is equal to at least 3 inches of insulation.

Another high-quality characteristic of these sidings is that they require only one-half to one-third as much paint as do natural wood siding boards. The paint goes on smoother and faster and it tends to last longer. Plywood, or hardboard siding, tends to hold paint without chipping or flaking. These siding materials often need painting only half as frequently as wood boards.

Before you make a final selection for exterior wall coverings, you should consider some other coverings. One of these is vinyl siding, which has largely replaced aluminum siding in many parts of the country. Masonry walls have been, and still are, highly popular and efficient.

Chapter 11 discusses vinyl siding, and Chapter 12 deals with brick walls. Stone masonry will be discussed in Chapter 14.

11
Vinyl Siding

VINYL SIDING IS ONE OF THE BEST WALL COVERINGS TO COME ALONG
in modern times. Exterior walls that receive constant sunlight and rainfall often will not
hold paint. Some type of siding, other than wood, is needed. One explanation for the
inability of certain walls to hold paint is that, particularly for walls on the east side of
the house, the rain or morning dew will still be on the walls when the sun rises. The sun's
rays are highly intensified by the drop of water, and one result is that the paint blisters.

Walls on other parts of the house are not as susceptible. By the time the sun hits these
walls, the heat of the day has already evaporated the moisture and no blistering effect
is created.

Whatever the reasons, some woods do not hold a coat of paint well. Even if you apply sealers prior to painting with some of the gels, they will not protect certain walls.
Masonite or other types of the newer lines of wall coverings will hold paint without any
real difficulty.

If you want to use the latest and best of the exterior wall coverings, you might want
to try vinyl. It has many positive characteristics and very few negative ones. One of the
drawbacks is that, although the actual siding is rather easy to install, the molding, and
particularly the curves and the corners, are very difficult to handle.

"Anyone with reasonable abilities in construction can put up the difficult parts of
a wall," one vinyl siding installation spokesman said. "The problem is that it takes a $1000
machine to give you the proper curvature or angles, and not many people are willing to
pay that much money for a machine that can be used for nothing but that one function."

The spokesman did have a possible solution for the home-repair person. "He or she
can put up the easy parts and then call a siding expert to complete the job," he said.

Will a siding team bring its equipment to a home to do only part of the job, particularly
if the home owner installed the early siding units solely to keep from paying the siding
team? Apparently many will accept even partial jobs.

144

The same spokesman said, "We encourage owners to do as much of the work as they can. We generally have as much business as we can handle and we welcome the shorter jobs where we do only those things that qualify us as professionals." While he might not be speaking for all siding installers, he speaks for some of them.

If you discuss this type job with a contractor, be sure to get the arrangements in writing and signed by both parties. One of the worst things that could happen is that the contractor might change his mind or prolong the time frame for completion of your project.

When you sign the initial agreement, have the document state that the siding contractor's firm will agree to install the molding, door and window siding, and other work that you cannot do (stipulate exactly what those parts of the job are so that there will be no mistakes). Get a date for the contracted work to be done so that you won't get pushed aside while other more lucrative jobs are completed. Above all, you do not want to be left totally without assistance. If you do not get the entire agreement in writing, you might find that none of the contractors will complete your job.

In the agreement, you should state what kinds of materials you want used. If you use one type of insulation panel or pad under the siding, make sure the other part of the house uses the same thickness. State in the contract if the contractor is to install siding over the window frames, the porch posts, and door frames. Get in writing that he will rebuild windows to keep frames aligned with the rest of the wall (if that is what you want him to do). Leave nothing to chance. Stipulate that he is to replace old and decayed wood with new wood on facia or eaves.

If you cannot get the previous information in writing, perhaps you had better reconsider your decision to do the vinyl siding work. It if seems that too much is being made over a small part of the job, remember that this one part of the job is by far the hardest and most demanding. Remember also, your unfinished house or unfinished wall will never be acceptable to you.

You can find a list of vinyl siding contractors in your local telephone directory. One strong recommendation is that you deal with a local person, if possible. Try to work with a company that has been in business for a long time.

Many contractors who formerly concentrated on aluminum siding have now switched to aluminum and vinyl siding work. The reason is clear: aluminum, while fading from the market as vinyl becomes more and more popular, is still needed on doors, window frames, porch posts, corners, and borders.

From a comparative viewpoint, many contractors who install aluminum siding report that their product is guaranteed for a period of 20 years, while vinyl siding carries a guarantee that is for your lifetime (often, they add a rider or qualifying clause—if you continue to own the house).

The problems that occurred with aluminum siding were not many, but they were serious. Other than the conductivity of the material, many complained that aluminum siding dented easily. A baseball, rock, or similar objects can do serious damage to a strip of siding. Another complaint is that if the wall is pushed against or shoved against by a heavy person or object, the siding will collapse.

Vinyl siding is reportedly far more satisfactory. Contractors who sell and install both aluminum and vinyl often admit they prefer vinyl overwhelmingly to aluminum. They argue that vinyl is stronger, more durable, and more attractive. One major complaint against aluminum is that it is "unforgiving." This statement means that, unlike many other building materials, it will not expand and contract during alternating hot and cold weather. Contractors say that if it does expand, it remains expanded, while vinyl will soon revert to its original shape.

If you need to hire someone to do part of the installation, choose your contractor with care. This is another reason for hiring someone who is a local businessman or contractor: you will want to know that the person will remain available to you in the event that problems occur later.

As we were gathering material for this book, we contacted two vinyl-siding contractors—one local and one who informed us that he had siding crews in the area for a short time. What we learned was invaluable to us in helping us reach our decision concerning our own house. This information can also be of value to you, in the event you encounter similar people.

The out-of-town siding installer visited our house, looked around the outside, and then quoted us a price of $18,000. He would lower this price considerably if we agreed to allow him to take and use "before and after" photos of the house and photos of work in progress. He did not measure any walls, and he did not look at part of the house. He nevertheless told us how many board feet of new lumber we would need. He further informed us that he would replace some windows and reframe others. The prices quoted to us for new windows were approximately twice what we would have to pay for similar windows at a local building supply outlet.

The out-of-town salesman had no business cards, no literature on his product, and no photos of previous work done. At no time did he supply a business telephone number or mailing address, although the request was made several times. The only demonstration of his product was to show us that a short segment of his siding would, when it was laid across two objects, support his weight.

When he was shown a siding brochure that had arrived in the mail earlier, he became hostile in his attitude toward a company that was apparently so unprofessional and unreliable. He did not even recognize the brochure as one sent out by his own siding company.

When he quoted us the final price, he insisted that he receive an answer immediately— before he left. Otherwise, the price markdown would be cancelled. He demanded an answer within fifteen minutes of the presentation.

On the brochure sent out by his company there was only a detachable card to be mailed in to the company. The name of the company and the address do not appear anywhere on the remainder of the brochure—only on the mail-in card.

Concerning the strength of the siding as indicated in the demonstration, we later showed that a short piece of badly damaged wood board would similarly hold our weight. While we had no real intentions of accepting the out-of-town offer, we wanted to hear the sales pitch so that we could better inform you what to guard against.

The local siding contractor's business was located through a large ad in the yellow pages of the telephone directory. The mail address was also prominently displayed in the ad.

When the company spokesman arrived, he brought with him many samples of materials and a huge array of "before" and "after" photos of his company's work. He further supplied names and addresses of other area customers who, when contacted, readily agreed to let us come inspect the company's work. His estimate of the cost of the work to be done was several thousand dollars lower than that of the previous caller.

If you choose to have your exterior walls covered with vinyl siding, your first step is to learn some of the unethical or borderline ethical ploys used by some siding companies. First, beware of companies that promise something for nothing. You might be told that your house has been selected as a special demonstration model and, consequently, you will be given a huge reduction in the cost of the siding installation. One brochure promises that "if your home suffers from very high fuel bills and needs periodic painting and repairs, then there is a good chance that it will be selected" for advertising purposes.

Second, learn the locations of work in progress and drive to the site to observe the installation processes. See firsthand how professional the workers are and examine the materials to compare them with other materials you have seen.

Third, talk with previous customers to see how satisfied they are with the company's work. Talk with customers whose work was done in the past month, year, and even five or more years earlier. Find out if the contractor indeed agrees to return promptly to correct problem areas and how much, if anything, he charges for return visits.

Fourth, read brochures or, even better, read one of the consumer publications in which comparative studies have been made of a particular type of siding. Your local library probably has several publications of this nature.

PREPARING FOR SIDING

Installing siding is only half the job. Preparing for the job is the tough task. In order to prepare, you have to take care of three major chores.

The first chore is to prepare the walls for the actual siding. If the house has already had wood siding on it, you will need to locate and remove all boards that have been gravely damaged by decay. This does not include boards that simply are old and unsightly because of flaking paint. If the wood in the board is still good and sound, leave it. If the wood is soft and spongy, take it down and discard it.

You might encounter difficulty in getting a board in the center of a wall free from the siding that laps it. Here is one possible solution: use 2 × 4, 2 × 6, or similar lumber as a pivotal point for your crowbar. Push the crowbar point under the defective board. Hold the crowbar so that the claws are pointed downward. Push the blade of the crowbar under the lap of the siding board that is directly above the defective board.

When you have inserted the point an inch or more under the lap board, place the 2 × 4, or similar material (the length should be no more than 1 foot), under the angle portion of the crowbar blade. Push downward on the crowbar until the lap board is pulled up at least an inch or two.

Now move 2 or 3 feet to another point and do the same thing. Keep prying and moving until the entire board no longer touches the defective board.

Probably there will be nails through the bottom of the lap board and top of the defective board. If so, you will need to remove them. One method you can use is to hit the lap board near the nails and force the lap board down. The force of the blow often will leave the nails protruding far enough for you to get the claws of a hammer or crowbar under the nail head so you can extract the nail.

Remove all of the bottom nails as you can. Next, insert the blade of the crowbar under the bottom edge of the defective board, and pry it away from the board under it. Remove the nails in the same way. The lap board should slip easily from the wall.

In this fashion, remove all decayed boards. Your next job is to take down any window framing that needs to be removed. You can decide whether the windows should be reinstalled in one simple way: decide whether you will install siding over the old wood, and whether you will install ⅜ inch insulation pads under the siding and over the existing siding boards. If you do so, you will be adding slightly more than an inch, including lap joints, to the thickness of the wall. Calculate what this extra inch, or slightly more, will do to the window frame alignment.

One of the great problems facing the siding installer is bowed walls. This misalignment is generally caused by studding nailed in, out of line, with the wall. Correction is difficult, short of completely rebuilding the wall.

Because vinyl siding conforms closely to wall lines, it will show any bows or curves in the wall. You can try one or two correctional measures. One possible remedy is to is to correct siding boards that were installed green and, in the course of time, have warped.

You can check board trueness by removing two or three boards where the curve seems worst. If the boards are true on the bottom and top of a wall but bowed in the middle, the cause is far more likely to be defective boards rather than improperly installed studding. It is extremely improbable that all of the studs bowed in the same place, so it stands to reason that the boards are at fault.

You can correct the problem by replacing the boards with new, true boards that have been cured adequately. Install new boards by reversing the process of removing old ones. You will want to allow the lap board above the new boards to remain out from the studs and wall line by 2 or 3 inches.

If you have only two or three boards to replace, first pull out any nails that might have remained in the top portion of the old board under the last board removed. Remove any fragments of old wood. Clean the area as well as you can.

You can drive two or three nails spaced 3 or 4 feet apart in the top part of the board under the new board to be nailed in place. Drive the nails in only far enough to support the weight of the new board while you install it. Start the nails at the same points, if possible, where final nailing will occur.

Place the new board in its proper location and abut it well against the corner boards. Let the bottom of the board rest upon the nails just installed.

With the board supported, drive nails into the top of the new board and into the studding or corner post. Sink the nails all the way. Make sure that the new board laps the old board properly. It should do so without difficulty if you started the support nails on a level alignment.

Fasten the top of the new board. When this is done, you can drive nails through the bottom edge of the new board so that they will also penetrate the top of the old board. When you come to the last new board to install, first check to see that all of the nails in the top board have been removed. Start the support nails as you did before, and slip the new board into place by tilting it so that the top can slip under the protruding edge of the board above it.

Check the new board for position and proper lap. When you are satisfied that the board is positioned accurately, drive the nails through the bottom portion of the top board so that they penetrate the top part of the board below. Be sure that the nails hit studs when they pass through the two thicknesses of boards.

If the trouble is in the studding, you will have to take down siding boards and realign the studding. If the trouble is in the sole plate (and the crookedness of the sole plate is causing the wall to be out of line), you will have to remove the studding, then take out the sole plate, and later install it as it should be.

This procedure is a big job, one that will require several hours of work and a virtual rebuilding of the entire wall. Rebuild only if the wall is so badly out of line that you have no choice.

To make the needed corrections, you will have to remove the siding boards, take out studding, and then remove the sole plate. The problem with this procedure is that if the rest of the house is completed and the wall is a bearing one, you cannot take the studding out without endangering the entire house.

If you have no choice, you can cut the sole plate and remove it in sections while leaving part of the wall intact. If the wall is 20 feet long, remove studding and sole plate in 4 foot sections. When one section is removed, immediately replace it with new sole plate and studding. Then go to the next section.

When the second section is reinstalled, you can strengthen the sole plate by nailing a 2 × 4 between the studs and over the joint of the plate.

Even if a wall is badly bowed, you probably will not have to replace the entire wall. You can usually determine where the major problem is located and remove only that part of the wall. It is extremely unlikely that the whole wall and sole plate are out of line. You can perhaps remove only the middle of the wall where the greatest bow is located.

You can pry siding boards free and, if you can work from the inside, remove and replace the defective portions of the wall. Then you can reinstall the wall section, refasten the siding boards, and start to install siding.

INSTALLING THE SIDING

Assuming that your wall needed no corrections or that all the corrections had been made, you can start to install the vinyl siding. Choose as a starting point a wall that is uncluttered. By uncluttered, we mean a wall that has no problem areas such as alcoves, recesses, odd wall lines, angles, bay windows, and other difficult sections to fit siding around.

Try to start with a wall that has no windows or doors or any other kinds of interruptions of the wall line. Save the more troublesome walls until you have gained a degree of experience. (See Fig. 11-1.)

As always, you need to start the first siding unit with a square fit on the corners and a perfectly level position. Siding is manufactured in a variety of ways, but one of the most popular styles is that of lapped siding with nailing rails attached to the top of each unit. Below the nailing rail there is a raised portion sometimes called a lap rail. Your next unit of siding will fit neatly over this raised portion to provide the lapped siding look and also to provide a good watershed effect. (See Fig. 11-2.)

Nail in the first section of siding so that it slightly laps the joint of the sill and foundation wall. You will probably be nailing the siding over the existing siding and the panels of insulation. The insulation, in addition to providing better temperature control over the house, also helps even walls. (See Fig. 11-3.)

Fig. 11-1. You might need professional help for areas such as the ones shown here. If you try to install siding in such places, save them for last, after you have gained experience.

With the first section in position, nail the siding in place. Your dealer can provide the proper nails. The siding also comes with installation directions. Follow these directions carefully.

When you have installed the first section, place the second section in its proper location so that the bottom laps over the lap rail. Then nail the top by inserting nails through the nailing rails and fastening the section to the wall. Proceed in this fashion up the wall. (See Fig. 11-4.)

When you reach the top of the wall, you can either round the corner or, if the wall is all that you plan to do at this time, you can install the corner molding, which is generally a thin strip of molding that fits neatly over the corners. You can buy molding for inside corners and outside corners. (See Fig. 11-5.)

Fig. 11-2. Siding units will fit together, much like lap siding, and it is self-aligning.

Fig. 11-3. Let the siding lap slightly over the foundation wall for better overall protection and appearance.

Fig. 11-4. Once you have made a true start, you can move rapidly and cover an entire wall.

Fig. 11-5. At the top of a wall, you can install molding and other specially-fitted sections of the siding.

You can saw vinyl siding with a circular saw or with a hacksaw. You can also saw the molding strips with a hacksaw. Because many of these molding units are made of aluminum, you cannot saw them with a regular handsaw. You can saw vinyl siding with a handsaw if you don't mind rather slow progress. (See Fig. 11-6.)

Vinyl siding is not nearly as expensive today as it was when it arrived on the market (pricing being comparable to the buying power of the dollar). You can buy a 12-foot section of siding 10 inches wide for about $4.50 per section. Ten pieces of this siding will make a square or cover 100 square feet. Total cost would be about $45 per hundred feet.

These pieces are manufactured so that they have the general appearance of two, 5-inch boards lapped. The narrow-plank effect is attractive, and each piece can be installed quickly and with perfect alignment. The self-aligning quality of this type of vinyl siding is one

Fig. 11-6. You will have to use aluminum for posts and some sections of molding. You can install aluminum in much the same manner as vinyl.

Fig. 11-7. When installing around windows, check to see that you have maintained your level trueness. You can use a story pole or simply measure with a tape.

Fig. 11-8. Once installed, your vinyl and aluminum combination siding will never rust or corrode. It will not fade, and it will never need painting.

of its best points. You do not have to make regular level checks. As long as you position the laps over the lap rails, the siding cannot deviate from a true horizontal. (See Fig. 11-7.)

You can install this type of siding only horizontally, so you are restricted somewhat in terms of your design flexibility. The siding will not rust, corrode, conduct electricity, or decay. Insects will not damage the siding, and the siding will not leak or absorb water even when submerged for prolonged periods of time. (See Fig. 11-8.)

Painting is not a necessity for vinyl siding. Usually you can wash the siding and clean it thoroughly. Abrupt weather changes do not exert an adverse effect on the siding. It will not chip, crack, blister, peel, or buckle as weather changes occur. The vinyl surface is far more durable than aluminum.

Vinyl is also comparable in price to other forms of siding. A 4-×-8-foot panel of rough-sawn pine sells for about $14 per panel. It will cost you virtually the same amount of money to cover 100 square feet with pine panels as it would to cover the area with vinyl siding.

Three-quarter inch insulating panels, 13⅝ inches wide, and 4 feet high, can be bought for slightly more than 50 cents each. Typically, these panels are sold in lots or packs of six at a cost of $3.50 or slightly higher per pack.

Because you can install vinyl siding yourself, much as you would install lap siding, you can install the siding at a very reasonable cost. The lifetime guarantee makes the siding one of the best bargains on the market today.

12
Masonry Wall Covering

THREE FINAL TYPES OF EXTERIOR WALL COVERINGS FALL INTO THE
category of masonry products: stone, cement blocks, and bricks. Although all three of
these products share several common qualities, all three are quite different in installation
and utility.

The common qualities are, primarily, that all three are the hardest substances to install
on exterior walls. All three require mortar and bonding, and all three require considerable
skill in installation. The three masonry materials are reasonably inexpensive to buy but
very expensive to have installed. For best results, all three require experienced and
professional craftsmen.

Although the beginning home-repair person can learn to nail up siding or paneling
in a short time, it takes years to become a good mason. Cement blocks are easiest to learn
to install, and rock or stone masonry probably are the most difficult to learn. A well-
known mason, a master craftsman who helped to rebuild many homes of Washington
politicians, who had bought and had overseen the dismantling of the homes in Europe,
and then had the homes reconstructed in the Washington area, once commented that the
only really difficult aspects of brick masonry were fireplaces and some of the circular
or oval constructions. "Anybody can stack bricks in a straight wall," he said.

The mason might have been guilty of a gross over-simplification. Laying bricks well,
even in a short wall, requires more than the ability to stack bricks.

The energetic and persevering amateur mason can, however, learn to lay masonry
products with a degree of success. Although it might be overly ambitious for you as a
beginner to attempt to build a fireplace and chimney, you can learn to lay the bricks or
other masonry products in a patio, outdoor grill, or even a wall.

You will need a few basic tools, and you will need to learn how to use the tools
effectively. You need to learn how to mix mortar and concrete, and you need to be familiar with the basic bonding patterns used in masonry.

TOOLS NEEDED FOR BASIC MASONRY

The minimum tools you need for any degree of masonry work, other than pouring a concrete slab, include tools used in spreading mortar, cutting bricks or stones, maintaining a straight and level wall, and constructing perfect corners (inside and outside corners included).

To spread mortar, you will need at least one trowel, one jointer, a mortarboard, a shovel, and a hoe. You will also need a mortar box or mortar pan in which to mix the mortar.

You use the shovel and hoe to do most of the actual mixing work. Use the mortarboard to hold fully-mixed mortar which is ready for application in the wall or other work area. You will use the trowel for "buttering" bricks and for spreading mortar beds on footings or previously-laid courses of bricks or other masonry products. To make joint finishes between the courses of bricks or between the bricks in a course you will use a jointer.

You can buy a shovel and hoe inexpensively at any hardware store. Trowels and other needed equipment also are available at such outlets. You can make a mortarboard and a temporary mortar box in a few minutes at a cost of less than one dollar.

To make a mortarboard, all you need is a 2-foot square section of plywood, or similar material, two 24-inch 2 × 4s, a hammer, and some nails. Stand the 2 × 4s on edge about 20 inches apart, and position the plywood section on top of the edges of the 2 × 4s. Drive nails through the plywood and into the 2-×-4 sections to hold the mortarboard together. (See Fig. 12-1.) If you do not have plywood, you can use 1-×-4 or 1-×-5-inch boards, set tightly together and nailed across the 2 × 4s.

You can buy mortar boxes or mortar pans; however, you also can build one out of a panel of plywood, some 2-×-12-inch boards, and some 2 × 4s. Again, if plywood is unavailable, you can use closely-fitted boards for the bottom of the mortar box.

If you will be mixing only small amounts of mortar at a time, you can use 2-×-8 or even 2-×-6 boards for the sides.

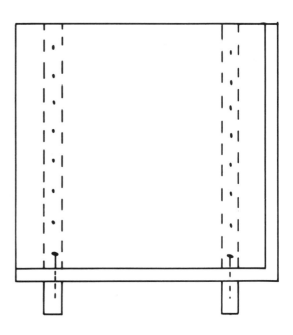

Fig. 12-1. You can make a mortar board in minutes by nailing a section of plywood over two 2 × 4s standing on edge.

Good dimensions for the mortar box are 4 or 5 feet long, 3 feet wide, and 8 or 10 inches deep. Start by standing two wide boards on edge and nailing the plywood, or the fitted boards, across them. Pull the boards crossing the wide boards as tightly together as you can, and nail them securely. When you have completed the bottom, nail on the ends.

A better way is to make a rectangle by nailing the wide boards together and then adding the bottom. Nail three lengths of 2 × 4s, just long enough to reach from side to side, to the bottom. You can lay the 2 × 4s flat, and nail one at each end and the other in the middle.

MIXING CONCRETE AND MORTAR

You can buy cement mixers that are portable and powered by electricity. These machines save a great deal of time and energy. Mixing concrete by hand is grueling work, but you can do it, particularly if you plan to mix small amounts at a time.

Many mortar and concrete mixes include hydrated lime. You can omit this ingredient if you wish. You will need cement, water, and sand for mortar. You will need to add gravel if you wish to mix concrete.

A good random mixture of mortar is one shovelful of cement to three shovelfuls of sand, plus enough water to mix well. Start by putting the dry cement into the mortar box. If you use five heaped shovels of cement, you will want to add two gallons of water and mix well. Do not just wet the cement. Use a hoe to work the water and cement together until you have a wet, plastic mix. Add as much water as you need to get the sufficient moisture. The mix, at this point, should be as thick as a heavy soup.

Add 15 heaped shovels of sand, three shovelfuls at a time. As you add the sand, stop and mix it thoroughly into the cement. Again, do not simply wet the sand. Mix the cement, sand, and water completely.

When you mix the first deposits of sand, add more, until you have mixed all 15 shovelfuls of sand. Add water, as needed, until the mixture is thick enough to hold its shape and plastic enough to work well. To test it, pull a trowel through and make a V-shaped groove. If the groove holds its form, the mixture is the right consistency.

You can buy a load of sand from any concrete supply outlet. Do not attempt to use sand shoveled from a creek bed or roadside because such sand will also have small gravel in it. You will find that it is difficult to lay an even course of bricks if the mortar is lumpy.

If you are mixing concrete instead of mortar, you can use the rougher sand. The small gravel in it will actually help make the mixture better.

Always start by mixing the cement and water, then add the sand (often called the fine aggregate). Always add the coarse aggregate (the gravel) last. As you add the gravel, the mixing chore becomes much more difficult. It is hard to pull the complete mixture with a hoe, which is what you need to do if you are to mix the concrete well. As you work the mixture, drop the hoe against the far end of the box, and chop it into the mixture. Pull the hoe through the mix, and bring it to the surface. As you heap the mix at the near end, push the hoe back through it. Repeat this process until every grain of sand and each tiny part of the cement is saturated fully.

If your sand is already wet, you will need less water. Always add less than the recommended quantity of water until the final stages of the mix. During the final stage, add as much water as you need to get a thick, plastic mixture. If the weather is hot, mix in the shade if you can. The first obvious reason to mix in the shade is the effect heat can have on you, especially if you are unaccustomed to hard work of this nature. The second reason is to keep the mix from setting up before you are ready to use it.

When you see that your mix is starting to harden in the box or pan, you can add a slight amount of water. Use just enough water to keep the mix pliable. You also can cover the mixture.

If you do not have access to good mason's sand, you can use the roadside sand, but you must screen it. Use a section of screen wire and pour the sand over it so that the screen wire will filter the sand. As the coarse bits accumulate on top of the wire, stop and discard them regularly.

Despite your efforts, some coarse sand or small gravel will find its way into the mixture. When you are laying bricks and a brick will not push into the mortar bed, use the point of the trowel to locate the trouble spot, and discard that part of the mortar.

If you add too much water and the mixture is too thin, you can add more sand to thicken it. If you need to add more than three shovels of sand, add a shovelful of cement so that the final mixture will not be too weak to hold well.

USING MASONRY TOOLS

The most important mason's tool is the trowel. Several kinds of trowels are available, including the buttering, the brick, and the pointing trowels. For general use, you will need the brick trowel, which is the largest of the three and has a diamond-shaped construction. (See Fig. 12-2.)

An easy way to hold and use a trowel is to curl your fingers around the handle and place your thumb on the top of the handle. This position allows you to move freely without awkwardness. When you pick up mortar with the trowel, if you are right-handed, use the left side of the trowel, scoop it sideways into the mortar heap, and lift straight up. You can lift enough mortar for five bricks at one scoop.

The purpose of this type of pickup is to minimize the number of times you will need to turn or bend to pick up mortar. While you are learning, you might be content to pick up enough mortar for only one brick at a time. As you gain expertise, you will be able to scoop up a full trowel of mortar, butter, and lay five bricks in one basic operation.

When you are laying a mortar bed (sometimes called a windrow) on the near side of the wall, pick up the mortar, turn the trowel away from you, and tilt it to a vertical point. The mortar will not slide off if it is mixed well. With the trowel point away from you to the front, hold it over the center line of the bricks. Spread the mortar by tilting the trowel slightly more and then pulling it back toward you. You can spread a foot to 2 feet of mortar in this fashion with one trowel load.

When you are spreading a mortar bed on the far side of the wall, load the trowel, tilt it to vertical, and hold it barely outside the brick line. With the bottom edge of the trowel parallel to the brick line, lower the trowel and pull it toward you at the same time.

Use the mason's hammer to break bricks or to split and rough break them. To break a brick, hold the brick in the palm of your hand with the narrow, long edge upward. This edge is called the *face* of the brick. Holding the mason's hammer in your other hand, with the chisel peen pointing downward, strike the brick at the point you want to break it. Hit the brick sharply one time with the chisel peen at right angles to the length of the brick. (See Fig. 12-3.)

Fig. 12-2. The diamond-shaped trowel is the most universal tool in masonry. It is constructed to make numerous moves in laying bricks or blocks.

You also can use the chisel peen and face of the hammer to break bricks into bats, quarter closures, three-quarter closure, king closure, queen closure, and splits. A *bat* is half a brick. A *quarter closure* is one-fourth of a brick. The *three-quarter closure* is, as its name suggests, three-fourths of a brick. A *king closure* is a brick with one corner broken away. A *queen closure* is half a brick split lengthwise, as opposed to the bat, which is broken in half. A *split* is a brick cut in half across the thickest part of the brick.

To cut bricks with the face of the hammer, stand the brick on a narrow edge (or face) and either mark or imagine a cutting line down the center of the face. When you are ready to begin, hit the brick just inside the cutting line. Follow this procedure all along the cutting line. As you strike, hit slightly at an angle toward you. (See Fig. 12-4.) When the brick chips away along that cutting line, turn it over and do the same thing on the other side.

Finish the brick by using the chisel peen to trim away the rough spots. Do not try to hold the brick as you do this work. You could injure your hand either through the force of the hammer or chisel peen, or a shard of brick could cut or penetrate your palm.

Use a jointer to rub along the joints between the bricks and between the courses to remove surplus mortar and also to add a design to the mortar joint. You can buy or obtain jointers that will give a straight joint or an interesting variation such as the grapevine joint. (See Figs. 12-5 and 12-6.)

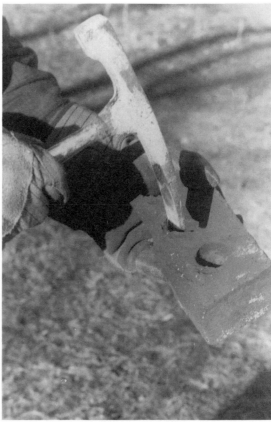

Fig. 12-4. To cut a brick, hold it firmly and chip at the edge of the brick with short, downward strokes of the hammer.

Fig. 12-3. Hold the brick in the palm of your hand and strike it at the desired breaking point by bringing the hammer down sharply. One blow usually breaks the brick.

ELEMENTARY BRICK LAYING

If you have a fully-framed wall and the sill is resting on a foundation wall, you might decide to lay bricks up the sheathed wall. At this point, you have poured your footings wide enough to accommodate the thickness of a brick wall. Start by clearing away any dirt or other debris that might have accumulated along the footing. When the footing is clean, start by laying a mortar bed alongside the foundation wall and wide enough to allow a brick to be embedded in it.

Lay the first brick by pushing it against the foundation wall and then slightly downward until the mortar is pushed out slightly from under it. The force of the push will cause mortar to enter the holes in the brick and stabilize the wall from the beginning. The brick should be flush with the end of the foundation wall at the corner.

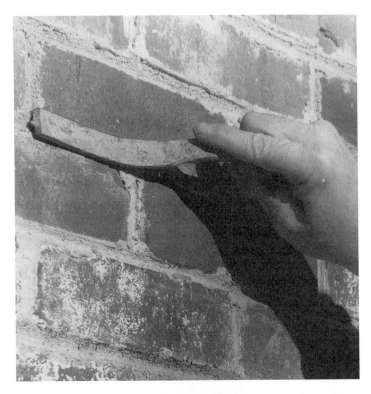

Fig. 12-5. Jointing is one of the necessary steps needed to create an attractive wall. Run the jointer through all mortar joints in the wall.

Fig. 12-6. The last step in finishing up a wall is brushing away all the crumbs of mortar pushed up by the jointer.

Go to the other end of the wall and lay a brick exactly as you laid the first one. You can lay a row of bricks without mortar along the wall to determine the spacing problems, if any, that you will encounter. Leave half an inch between bricks as you lay them temporarily beside the mortar bed.

Stretch a taut guideline over the tops of the first bricks in the mortar bed. You can use a thin shim of wood (the approximate thickness of the stick in an ice cream bar) under the cord and on top of both end bricks.

Now lay the bricks into the mortar bed. You can butter the end of each brick slightly as you work. Use the trowel and leave a thin spread of mortar on each end corner. Push the brick against the first one with sufficient force to cause the mortar to be slightly compressed (but not hard enough to dislodge the first brick). Each brick should be slightly lower than the guideline you have stretched across the end bricks.

Complete the course. When you reach the end, lay a short bed of mortar and several bricks along the adjacent walls. The first bricks in the new wall line should extend far enough to be even with the outside edge of the first bricks. The purpose of this arrangement is so the corner bricks will be bonded. In subsequent courses, tie each brick on the corner to the bricks above and below it.

Because you have a sheathed wall behind the bricks, you do not need to worry about keeping the wall vertical. As long as the bricks are barely touching or uniformly distant from the wall, your wall line is all right. You should keep a level and a straightedge handy. Use them regularly to be sure that you are maintaining mortar joints of a uniform thickness and that one end of a brick is not higher than the other end.

It is very easy, unless you use a guideline, level and straightedge, to allow the bricks in the middle of a course to sag or rise. When this flaw occurs, you will have to correct it in subsequent courses by thickening or thinning mortar joints to compensate for the error. Such changes in joints are unattractive and should be avoided when possible.

One of your greatest tendencies will be to allow the brick wall to lean outwards. Guard against this problem by keeping a careful check on the proximity of the brick line to the framing wall behind the brick wall. When you see a mistake, correct it immediately. Do not try to compensate by edging the brick line back to a normal position. All this will do is create a bowed wall which is dangerous and unstable, as well as unattractive.

You can buy, very inexpensively, metal ties that you can fasten to the framing wall. Embed these ties in the mortar joints, so that you connect the brick wall to the framing wall at several points. (See Fig. 12-7.)

When you start the second course, be sure to lap or bond the end bricks to the bricks below. By doing so, you will not need to break a brick to end the course correctly.

Maintain the same pattern as you continue to lay course after course. Lay a bed of mortar, lay the corner bricks, then butter and lay subsequent bricks. Your speed will increase greatly with a little practice.

You can keep a stack of bricks beside your work area, or you can place the bricks just beyond the mortar bed. As you lay one brick, you can reach slightly to one side and pick up another. As you pick up the brick in one hand, hold the trowel, loaded with mortar, ready to butter the next brick. In this fashion, you need not lay the trowel down except when you pause to check the level or trueness of your wall.

Fig. 12-7. If you are laying face bricks over an inner wall, you can install metal ties to the inner wall and then spread these in the mortar of the outside wall.

When you butter the fifth brick with one trowel of mortar, place any leftover mortar back on the mortarboard. You can snap the trowel slightly over the board, and the mortar will fall away instantly.

You might need to wet the bricks, particularly if the weather is hot and dry, before you place them in the mortar. A dry brick has a tendency to absorb excessive amounts of water from the mortar, leaving it weak and unstable.

After you have laid three or four bricks, take the side of the trowel and run it along the face and back of the wall to scrape off excess mortar that has been forced from the joints. Snap this mortar onto the mortarboard, and use it later.

Remember that wetting bricks serves four basic purposes. Any mortar containing Portland cement needs to stay wet as long as possible, within reason. Portland cement can harden properly only if there is enough moisture present to cause the hydration of the cement. If the bricks absorb the water too quickly, the proper amount of hydration cannot occur.

A second reason for wetting bricks is to remove the dust and dirt from the side of the brick. If there is a dust or dirt cover between the brick and the mortar, no real bonding can occur.

If the bricks are wet, the mortar will spread more evenly under the brick. A wet brick will create a stronger and longer-lasting bond between the brick and the mortar.

At the end of a day's work, clean your trowel, mortarboard, mortar box or pan, and all other tools that have been in contact with mortar. Your last task for the day is jointing the work done that day. You might need to stop during the day, if you work a long day, to do the jointing. This work needs to be done while the mortar is starting to set up but while it is still soft enough to be scraped by the jointer.

To joint, lay the flat portion of the jointer inside the mortar joint and, starting at one end, pull the jointer across the course. Exert enough pressure to cause the mortar joint to be indented until it is at the deepest point, at least half an inch back of the brick face. Joint also between bricks. Jointing will result in a far more aesthetically appealing wall.

Try to work out the end of the day's work by using up all of the mixed mortar. If you run out of mortar near the end of the day, do not mix more than a small amount, because any mortar that is leftover will harden overnight and be useless.

LAYING CEMENT BLOCKS

Laying blocks is much like laying bricks, except that the blocks cover a great deal more space in less time. The blocks also weigh a great deal more than bricks. You also have a fairly wide range of block sizes from which to choose.

Nominal dimensions of typical blocks are 8 × 8 × 16 inches. The actual size of the block is 7⅝ × 7⅝ × 15⅝ inches. The mortar joints added to the block size bring the blocks to nominal dimensions.

You can also buy blocks that are, nominally, 8 inches wide, 4 or 6 inches high, and 16 inches long. Solid blocks 4 × 8 × 16 are also available. Partition blocks are 4 inches thick, 5 inches high, and 16 inches long. Other sizes are also available, including solid bricks 2¼ inches high, 4 inches wide, and 8 inches long.

Blocks also come in special designs. Corner blocks have two square corners on one end and the other end is recessed. Double corner blocks have square corners on each end. Stretcher blocks have two recessed ends and no square corners. Numerous other possibilities are available, including blocks that have cutouts for headers, beams, and lintels.

When you start to lay blocks, you need to lay a full mortar bed, wide enough to hold the width of the blocks. Use the point of the trowel to furrow the mortar to help create a better bond. When you lay the first block, use a corner block. Use stretcher blocks for the rest of the first course (these are the blocks with two recessed ends) except for the corner block at the other end of the wall line. (See Fig. 12-8.)

Lay the stretcher blocks (and all other blocks) with the thicker end of the face shell upwards. You can immediately see the difference in the thicknesses if you will compare both top and bottom of a block. The purpose of having the thicker end up is so that you will have a wider base for the mortar bed.

Use the guideline for all block courses. To make the work handier and easier, once the corner or end blocks are laid, butter one end only of the stretcher blocks. Stand them upright and in a row along the wall line. Then, as you lay one block, you can pick up the next one, slip it into place, and then proceed until all stretcher blocks are laid. (See Fig. 12-9.)

It is helpful to build up the corners first. You can have the corners five or six courses higher than the middle of the wall. Once you lay the end blocks and the first course, round the corners and then keep building up corners. Each corner will require that you move further and further out onto the wall line. Soon the wall line will be only a matter of filling in the blocks between the corners.

You can use the story pole again with brick or block laying to help you maintain an even-course line. You need to check the level of each corner block in three directions: across the width of it, across the length, and up and down for vertical trueness. In addition, you need to double check for squareness.

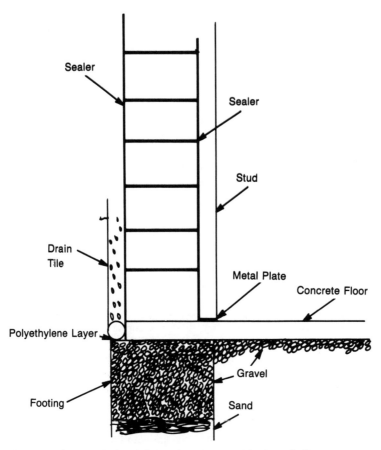

Fig. 12-8. Here are the basic ingredients in a cement-block wall. Be sure to use a good bed of sand and gravel, and pour the footing concrete bed wide and deep. Install drain tiles and metal plates before starting on the wall.

To fill in the blocks between corners, stretch the guideline so that the top, outside edge of each block is barely in contact with the guideline, or mason's line. Be sure that the entire block is in contact with the line or that the entire block is exactly the same distance from the line—preferably $\frac{1}{16}$ inch or less.

From time to time, check the horizontal spacing of blocks. Do this check by holding a straightedge diagonally so that it is in line with the corners formed by block courses from corners of the wall. If each block is not fitted properly, remove the block and position it properly.

As you did with bricks, cut off excess mortar, flip it back into the mortar on the mortar board, and work it into the fresh mortar. Any mortar that has started to dry is considered "dead" and should not be used.

LAYING STONE MASONRY WALLS

Stone masonry, as described here, is made up of natural stones found in fields and stream beds. We do not refer to the stones that are machine cut to perfect dimensions.

Fig. 12-9. If you use a guideline, you can keep blocks in perfect alignment and keep the wall straight.

Generally, the stones are not shaped at all, other than the chipping off of a narrow neck or completing the breaking of a cracked stone.

Coursed rubble walls are made up of stones that are as nearly squared as you can find them. Random rubble stone walls are made up of stones of varying sizes and shapes without regard to any effort to maintain a uniformity of surface or courses.

One of the guiding lights of stone masonry is that the stones should be plentiful, cheap, strong, and durable. Most of the time, you can find an abundance of stones in rural areas, particularly along dirt roads where road grading is a predictable aspect of state road maintenance.

You can use limestone, sandstone, granite, and field stone. Use a mortar of one part Portland cement and three parts sand, mixed with appropriate amounts of water. Start a wall by laying the first course on footings poured of concrete. The stones should be at least as long as the footing is wide.

When you lay a stone, leave its broadest surface down. Lay the largest stones at the bottom of the wall saving the smaller ones for the top. As with bricks, you might need to wet the stones to keep them from absorbing the water from the mortar mixture too rapidly.

Space the stones so that they fit together as well as you can arrange them. If large gaps exist between the stones, particularly where angles are formed, you can fit smaller stones into the gaps after first packing mortar into the spaces.

As you work, lay bond stones every 3 or 4 feet so the wall is not totally dependent upon mortar and trueness for its strength and durability. After the mortar has set you can point or joint the mortar spaces.

If you wish, you can vary colors, sizes, and shapes of rocks for a more appealing geometric pattern. You can break rocks that are too large, especially if they are flat and have a near-square or rectangular shape. To do so, place a chisel against the rock surface and tap lightly. Move the chisel over an inch or two and tap again. Move back and forth across the rock until the tone of the sound changes when the hammer hits the chisel.

You can also use a mason's hammer and achieve the same affect. The stones will not break as clean and as straight as do bricks. Smooth the broken surface of many rocks or stones by using the face of the mason's hammer. For softer stones, you can use the chisel-peen part of the hammer, once the stone has been broken.

Start with areas where you have a straight and clean wall line. If you must cross window or door frames, use a strong metal bar across the framing. Never attempt to cross a window or door line by using only rocks, unless you have one strong stone that will completely span the opening and also fit into the wall line properly.

When you complete the exterior walls, you will need to move indoors to complete the walls constructed there. Chapter 13 details how to hang wallpaper and other wall coverings of paper, cloth, or fabric.

13
Hanging Wallpaper

WALLPAPER, OR PAPER TAPESTRY AS IT WAS COMMONLY CALLED, came into general use as a practical and less expensive substitute for covering walls in the seventeenth century. The earliest records and discoveries reveal that prehistoric cavemen filled their cave walls with decorations. These early artists used rich, bright colors in their drawings of mainly wild animals. Although materials and techniques have changed through the years, the desire to decorate our surroundings has remained with civilizations over the centuries.

From the beginning, wallpaper, whether printed, painted, woven, or embroidered, closely imitated the more expensive tapestry hangings, painted cloths, leather, and wood paneling. Wallpaper was accepted quickly.

The modern wall covering markets offer an overwhelming variety of fabrics ranging from natural fabrics to water-resistant vinyls. Infinite numbers of patterns, colors, and designs are available. Almost all wall coverings also are suited for use on ceilings. Whatever wall covering you choose, it will generally cost more than paint, and hanging the wallpaper will take a little longer to do than painting.

Changing plain walls into a colorful room with patterns that are designed to mix and match has become an easy process. By being your own decorator, you can achieve the overall decorating scheme you desire with the option to accept or reject any color, design, or pattern you like. If you decide on pastels, follow through with a soft decorating scheme. If you choose an accent color, select a color that is very visible in your wallpaper as well as throughout the entire room. If you like prints, choose one. Also select a contrasting print in a reverse color to give your room special decorator affects. (See Fig. 13-1.)

If you should have questions while you are shopping for wallpaper or papering supplies, do not hesitate to request help from the store personnel. Their knowledge is available for the asking, whether you have questions about the amount of materials you need to buy or about your use of a particular pattern or color in a certain area of your room. Many

Fig. 13-1. Plain walls in a room can easily change to bright, colorful ones with the use of wallpaper. The many patterns and textures of wallpaper available make decorating a process that anyone can achieve.

wall-covering suppliers offer classes and demonstrations in techniques free. They also make available pamphlets and videos on the wide variety of materials that they offer.

TYPES OF WALLPAPER

Manufacturers offer many different types of wall coverings with different properties. Before you visit your wall-covering supplier, become familiar with these coverings and their properties. Three broad categories with various types of wallcoverings are available in each. A brief description is given here.

The paper categories include coverings termed relief wallpapers, flocks, duplex papers, wood-chip papers, and grounds. *Grounds* begin as plain, white paper similar to ordinary lining paper. It is later colored or printed. Selections available in the grounds category are small usually. Grounds are a little more difficult to work with. They are more easily torn than many other types of paper when you are pasting the strips, during the hanging process.

Relief wallpapers have a textured surface of some type with a deeply embossed design which might be a formal pattern, a rough plaster appearance, a sand-paint texture, or a traditional tile design. Although reliefs are available in self stick papers, most traditional reliefs are made from heavy paper and require hanging with special adhesives. Once hung, you can paint reliefs later. Some types of reliefs offer the advantage of being scrubbable. Traditional relief wallpapers are very difficult to strip from the wall.

To simulate Italian velvet hangings, flocks were introduced to the wall-covering market. In the design of flocks, special materials are used. They include chopped silk, rayon, or other fibers to give the paper a raised-pile effect. Although flocks give walls a very elegant treatment, they are expensive and require very careful attention to the pile of the pattern during the hanging process.

Wood chips are incorporated in the texture of this paper and the finished product has an oatmeal appearance. Because of the textured effect, wood-chip papers are a good choice for older homes or for any wall that has an uneven or poor surface. You can purchase these wallpapers in white and paint them after hanging them to complete the decor, if desired. The price of wood-chip paper is much less than other traditional papers.

For a stronger paper, you might wish to consider the duplex papers. These papers are made of several layers for a base and then embossed to produce a textured effect.

The second category covers the various vinyls and the Mylars which have a silver-foil ground. The vinyl group includes the basic vinyls, the flock vinyls, textured vinyls, and metallic vinyls.

Manufacturers fuse a layer of vinyl onto a heavy paper backing or cloth backing to produce the vinyl wall covering. If a design is used on the covering, it is also in vinyl. Vinyls are similar in appearance to traditional wallpapers, although the color in vinyl tends to be brighter. Vinyls are popular for use in areas where upkeep requires a lot of attention because vinyls are moisture resistant and can be cleaned easily.

Although they have a beautiful pile surface, flock vinyls are spongeable and you can clean them just like the other vinyls. A flock-vinyl wall covering adds elegance and charm to any room. This vinyl is available in a wide array of colors and designs.

Textured vinyls achieve the look of a fabric wall covering but are available at a considerably lower cost than fabrics. Most textured vinyls have a basically plain color, but the covering is textured to give the appearance of burlaps, linens, or silks. Another technique with textured vinyls employs spun strings to give the look of string cloth. (See Fig. 13-2.)

One of the latest vinyls offered to do-it-yourselfers is the metallic vinyls. These vinyls are usually more expensive than the previously mentioned vinyls, but they are very spectacular in their appearance and well worth considering in your decorating schemes.

Other vinyls include sculptured-vinyl wall coverings that have designs that appear to be sculptured over the basic paper and Oriental collections to compliment any decor of that nature.

Although *Mylar*, paper with a silver-foil background, requires a little more careful handling during their hanging process, they are practical because they are washable. You can purchase Mylars plain or imprinted. They present a striking effect on any wall or ceiling where you use them.

The fabric category includes the chintzes, silks, linens, felt, and grass cloth. Do-it-yourselfers select few of these fine materials because they are difficult to hang. Professional

Fig. 13-2. One type of textured-vinyl wallpaper uses spun strings throughout the surface of the paper to give the look of string cloth.

decorators usually are called in to hang fabrics; however, an alternate is available for the home decorator and is much easier to hang. This alternate includes the paper, or fabric-backed specialty wall coverings which are found in felts, paper-backed silks, grass cloth, cork, and burlap.

You can find felt that is paper backed in a wide range of colors. It has wonderful insulating properties against heat loss and noise. Whether you use felt on one wall or to cover an entire room, the effect makes an immediate impression and adds a coziness to the room.

Paper-backed silk is more difficult to hang than vinyls or regular wallpaper and is very expensive. Covering a small area with this material is more advisible. The silk does offer a feeling of luxury to the adjoining surroundings. The lustrous sheen of the silk paper and the variety of the weave in the silk have an attractive natural effect.

Grass cloths usually are available in their natural green and brown tones with a variety of patterns established by the weave of the cloth. Although grass cloths are trickier to hang than most wall coverings, with a little patience and more persistance, you can

172

achieve the atmosphere you desire with a grass cloth covering. The grass cloths have a tendency to lose their shape during the hanging process if not handled carefully.

Brown is the predominant color of most cork wall coverings, but newer techniques in the industry allow corks to be found in various shades of brown. These shades range in color from the very dark to delicate pales. You can find a few colored or metallic backgrounds for special effects.

Paper-backed burlap is the most popular fabric covering and probably is the easiest to hang. You can use burlap effectively in small areas or over entire rooms. An almost infinate range of colors is available from suppliers, but a small caution is in order with the use of certain colors in certain areas. Do not use boldly-colored burlaps in a bright, sunny room where the colors will eventually dull. Otherwise, paper-backed burlap is a wonderful material to use. The natural shades are least likely to fade.

Lining papers are discussed because they can be a very important aspect of your papering project. Lining papers are made from an off-white paper. You must brush an adhesive on the back of the paper in order to apply the paper to the wall. Apply lining paper where it is needed to absorb excess moisture from paste when extra fine wall coverings (such as silks or grass cloths) are being used for the wall covering. The lining paper helps control the adhesive moisture and blots the paste, reducing the chance of damage to the wall covering. You also can apply lining papers to walls with slight irregularities on their surfaces. These papers will not eliminate all problems from all walls, but they will greatly improve many problems that otherwise would not be hidden. Lining paper is not difficult to apply to walls. You do not overlap the seams of lining paper, as compared to some areas of wallpapering, but you do make a close joint. Also, you do not extend the paper completely to the ceiling or the floor as you would with wallpaper. You do use the same care when hanging lining paper as you would when you hang other coverings.

WALLPAPER DESIGNS AND COLORS

You can create special effects in an area using a particular design or color of wallpaper on the wall or the ceiling of a room. To raise a ceiling, select a stripe or use a pronounced vertical pattern on the walls. To make a ceiling appear lower, select a bold print or use a horizontal stripe. A narrow room appears wider with the use of bold prints or horizontal stripes also. For a dramatic effect, use darker colors. Big patterns fill up rooms while small, nonmatched patterns unify open areas.

Specific collections, available from suppliers, can help you achieve the style you wish to establish. Your choices range from traditional decor, country look, casual living, contemporary setting, children's rooms, to combinations of any of the above.

Wallpaper is available in prepasted or unpasted varieties. The latter type requires an adhesive in order to hang it. Many coverings are washable and easily cleaned. An important aspect to look for when purchasing wallpaper is whether the paper is *dry strippable*, which means the covering can be removed easier when the covering has served its time and you are ready to replace it. Whatever your preference, you want the best wall covering your money can buy, along with ease in hanging the material, as well as quick clean up, and maintanence in time to come.

Although you will spend more time in shopping, visit many suppliers or wallpaper showrooms. Borrow, if possible, sample books of wallpaper which you can take to the walls you plan to cover. If the sample books are not accessible, ask for sample swatches of several papers you particularly like, and try these in your room.

Although the technique for hanging all types of wallpaper is basically the same, advantages and disadvantages should be considered before you decide on a particular wallpaper. If you select a wall covering that is not prepasted, you have a few more steps during the hanging process, as you must apply the adhesive to the back of the wallpaper in order to hang it. On the other hand, you must soak a prepasted paper in a waterbox before you apply the paper to the wall. You must also consider other advantages. The prepasted wallpaper requires less work, less working room, and fewer tools; however, the unpasted paper will be less expensive, and applying the adhesive to the unpasted paper is not difficult, nor does it take much longer to prepare. Many do-it-yourselfers, nevertheless, enjoy the convenience of the prepasted paper.

NECESSARY MATERIALS

Hanging wall coverings can be an easy and enjoyable project, especially if you take a few preparations into account. Before you buy your wallpaper or other covering, take the time to measure the dimensions of each wall to be decorated. In addition, you should make a small sketch of the room showing all windows and doors. These sketches are helpful not only in determining how many rolls of wallpaper you need to buy, but also in determining what size design or pattern you can use for the particular area you wish to decorate. You should keep in mind special areas, such as dormers. These would require extra material. Fireplaces require less material. If you have decided on a wallpaper that has a certain design, you need to purchase a little extra material in order to meet the matched points.

Deciding how much wallpaper to buy can be calculated through a relatively easy process. Some single rolls of wallpaper contain enough paper to cover 35 square feet while others cover only 27.7 square feet. The amounts are stated on each roll of wallpaper. Remember, you must allow for some loss when trimming the paper during the hanging or matching points if the paper has a certain design. On this basis, allow each roll to cover approximately 5 square feet less than the given total amount stated on the roll.

Begin your measurements by getting the total length of each wall in feet and multiply that figure by the total height of each wall in feet. The next step is to add the square footage of all walls and divide that figure by the square footage each roll of wallpaper would cover. You now have the number of rolls of wall covering you would need to cover completely the walls of your room. At this point, you should subtract one single roll for every two regular size openings in the walls of your room, such as windows, doors, archways, or fireplaces.

If you want to paper the ceiling of the same room, again multiply the width by length, in feet, of the ceiling, and divide the figure by the square footage stated on the roll. Add this figure to the amount needed for your walls for the overall total of rolls of wallpaper needed to do the entire room.

The sales personnel can help you with any questions you have concerning possible problem areas. Take your room dimensions and sketches with you any time you visit your supplier.

174

TOOLS FOR HANGING WALLPAPER

Special or complicated tools are not needed in wallpapering in order for you to do a professional-looking job. In a short time, an entire room can be done with a few tools you probably have around the house now.

Start by gathering a yardstick and a pencil for measuring and marking the paper, a carpenter's square for marking precisely the cutting line on the wallpaper, a plumb bob or weighted string with colored chalk for making a plumb line, a pair of straight-cut scissors, a single-edge razor blade or razor blade knife for cutting and trimming, a waterbox for soaking prepasted paper or a bucket and an inexpensive brush for applying adhesive to unpasted paper, a sponge for smoothing and rinsing the paper after you apply it to the wall, a sturdy stepladder or stool for reaching the upper portions of your room, and a screwdriver for removing switch-plate covers. You also will need a large, flat surface, whether the floor of a large room or the dining room table, on which to cut and to paste the paper. Two carpenter's sawhorses covered with a full sheet of plywood would be perfect for the job, too. Drop cloths are convenient to place around the area where you are working to ensure that the floor is not marred with water or adhesive.

Other tools that are very helpful but not an absolute necessity are seam rollers, smoothing brushes, a wide-wall scraper, and a wide-bladed putty knife. A pastry rolling pin is a good substitute for the seam roller for pressing seams. Sponges are excellent for smoothing the entire length and width of strips of wall covering instead of having to purchase smoothing brushes. You can use anything with a straight edge and made of durable material for trimming and cutting with a razor blade in close areas, instead of a wide-wall scraper or a wide-bladed putty knife. We mentioned the waterbox previously in the necessary tools, but, you can use your bathtub if you absolutely must. The bathtub is not as convenient as a waterbox since the box will be located at your worksite. The possibility exists of marring the floors with dripping water when you carry the paper from the tub to the wall of your room. You can still get the job done well with careful working habits and patience.

WALL PREPARATIONS

Possibly the most important step during the entire wall-hanging process is preparing the wall to be covered. Different types of preparation are necessary for different types of wall surfaces. Anything that is loose, whether it is loose paint, old wall covering, dust, or grease, will lead to trouble and must be removed from walls.

For previously papered walls, you should, if possible, remove all of the old wall covering. Soak ordinary wallpaper with water until you can scrape it off the walls. Dry-strippable wall coverings are easier to remove because you do not need to soak them to remove them. With metallics, flocks, foils, or embossed patterns, you must remove them completely because they cannot be covered. If you have used a vinyl covering, you can leave the backing paper as a base for the new covering if you are able to remove the face of the old vinyl.

After you remove the old wall covering, clean your walls with a mild detergent. Work the adhesive from the old wallpaper completely off the wall. If necessary, use a gentle motion with an abrasive pad. Rinse the walls and dry them thoroughly before you begin hanging any new coverings.

If you cannot remove the old wallpaper without damaging your wall, then leave the paper in tact. Clean and seal the old covering by covering it with a coat of wall-covering sealer. Apply the sealer with a brush or a roller. Sealers are available in white, which is the best color to use under most new wall coverings.

If you have old wallpaper that has been painted or varnished, you will have more difficulty removing the paper because the water cannot penetrate the paint or varnish and loosen the paper. Commercial wallpaper removers are available that would help with old, painted paper. Most cities have stores that rent steamers for wallpaper removal if you have large areas to prepare.

If the surface to be covered has been painted with a water-based paint, age the paint at least one month before you hang any wallpaper on it. If the proper time has passed, you might need only to wash the walls with a mild detergent to remove any dust or grease. Then rinse the walls well.

If a wall has paint that has begun to crack or chip off, you need to scrape off as much paint as possible. The new covering needs a sound surface for successful adhesion, or it will only pull loose after a short while.

Wash painted surfaces that are covered with an oil-based paint with a detergent. If the surface is a glossy one, you have further steps you need to take. While the surface is still wet from the washing, rub it down using abrasive paper. Or, you can use a small sander with fine sandpaper, and sand the surface until it appears dull. Rinse the sanded surfaces with warm water to remove any dust.

Dry out plastered walls for at least one month before you apply any wallpaper to them. The moisture content of plastered walls does not allow the paper to adhere properly if the plaster is not aged before papering begins.

If you have old plaster that has been repaired, you must allow the surface to dry thoroughly before you begin new work. If you have plastered walls that you removed wallpaper from, you need to wash the walls with a detergent to remove any paste residues of the old wallpaper.

If your walls are wallboard or plasterboard sections, you should check all joints and nailheads to be assured these areas are smooth and that no gaps exist where the sections meet. Small irregularities of only a fraction of an inch can lead to many troubles later if they are not corrected before the wallpapering is started, especially if you want a design or pattern in the paper since these must be matched. Cover gaps between sections of wallboard with a paper tape which is bonded by spackle or similar compound termed "mud" by many suppliers. Fill nail holes with spackle, and smooth them before the spackle dries. If a nail head is protruding in a dry wall, drive it below the surface and repair it with spackling smoothed over the indentation.

You can paper walls of plywood with relative ease. Use a fiberglass mesh to conceal the joints of plywood sections instead of the paper tape used with plasterboard. Seal nail heads and holes using the same procedure as plasterboard in order to have a smooth surface for the wall covering.

You should apply a product called wall size to all surfaces before preparing for smooth, satisfactory adhesion of the wall covering. Taking the time to apply a coat of wall size assures you that you will have a surface ready for the adhesion of your new wall covering. Wall size will eliminate any areas of inconsistency in the wall covering remaining on the wall. Several types of wall size are available, but the synthetic type with a mold inhibitor is generally recommended. You run the risk of mildew if you cover walls with material that does not breathe well, such as foils and vinyls. You can purchase powdered wall size more economically. All you do is mix the contents with water to a smooth consistency, and then brush the mix on your walls.

You can also buy convenient, ready-mixed wall size. Once you open or mix your size, you should use it within 48 hours or in accordance with the manufacturer's instructions. Dealers also have information concerning sealers, sizings, and other products you will need to know about before you hang your first wallpaper.

HANGING THE WALL COVERING

After you have measured your walls, selected your paper, and prepared the walls, you can start hanging wallpaper. Only two simple steps remain before you begin cutting and pasting.

The first step is the *plumb line*, which is a marking or guideline on your wall. The plumb line must be a true vertical. It serves as the guide for your first strip of paper. Align all subsequent strips of paper with this first strip and with the plumb line.

You can buy a plumb bob economically, or you can use a weighted chalk line. Measure from a corner of the room, or from a door frame edge, to a point 1 inch less than the width of the wallpaper. If your wallpaper is 27 inches wide, measure 26 inches from the corner. At this point, make a mark at the ceiling. Drop a plumb bob from the mark and suspend it just above the floor. Wait until the string has stopped moving. Then hold the string tightly near the baseboard with one hand. With your other hand, snap the string against the wall. This mark is your starting point for the first strip of paper.

If you are using unpasted paper, one other step remains. Get the paste or adhesive ready to use on the back of the paper. To mix, you need a bucket and some water. The bucket should be wide enough for your brush to enter easily. Mix the paste according to the supplied directions.

Measure the length of the wallpaper in one of two ways. You can measure from ceilings to baseboards, but often there will be slight differences from point to point in a room. Learn the maximum height of the wall and add 4 inches. All strips for full walls should be this same length.

Another way to measure is to take the entire roll of wall covering to the wall and, starting at the ceiling, unroll enough paper to cover the wall and allow an extra 2 inches at both top and bottom. Mark and cut the paper at the bottom. Reroll it from the bottom up with the design on the inside. The way you reroll the paper is extremely important, especially if you have a matched pattern. By cutting only one strip at a time, you can keep check on your pattern easily and you will have less chance of cutting a piece that does not match the previously pasted piece.

If you are using a paper with an unmatched pattern, you simply measure and cut each strip as you need it. The procedure varies slightly at this point, depending upon whether you have prepasted or unpasted paper. If you have unpasted paper, you need to take the strip of paper to the table or working area. Be sure to cover your work area with old newspapers or large sheets of plastic to protect your floor or table from paste smears. At the work area, cover completely the back of the strip of wallpaper with paste. The pattern side should be down or next to the work surface. With the brush, apply the adhesive, making certain you brush over each edge of the paper. You do not want any loose seams running down walls or loose pockets at the top and bottom of the strip. For best results, begin brushing from the center of the strip, and continue to the edges.

Many professionals suggest letting the pasted strips have a rest period of about five minutes before hanging the paper. You can test the stickiness of the backing by touching it to determine when the paper is ready to hang.

Do not reroll the strip at this point, but fold it wet side to wet side and top to bottom in order to carry it more easily to the starting point of your wall. Do not allow any creases or severe folds to occur in the strip as you fold and carry it.

Measure, cut, and reroll prepasted paper in the same manner as unpasted paper. When using prepasted paper, you need to ready the waterbox for use. Place the waterbox directly under the area where you will apply your first strip. Have some type of protective covering, either a drop cloth or plastic sheeting, under the waterbox which should be placed at the baseboard. Fill the waterbox two-thirds full of tepid water so the rolled-cut strip of wallpaper will be completely covered when it is placed in the waterbox. Plan to change the water every five to six strips in order to prevent excessive accumulation of the paste in the water. You want your colors and designs to remain clear and free from debris.

Place the strip of wallpaper totally under water in the waterbox. Allow the strip to soak evenly, and check it frequently to see that the strip stays submerged. Time for soaking papers might vary from 15 seconds to 60 seconds. For best results, follow the time table suggested by the manufacturer for the particular type of paper you are using.

When you have completed the soaking period, slowly pull the paper up to the ceiling. Keep the paper clear of the wall, and overlap the ceiling joint with the 2 inches you allowed when you measured the strip. This step is the same whether you use unpasted or prepasted paper.

The plumb line is your next point of attention. At this time, you need to line up the right-hand edge of the paper with the plumb line, or chalked line, you made earlier. Lap the left-hand edge of the paper into the corner of the wall or against the door frame, depending on where you started your measurement for the plumb line.

In order to get the right-hand edge perfectly aligned, you can slide the wallpaper strip around until you have it where you need it. While the paper is still moist, you can lift it and move it until the edge is properly aligned.

Next, begin smoothing the strip at the ceiling line with a few horizontal strokes to the upper section with a wet sponge or wallpaper smoother. Continue pressing the paper in place gently by working down the center and to the sides. Smooth out any wrinkles or large bubbles. Be careful when working near the edges in order to avoid stretching the strip of paper. Check the left-hand edge to be sure it is firmly secured in the corner.

Trim away any excess wallpaper at the top and bottom of the strip. Use a wall scraper or wide putty knife blade as a guide for your razor knife or blade. To prevent slips from occurring and marring your work, cut on the side of the scraper or straightedge away from the wall.

If you plan to paper the adjoining wall to the left of your strip, leave the corner overlap. If you do not plan to paper the wall, carefully trim away the excess. With the strip in place and trimmed to fit the area, rinse the entire strip with a fresh sponge in order to remove excess paste that might be left on the wall during the hanging process.

Proceed with the second strip in the same manner as you did the first. Take the entire roll of paper to the wall again, and match the pattern, if necessary, to the edge of the first strip. You might have to waste several inches at the top in order to match the patterns. Remember to allow 2 extra inches at the top and bottom after you match the pattern. The roll consists of extra material to allow for matching of patterns, so you have a built-in allowance.

After pasting your second strip or soaking it, line the edge of one strip against the other. Match the pattern as you work. Do not overlap the strips. Abut the edges, and use great care at the seams.

Do not stretch the seams. Stretching them will cause them to come loose, and your professional look will be lost. To ensure that your seams are well pressed, you can roll them lightly with a seam roller or pastry rolling pin. If you are hanging a textured paper, flocks, or other delicate paper, you can tap the seams down with the bristle tips of the smoothing brush. Do not roll these types of materials. Properly abutted seams result in a seamless appearance. Trim and again sponge the second strip as you did the first.

After hanging the second strip, move several feet away and look over the strips. Make any necessary corrections. Check to see that both strips are the same shade. If you find any variance in color, report the discrepancy to the dealer.

Continue matching, measuring, cutting, hanging, and trimming all strips for the entire wall. Remember to smooth each strip with a freshly-washed sponge, and keep the water in the water box clean.

When you have papered the entire first wall and are at a corner, do not try to wrap any of the full strip you are working with around the corner. This procedure is especially true of all inside corners. Corners are rarely totally straight. A pattern or a stripe in the paper will reflect this defect even more at corners. You also are more likely to have wrinkles or creases in the wall covering if you try to wrap them around corners by more than 1 inch of material.

To paper the inside corner, measure to check the width that remains between the last full strip hung and the corner. You will probably not need a full width of the strip. After measuring, add 1 inch to the width. Cut the proper length for the room and lay it on your table or floor. Now mark and cut the strip lengthwise to the width you need. Hang the strip in the same manner as before, but allow the extra inch to extend around the corner of the next wall. Apply the narrow strip by aligning the right edge of the strip with the plumb line. Fit the left edge into the corner to overlap the previous strip. If you have a little pattern loss, it will not be noticeable. (See Fig. 13-3.)

It is easier to handle outside corners than inside ones since you can wrap outside corners. You can have a smoother wall, though, if you do not wrap a large section of paper around a corner. You might have a small overlap with the remainder of the material if you choose to trim and repaste a width of the material around this corner also.

HANGING WALLPAPER IN SPECIAL AREAS

When you are working the areas around the room, you should not skip any doorways or windows. It is important to keep working straight around the room. Instead of trying to cut the wallpaper to fit around windows or doors, you hang the pasted strip-over them. Trim the strip away from the window or door by making diagonal cuts up to, and a little

Fig. 13-3. Hanging wallpaper in an inside corner is an easy task if walls are true and square. By allowing only an inch of paper to extend around the corner, the hanging process is made less difficult.

beyond, the corners. Trim the excess material away from the window or door by using a razor blade and wide scraper as a cutting guide. Press into place the sections above and below the window continuing carefully to match patterns, if necessary.

Cover a heating or cold-air grille with the initial hanging of the wallpaper. Do not attempt to cut the paper to fit these fixtures before you hang the paper. When you have the strip in place, first trim around these fixtures, then, using the diagonal cuts, trim the excess paper at the ceiling and the baseboards.

For a neater, smoother appearance without signs of a break in the surface, remove electric switch plates, outlet covers, wall lighting fixtures, thermostat covers, and similar objects before you apply the wallpaper to that area. By doing so, the edges where you trim away the excess wall covering will not show when you restore these fixtures to the wall. (See Fig. 13-4.)

Before you begin your work in these areas, turn off the electricity. Remember, the wallpaper paste has a high moisture content and the prepasted paper is soaked in water before hanging. You do not want any moisture to come in direct contact with live electrical connections. When you hang a strip over an outlet, smooth the paper in the usual manner. Then cut an opening large enough for the electrical connections to be exposed but not in contact with the trimmed edges of the wallpaper. Cut carefully so that the opening is

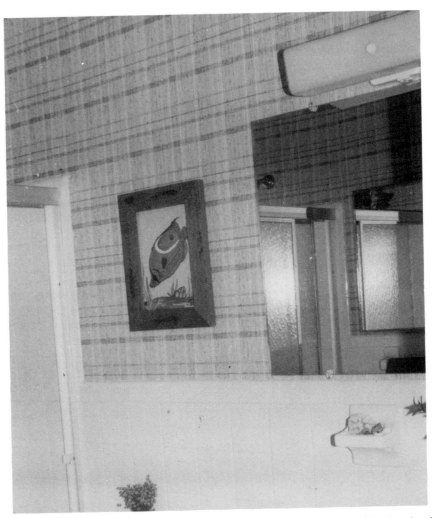

Fig. 13-4. Smoother, neater appearances are accomplished when visible breaks do not exist in the surface of the wallpaper. Simple hanging techniques make corners, edges, fixtures, and other similar objects present no difficulty.

a little smaller than the face plate. You also can cover the plate with the same wallpaper by applying a matching strip over the face of the plate. Trim the areas where the electrical switch or receptacle emerges through the plate. You must allow the wallpaper adhesive to dry completely before you reinstall the plates and return the power to the outlets. Do not cover any electrical outlets if you are using a foil.

If you plan to cover the ceiling, do so before you cover any of the walls. It is much easier to cover ceilings if you have a second person to assist you.

HANGING FOILS AND MYLARS

Foils and Mylars are special coverings and require a little more work in their application, but they are well worth the extra effort because of the impressive look they exude. Because these coverings reflect light, imperfections in the wall are clearly evident. Therefore, a wall surface that is nearly perfect is necessary for these materials.

If you apply lining paper first to the wall surface and then cover it with foil or Mylar, you will have a more satisfactory result. Lining papers help cover many irregularities in wall surfaces. One precaution to take early in this project is to hang the lining paper horizontally so that the seams of the lining paper and the seams of the foil, or Mylar, will not overlap. If you do not hang the lining in this way, the seams will appear bulky and will produce a noticeably negative effect.

Hang Mylars and foils the same as you would any other wall covering. Use extra care when applying these materials around any electrical fixture. Be sure to trim away any excess material in these areas. Again, turn off electrical current while you hang these wall coverings.

Carefully fold the foil strips while you are working with them, and never allow them to crease or bend at sharp angles. You should again line up the right edge with the plumb line. To remove bubbles from the surface, use a plastic smoother to avoid scratching the foil or Mylar. Use sharp scissors to do all cutting and trimming rather than a razor blade to ensure a straight, clean cut rather than a frayed edge.

Whether your pattern is subtle or refined, you will find that the wall coverings bring special character to any room. Whatever your decorating preferance, you are certain to find the color and design you desire in the many wall coverings available in your supplier's showroom.

14
Finishing Touches

WHEN THE EXTERIOR WALLS ARE COMPLETED AND THE INTERIOR
walls are covered, you have two major tasks remaining: installing the molding and
baseboard and then painting or staining the woodwork. You can do the molding with a
modest amount of work and materials. The painting or staining requires more time, a little
more patience, and careful work.

You will need a drop cloth of some type for the painting. You can use old newspapers
if you have no canvas or plastic sheeting. Unless you are painting ceilings, you will have
very little need for a wide drop cloth. If the floors have not been finished yet, and if there

Neither job requires a great deal of equipment. When you are installing molding, you
will need a saw, hammer, straightedge, and some nails. Very little else is necessary. For
the painting and staining jobs, you will need a wide brush (4 inches or wider), a narrow
brush (2 inches wide), and perhaps a paint roller and a roller pan.

You will need a drop cloth of some type for the painting. You can use old newspapers
if you have no canvas or plastic sheeting. Unless you are painting ceilings, you will have
very little need for a wide drop cloth. If the floors have not been finished yet, and if there
is no furniture in the room, the danger of damage from paint drippings is even less.

You might be wise to complete all painting work before you install the molding. You
can even paint the molding before you nail it up. When it is in place, you can spot paint
over the nail heads, if you wish, but this is not necessary.

CHOOSING PAINTS

You will make your paint selection in terms of what kinds of surfaces you need to
paint. Wood, masonry, and metal often need different types of paint. The quality of the
surface of the work to be painted also affects the kind of paint you buy.

Your paint dealer can help you make your selections by showing you color charts
and by telling you what types of paint work best with specific surfaces. The two major
types of paint are oil-base and latex. Oil-base paint usually contains linseed oil with either

turpentine or some type of mineral spirits mixed with the actual paint. Latex paint is a water-base type of wall covering. Water is the primary thinner, with tiny particles of resin emulsion suspended in water.

For comparative purposes, oil-base paints smell considerably stronger than water-base or latex paints. If you are sensitive to oil-base ingredients, you might prefer to use latex paint. Some people are allergic to the oil-base paints and suffer from degrees of respiratory distress when exposed for long periods of time to the fumes.

Oil-base paints are, generally, harder to apply, longer-lasting, and far more difficult to clean up, particularly after the paint dries. Latex paints are much easier to apply, they dry faster, they tend to hold the original color tones better and longer, and they resist chipping and flaking better than do the oil-base paints.

One of the great advantages to latex paints is that you can apply them in damp or rainy weather indoors and in very humid weather outdoors. You can clean brushes and pans with water, and a damp cloth will clean up any spots of paint that fall to the floor. Until the paint dries, it is very easily damaged. After it dries, it is highly durable and attractive. The fumes associated with oil-base paints are absent in latex paints. Some of them even have a rather pleasant smell.

A third type of paint is a water-base basic paint with a linseed oil additive dissolved in water. The primary advantage of this paint is that it combines the best qualities of both water-base and oil-base paints and has few of the disadvantages.

When you are using oil-base paints, you will need to clean brushes with varsol, paint thinner, or similar substances. These cleaning agents often are irritating to eyes and nose and can cause upper respiratory discomfort to many people.

Some paints are nonchalking. Be sure to specify that you need a nonchalking paint if you are going to apply the paint above surfaces such as bricks or stones. The chalking activity of some paints will cause the chalky film to run down across the bricks or stones and create an unattractive surface. Some surfaces are already chalky as a result of previous painting jobs. It is better not to use a latex paint over such surfaces.

You can also specify that you want lead-free paint if you are going to be painting indoors for hours at a time. The fumes from this type of paint seem to bother sensitive people more than any other types of paint.

Before getting involved with specific paints, you should consider several factors. First, always purchase a high-quality paint. Some of the very cheap paints do not cover well. You will need at least two, three, or even four coats before you can produce a solid cover. You have not saved money if you have had to buy twice as much paint and use twice as much time and effort to apply it. Inferior paints also last a very short time. You might have to paint every three or four months as opposed to every three years.

Second, prepare the surface before you begin painting. If you try to paint over flaking paint, the new paint will chip off when the old paint flakes.

Third, follow instructions. Mix and apply paint according to manufacturer's directions. House paint is considered to be any paint that is formulated for exterior use. Interior paints are not considered to be "house paints."

For wood surfaces, you can use the latex, oil-base, or the combination of oil-base latex paints. You can also use virtually any type of stain for wood surfaces. If you are painting windows and door frames, you will want to use a brush, but, you can spray paint wood siding, or you can use a brush.

If the siding and windows are aluminum, use special aluminum paint. You also can use house paint if you apply a primer coat first.

You can paint masonry walls with house paint after you apply a primer, if you use oil-base paint. You can use a rubber-base paint on masonry without applying a primer first.

You can use aluminum paint on metal siding and other metal surfaces, if you first apply a primer. Also, you can use regular house paint on copper, iron, metal siding, and galvanized metal, if you prime the surface first.

For best results, use exterior trim paint for window frames, door frames, and shutters. Purchase exterior trim paint in an oil-resin mixture with alkyd added to the enamel. This type paint has a high-gloss finish, and it does not chalk. You can use house paint, but the gloss does not last as long and some chalking occurs.

For wood siding, the first choice normally is an oil-base paint. You can use latex, but many professional painters feel that it does not penetrate the wood pores and seal as well as the oil-base paints do.

For masonry, exterior latex paint is an excellent choice. You do not need to seal or prime if you use the latex surface.

One aspect of painting that we want to stress is that you should not paint except when necessary. Too much paint can cause a build-up that will create thickening around the seams of joints of wood and in corners. This build-up can freeze in cold weather and expand in hot weather, and thus cause large flakes of the paint to fall away from the wall.

PREPARING SURFACES FOR PAINTING

As with many household chores, getting ready to paint is almost as important as the finished work. At times, the preparation is even more important. Take the following steps before you open the first can of paint.

The primary rule of painting is that you should clean and dry all surfaces. By clean, we mean that you should not have amounts of dirt, dust, cobwebs, or other foreign matter adhering to the walls. If the walls are grimy as a result of months of weathering, the paint will cover the dirt, but you should remove anything loose before painting.

If the paint is starting to flake, scrape the loose paint free by using a wire brush, a putty knife, or a short-handled hoe. A hoe is exceptionally good to use if the flaking is bad. Remember, any paint that you can knock or pull loose before painting will break loose after painting, and you will be down to the bare wood quickly. (See Fig. 14-1.)

When you are painting wood walls, find and seal and knotholes with a sealer after first cleaning the area with turpentine or similar cleaner. You can use a good household detergent to clean any extremely dirty areas. Let the walls dry before starting to paint.

Use a caulking compound to seal any cracks that exist between window frames or door frames and siding. If siding boards are not seated firmly against the wall, use extra nails or fully drive in any nails that are not seated all the way. If nail-head rust has discolored the wall area, use sandpaper to clean away the rust spots. It is better to use nonrusting nails on exterior walls if the nail heads will show.

Where huge portions of a wall are down to bare wood, clean the wood and prime it before painting the entire wall. If segments of paint have chipped away and left a noticeable edge, sandpaper the paint edges until they gradually smooth into the wood. This procedure is called *feathering*. Feather any surfaces that will leave a clear paint mark when the paint dries.

Fig. 14-1. For scraping walls, a hoe does an excellent job in removing the larger paint flakes.

Fig. 14-2. You can paint ceilings and other hard-to-reach areas easily by using a roller with an extension handle.

For all metal surfaces, clean the surface thoroughly. Many metal products come from the manufacturer with a coating or glaze that you should remove so paint will adhere properly. You can remove the residue with a strong vinegar solution.

Clean all masonry surfaces before painting. If the wall is a new one, let it weather for several weeks before you paint it. Let it stand until the chalking process has stopped, before you paint.

Use a sealer for masonry surfaces if you intend to use an oil-base paint. If mortar cracks, caused by shrinkage exist, fill these cracks with caulk or compound. If any blocks have cracks larger than hairline cracks, caulk or compound these.

Anytime you find inferior materials in a wall, whether the material is wood, masonry, or metal, remove or repair the weak area before attempting to paint. Take all spongy wood out. It will only absorb paint and it will not remain in the wall long enough to pay you to paint it.

PAINTING TOOLS

You can apply paint in three major ways: with a brush, with a sprayer, or with a roller. All three methods have advantages and disadvantages.

By far the fastest way to paint is with a sprayer. You can usually paint a wide, clear surface five times faster with a sprayer than you can with a brush and twice as fast as you can with a roller.

The major disadvantages to the spray painting are that you will use a great deal more paint this way and, therefore, increase the cost of the job significantly in one respect. You cut the labor time considerably, too, and, in that respect, the sprayer is efficient. When you are painting masonry, the sprayer might be the best bet, because the sprayer will cause the paint to penetrate deep into the pores of the concrete and deliver a smoother and better-finished product.

A brush is by far the slowest method of painting, but, some places require very careful work (such as the trim around windows and doors or the inside wood portions of windows). You can tape the glass around these areas and then use a sprayer, but the time saved by using the sprayer will be negated by the time required to do the taping and later removing the tape. A sprayer is wonderfully efficient at those times when you can take down the door or shutters and paint them outside. You must, however, either own, rent, borrow, or buy the spray-painting equipment. You might need to invest a considerable amount of money, no matter which route you choose, unless you already own the equipment or can borrow it. Remember, when you rent from a commercial establishment, you might have to pay by the hour. You are paying as much for the drive to and from the rental agency as you are for the time the sprayer is in use.

Rollers, while deficient in some respects, also have their major advantages. The primary advantage is that you can cover a large amount of wall space quickly and with very little labor. You can obtain an extension handle for the roller and easily reach very high ceilings. While you are painting your masonry walls, you can, if you have a thick pile on the roller cover, cause the paint to penetrate the pores very well. Do not use a worn-out roller cover for this kind of work. (See Fig. 14-2.)

One problem with rollers is that you cannot do trim work with them. Often the trim paint applied with a brush is noticeably thinner than that on the nearby wall, because the roller carries a greater paint load than does a brush. Another disadvantage is that the roller is more likely to use a greater amount of paint. You can load the roller more lightly. Then apply greater pressure on the roller as you push it along the wall and thus cut your paint usage considerably. The extra effort is self-defeating, for the most part, because you could just as easily use a brush if you are going to slow your work in such a fashion.

The brush is the slowest method of applying paint. The finished results are, if you are a capable painter, highly pleasing, but, if you are not a good painter, you might leave brush marks and thin areas. With a brush, you can trim efficiently and you can cover door and window facing beautifully. One other major advantage is that a brush is very inexpensive. One that is of medium quality will last for weeks.

STARTING THE PAINT JOB

Once the surfaces are clean and you have the necessary equipment, your first job is to see that the paint is thoroughly mixed. When you buy the paint, the dealer will mix it for you, but if you do not use it within an hour or so, you will need to mix it again. If the paint has been mixed recently, the easy way to mix it for application is to secure another bucket, one that will hold as much as the paint bucket will. Open the paint-can lid and pour the paint into the other bucket, which must be clean. Let all of the paint run out. Then lift the new container, with the paint in it, and pour the paint back into the original bucket. Repeat this process until all of the paint is of the same consistency.

To mix paint that has been sitting on a shelf for several days, again find a second container and pour half the paint into the new bucket. Use a paint paddle or clean stick—one that has a flat side and a square end. You will need to pull the paint paddle through an inch or so of very thick paint at the bottom of the can. Stir until you mix all of the accumulation at the bottom in with the rest of the paint. Then pour the paint back and forth for greater consistency.

If you are using an oil-base paint, you will perhaps need to thin the paint slightly. Several paint thinners are available on the market and none seems to have a great advantage over the others. Ask your dealer to recommend an adequate paint thinner. Pour only a small amount of thinner—a cupful or so—into the paint at first. You will need to pour some of the paint into a second type of container in order for the bucket to hold the extra liquid. Mix the paint carefully, and then pour it back and forth. Add more of the thinner if it is still thicker than undiluted soup.

If you plan to use paint that has been sitting on a shelf for a month or more, the day before you shake the can vigorously, and then turn it upside down on the shelf 24 hours prior to using it. The accumulation on the bottom will filter into the rest of the paint and make mixing easier. Do not shake latex paint. You can cause it to foam.

When mixing latex paints, you can stir with a paddle. If the paint is too thick, add a little water. Do not add water to an oil-base paint.

You probably will need one wide brush and one 2-inch trim brush. Some professionals and experienced painters can trim with a wide brush, but most people get along better with a narrow brush. If you decide to trim with a wide brush, one easy way to do it reasonably effectively is to fully load the tip only of the brush. Place the brush in touch with the window partition or other wood, about an inch from the glass or other surface you do not want to damage. Press down slightly and force the bristles in the brush to curve away from the direction you plan to move the brush.

As you do so, a bead of paint will form just ahead of the brush. Move the brush until the bead is barely covering the wood surface. Keep exerting pressure as you move the brush so that you are, in effect, pushing the bead across the partition. Push it all the way to the corner, and then cut away with the brush sharply. This method works very well.

When you stop for lunch or a prolonged break, you should leave the paint bristles in paint. If you do not, they will dry and be too stiff for effective painting. One way to keep the bristles properly moistened is to drill a small hole through the handle of the paintbrush and then pass a wire through the hole. Let the wire rest along the rim of the bucket. The wire will keep the entire brush from being immersed. When the paint in the bucket is too low for the bristles to touch it, bend the wire slightly or as much as needed.

When you start a wall, begin at the top and work your way down. If you must use a ladder, make certain that the ladder is standing safely with all legs or feet upon the floor. Do not let the ladder tilt except to lean against the wall. Do not lean the ladder at a precarious angle or have it stand too straight. If too straight, the ladder will easily tilt backwards with your weight on it. If the ladder leans too much, as you climb higher, there is a danger that the feet of the ladder will slide away from the wall and the ladder (and painter) will fall. It is best to have some type of anchor against the feet of the ladder if it is convenient to nail one to the floor. You would not want to do this with a finished floor, but if only the subflooring is installed, you can nail a small 2 × 4 to the plywood and let the feet of the ladder rest against it. (See Figs. 14-3 and 14-4.)

Before painting, assure yourself of good ventilation. Never paint in a completely enclosed room for prolonged periods of time. Do not paint in a room where there is an open flame. Not all paints are highly flammable, but some paints emit flammable fumes.

When working on a ladder, if you cannot reach the higher parts of the wall, use an extension handle for the brush or roller or get a longer ladder. Do not stand on the very top rung, or step, of the ladder and try to overreach. (See Fig. 14-5.)

Before painting windows, mask the glass fully. If you do not want to use masking tape, as suggested earlier, you can buy liquid masking which is somewhat easier to use. One very simple answer to the problem is to put wet newspapers over the windows. The newspaper will cling to the windowpanes and the moisture in the papers will keep paint from being absorbed and eventually sinking through. When you have finished the painting, let it have a minute or two to set. Lift the wet newspapers by lifting gently at one corner and then peeling the entire section from the glass pane. (See Fig. 14-6.)

Fig. 14-4. If the ladder must lean excessively, stakes, driven into the ground behind the legs, will keep the ladder from sliding.

Fig. 14-3. When painting outdoors, rest the feet of the ladder on a strong, level, and stable surface.

Fig. 14-5. Instead of climbing too high on a ladder, use a roller with extension handle for easy paint work, but not for trim.

Fig. 14-6. Instead of taping windows, cut old newspapers and wet these so that they will cling well to glass. Fit the old papers into the window and then paint. You can lift the papers out easily, or, when they dry, they will fall out.

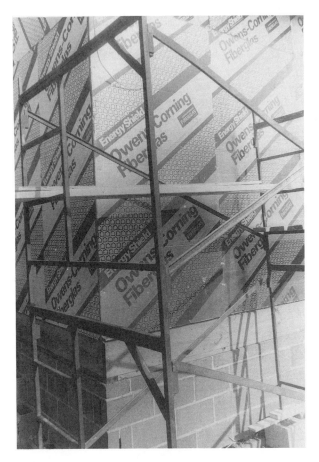

Fig. 14-7. For all difficult paint work at heights, use a scaffold if one is available. You can cover more wall surface and have room to walk around, in addition to being safer while you work.

You do not need to soak the newspaper. All you need is just enough moisture for the paper to adhere to the glass. Paper that is too wet becomes fragile and more difficult to remove. You can measure the pane and cut the newspaper accordingly. You can use several thicknesses for greater protection.

For safer painting of the higher wall areas, use a scaffold if you have ready access to one. You can spread thick boards between the scaffold ends and have a comfortable platform on which to work. (See Fig. 14-7.)

COMPLETING THE PAINTING

The best painting is done when the temperature is in the comfort range. If the room is too cold, the paint will be stiff and hard to apply. If the room is too hot, the ceiling area will be very uncomfortable as the heat rises.

The more ventilation you have, the faster the paint will dry. Oil-base paints typically need 24 hours to dry, but latex paints will dry in three or four hours sufficiently for you to apply the second coat, if one is needed.

Remove all furniture and other obstacles that block the room. You might drip paint on sofas and chairs, and you also run the risk of having an accident while you try to work over and around them. Take off wall outlet cover plates and switch cover plates before you begin to paint.

Dip your brush one-third deep into the paint. Never plunge the brush up to the handle. An overloaded brush will become very difficult to use, particularly if you are working above your head and the paint seeps through the bristles and runs down the handle. If this happens, stop and clean the brush handle.

With the brush loaded, paint with the grain, in back and forth strokes. At the end of each stroke, lift the brush lightly to create a feathering effect. Completely cover one area before you move to the next. After you move, when you start to paint the new area, you should overlap the first area slightly.

When using latex paints, stop occasionally and wash out the bristles. Latex dries quickly and soon you can have a thick crust of paint at the upper ends of the bristles, and this accumulation is very difficult to remove.

Start at the top of the wall and, if you are using a roller, trim or cut in the corner with a brush. You need to paint about a 2-inch strip along the ceiling and down the corner angle of the wall. You can use your roller freely after you have painted the border strip.

Paint window and door facings as well as baseboards and corner molding last in a room. You might want to use a semigloss paint on interior framing and molding and a flat paint on the wall area. Light-colored paints can make a small room appear larger, while dark paints have the opposite effect—a large room can be made to look smaller.

Always stop and clean up dripped paint. You even can clean oil-base paints easily while they are still wet. Latex paints also are easier to clean while they are wet. Some painters like to use a cloth dampened with paint thinner for oil-base paint cleaning. A soft cloth moistened with water will clean up latex paint spills. After you have completed the painting, be sure to dispose of the cloths properly. Oily cloths are highly flammable and can result in spontaneous combustion if they are stored carelessly.

INSTALLING MOLDING

Do not install molding or baseboards before you paint. When the room is painted, you can cut and fit the molding and baseboards, and then paint them before installation. If you want to cover nail heads, you can do so with a wadded cloth, dipped lightly into the paint used on the wood.

Installing baseboards is fairly easy. You might choose to use 1-×-4 or 1-×-5 boards, perhaps wider ones. For easiest installation, measure the longest wall line, and cut one board to fit snugly, but not too tightly, in the space. If the fit is too snug, you might have to force the ends in place and you might scar the walls.

Nail in the first baseboard section by sinking nails through the board and into the corner posts on each end and into the studs along the wall line. Next, measure and cut a baseboard for the wall opposite the one you just completed. Nail this second board in place as you did before.

Install the third baseboard so that the ends fit between the first two baseboards installed. If there are doors in a wall line, cut the baseboard to fit snugly against the door molding or door facing.

In rooms with recesses or alcoves, install one section of the baseboard so that the end is flush with the corner. Fit the second piece so that its end is flush with the edge of the first piece.

Nail in the baseboard on the two opposite sides of an alcove first, and then install the end section last. On outside corners of an alcove, you might wish to bevel the ends of the baseboard sections so that a neat fit is visible throughout the room. A butt-joined baseboard corner leaves one board edge fully exposed and some people find this unattractive.

You can use your miter box to bevel ends of baseboards for both inside corners and outside corners. All you need to remember is to reverse the angles for the two corners.

Molding is slightly more difficult to install. First, you have ceiling molding and corner molding, if you plan to use any in the corners. If so, choose ceiling molding that will fit or blend well with the corner molding.

Start with the ceiling. Measure and cut the first long piece of molding to extend along the longest wall. Square cut the ends at first until you decide how you want the ends to be fitted. You can bevel the ends by using the miter box, or you can try one very easy way of fitting molding.

This way is simple. Nail the first molding in place. Let the square-cut ends fit snugly into corners. Then take a scrap piece of the same molding and hold it against the end of the next long piece you plan to install. Hold it so that the end of the scrap piece abuts squarely into the long piece you plan to use to abut against it. While holding the scrap piece steadily, use your other hand and a pencil to mark along the line of the inside edge of the scrap molding. Keep the pencil point as close to the edge of the pattern piece as possible.

When the marking is complete, saw along the line. Cut the new piece to length and mark and cut the other end along a similarly marked line. Nail the molding in place. You will find that the fit is surprisingly good and looks very much like a mitered cut.

You can measure, cut, and install the rest of the molding in the same way if the room is a rectangle. Many rooms have alcoves and recesses created by closets or other conveniences, added to the room after initial construction.

When you are installing molding around outside corners, you will need to miter the corners for a good fit. Cut one length, and then miter the end that is to protrude past the alcove corner. The piece must be at least 1½ inches longer than the wall line for the recess.

Nail the piece so that the mitered end extends past the corner. Now miter the piece that will fit against the one you just installed. When the two mitered edges are end-matched, the fit should be neat and snug.

Miter inside corners just the opposite way the outside corners were cut. Match the ends, and nail these molding pieces in place.

When all ceiling molding is in place, you are ready for the corner molding. It is not necessary to install corner molding if you have gypsum board or plaster walls with smooth corners. If you use board wall covering or paneling, you will want to use some type of corner molding. Most supply houses can sell you corner molding to match the paneling of your choice.

To install corner molding, all you do is measure and cut to length so that the molding unit will fit between the baseboard and ceiling molding. The molding has two flat sides to align with the walls of the corner. Use small finishing nails to install it.

Your final step in the room will be to nail in some quarter-round molding, if you choose to use such an addition. This type of molding fits on top of the baseboard and the other flat side is aligned with the wall. You can miter-cut the ends of the molding as you did for the ceiling molding.

Install the molding for alcoves and recesses as you did with the ceiling molding. Follow exactly the same basic procedures.

Now your wall is completely constructed, inside and out. You have sturdy siding, a strong studding system, adequate insulation between studs or over the exterior wall, sheathing, and interior wall covering.

The job has been a rather long and often difficult one, but you saved yourself hundreds of dollars and gained a new respect for your own abilities and for the skills of the professionals who earn every dollar they charge for their services. With the skills you acquired during your many projects, however, you might have convinced yourself and others that you will seldom, if ever again, need to pay for such services. If so, you are several major steps closer to complete self-reliance.

Index

Other Bestsellers From TAB

☐ **KITCHEN REMODELING—A DO-IT-YOURSELFER'S GUIDE—Paul Bianchina**

Create a kitchen that meets the demands of your lifestyle. With this guide you can attractively and economically remodel your kitchen yourself. All the know-how you need is supplied in this complete step-by-step reference, from planning and measuring to installation and finishing. 208 pp., 187 illus.

Paper $17.95   **Hard $23.95**
Book No. 3011

☐ **MASTERING HOUSEHOLD ELECTRICAL WIRING—2nd Edition—James L. Kittle**

Update dangerously old wiring in your house. Add an outdoor dusk-to-dawn light. Repair a malfunctioning thermostat and add an automatic setback. You can do all this and more—easily and safely—for much less than the cost of having a professional do it for you! You can remodel, expand, and modernize existing wiring correctly and safely with this practical guide to household wiring. From testing to troubleshooting, you can do it all yourself. Add dimmer switches and new outlets . . . ground your TV or washer . . . make simple appliances repair . . . set up outside wiring . . . put in new fixtures and more! 304 pp., 273 illus.

Paper $18.95   **Hard $24.95**
Book No. 2987

☐ **BUILDING A LOG HOME FROM SCRATCH OR KIT 2nd Edition—Dan Ramsey**

This guide to log home building takes you from initial planning and design stages right through the final interior finishing of your new house. There's advice on selecting a construction site, choosing a home that's right for your needs and budget, estimating construction costs, obtaining financing, locating suppliers and contractors, and deciding whether to use a kit or build from scratch. 302 pp., 311 illus.

Paper $12.95   **Hard $14.95**
Book No. 2858

☐ **ADD A ROOM: A PRACTICAL GUIDE TO EXPANDING YOUR HOME—Paul Bianchina**

Overflowing with helpful diagrams, photographs, and illustrations, this indispensable guide focuses on the professional details. It's far more than a volume of plans or architectural ideas . . . it's a complete how-to-do-it manual that leaves no question unanswered. Using this guide, you can build a garage, a room on top of your garage, a sunspace or greenhouse, a family or rec room, a bathroom, and many others. 400 pp., 360 illus.

Paper $19.95   **Hard $27.95**
Book No. 2811

☐ **BATHROOM REMODELING—A DO-IT-YOURSELFER'S GUIDE—Paul Bianchina**

This complete step-by-step remodeling reference addresses all aspects of bathroom design. The author's expertise will help you construct the space you need, or improve your use of the space you have. The selection and installation of all traditional bathroom fixtures are covered, and detailed information on contemporary "luxury" bathroom options is presented. 208 pp., 200 illus.

Paper $17.95   **Hard $23.95**
Book No. 3001

☐ **PRACTICAL STONEMASONRY MADE EASY—Stephen M. Kennedy**

The current popularity of country-style homes has renewed interest in the use of stone in home construction. Now, with the help of expert stonemason Stephen M. Kennedy, you can learn how to do stonework yourself and actually save money while adding to the value, charm, and enduring quality of your home. This book provides step-by-step guidance in the inexpensive use of stone for the relatively unskilled do-it-yourselfer. 272 pp., 229 illus.

Paper $19.95   **Hard $24.95**
Book No. 2915

☐ **SUNSPACES—HOME ADDITIONS FOR YEAR-ROUND NATURAL LIVING—John Mauldin, Photography by John H. Mauldin and Juan L. Espinosa**

Have you been thinking of enclosing your porch to increase your living space? Want to add a family room, but want the best use of the space for the money? Do you want information on solar energy and ideas on how you can make it work in your home? If "yes" is your answer to any of these questions, you'll want to own this fascinating guide! 256 pp., 179 illus.

Paper $17.95   **Hard $21.95**
Book No. 2816

☐ **HOW TO PLAN, CONTRACT AND BUILD YOUR OWN HOME—Richard M. Scutella and Dave Heberle, Illustrations by Jay Marcinowski**

After consulting the expert information, instruction, and advice in this guide, you'll have the basic understanding of house construction that you need to get involved in all the planning and construction particulars and pre-construction choices entailed in building your home. Best of all, by learning how to make these decisions yourself, you can make choices to *your* advantage . . . not the builder's. 440 pp., 299 illus.

Paper $13.95   **Hard $15.95**
Book No. 2806

Other Bestsellers From TAB